More Praise for *The Message of You*

"You will read and exclaim, 'How does she know that's EXACTLY what I need to know?' And she holds you accountable to get things done . . . in a fun and friendly way. This is a 'must read' to find the message of you."

—Cyndi Maxey, professional speaker, speaker coach, and author *of Fearless Facilitation, Present Like a Pro,* and *Speak Up!*

"Judy's third book is her best yet! I have been a comedian/speaker for three decades, and very successful at what I do, but after reading *The Message of You* I realize that there is room for even more success for myself and just about anyone who truly wants to speak for a living. I recommend this book to everyone—even if you think you really have nothing to say—YES YOU DO! Judy has a way of putting all of us in touch with our true selves, our message, our commitment to life, and to even make money at the same time!"

—Geri Jewell, comic, speaker,
and author of *I'm Walking as Straight as I Can*

"As a producer and writer of many TV comedies, I know how important it is to not only have the jokes, but to have a message from the heart as well. Judy shows you how to do both better than anyone I know."

—Ellen Sandler, former co-executive producer, *Everybody Loves Raymond,* and author of *The TV Writer's Workbook*

"Judy's book is invaluable for anyone who wants to be an expert on TV. As a reality show producer, I'm always looking for people who have a clear message and point of view, and can express themselves succinctly and with humor. Next time anyone asks me how to prepare to get on TV, I'm just going to say, 'Get Judy Carter's book.'"

—Gina Rubinstein, Emmy-winning
writer/producer of reality TV shows

"As a WWE wrestler, I originally contracted Judy to become funnier while cutting promos in the ring. While she was helping me punch up my wrestling promo delivery, something bigger happened: Judy helped me find a message that is very meaningful to me and turn it into a speech called, 'Find Your Strength.' I'm now able to give back to my fans by speaking at schools. With Judy's help, I'm truly making a difference in young people's lives and, along the way, my own."

—John Hennigan, formerly known as
WWE Superstar John Morrison

"Judy Carter's new book is a rock star of the 'How to be a Great Speaker' genre. She offers insights into the foundational practices that make for a great platform presentation. Polishing the nuggets of one's core life experiences is just the starting point of an exceptional and moving speech. Her Seven-Step Method is a road map to speaking success. Read Judy's book and get moving on your speaking career NOW!"   —Jonathan Wygant, CEO of Big Speak Speaker Bureau

"When I first started standup comedy I didn't know what to write about. Thanks to Judy Carter I learned that the best material comes from your personal experiences and what sets you apart. That philosophy has helped me build a successful career as a standup comedian and become a TED speaker. Thank you Judy!"   —Maz Jobrani, comedian and member of the "Axis of Evil" comedy group.

"As someone who has been booking speakers for over twenty-five years, I've seen thousands of speakers and consulted with just as many event planning clients to find the right talent for their events. There are many books on the market geared toward helping people launch a speaking career, improve their presentation skills, etc.—but none go as deep as Judy's book. Judy describes how to turn your life's work and experiences into an inspiring message that can have a positive impact on everyone! That is what speaking is all about— sparking a tangible, real, and potentially life-changing connection with other people; whether the audience is twenty-five or ten thousand. You can be the best presenter in the world, but if you don't have the message and content to touch others, you'll fall flat. Judy helps her readers avoid years of trial and error on the speaking circuit and gets right to the heart of the matter. Earn your Ph.D. in speaking with one simple book. Judy will help you hone your message and craft so that not only will you become a financially successful speaker, but you will also be living your passion with an authentic message for others."   —Mike Frick, president of Speakers.com speakers bureau

"Judy Carter is an expert at connecting to an audience. If you are looking for your message this book will be your guide."
          —Patricia Fripp, past president, National Speakers Association.

"Judy Carter taught me how to *be* the story, rather than to just *tell* a story. Every time I go to a network to pitch a TV show, I remember what I learned from her because when I can make people laugh, they tend to hire me."
          —Rob Lotterstein, TV writer, producer, and creator of *Boy Meets World, Suddenly Susan, Ellen, Will and Grace*, and *The War at Home*.

THE MESSAGE OF YOU

THE MESSAGE OF YOU

TURN YOUR LIFE STORY
INTO A MONEY-MAKING
SPEAKING CAREER

JUDY CARTER

St. Martin's Press ⚏ New York

THE MESSAGE OF YOU:

TURN YOUR LIFE STORY INTO A MONEY-MAKING SPEAKING CAREER.

Copyright © 2013 by Judy Carter. All rights reserved.

Printed in the United States of America.

For information, address St. Martin's Press,

175 Fifth Avenue, New York, N.Y. 10010.

www.stmartins.com

Design by Maura Rosenthal/Mspace

Library of Congress Cataloging-in-Publication Data

Carter, Judy.

The message of you : turn your life story into a money-making speaking career / Judy Carter.—1st U.S. ed.

p. cm.

ISBN 978-1-250-00710-0 (hardcover)

ISBN 978-1-250-02087-1 (e-book)

1. Public speaking.   2. Motivational speakers.   I. Title.

PN4193.B6C37 2013

808.5'1—dc23

2012037792

10   9   8   7   6   5   4   3   2

To my sister, Marsha Carter,
who, in spite of not being able to speak,
was a great communicator

CONTENTS

PART THREE
TAKING YOUR MESSAGE TO THE WORLD

ACKNOWLEDGMENTS

Much gratitude goes out to all the speakers, meeting planners, and speaker agents who shared their expertise for this book. Special thanks to speaker agents Jonathan Wygant of BigSpeak, Inc., Brian Lord of Premiere Speakers Bureau, Kelly MacDonald-Hill of Speakers' Spotlight, Mike Frick of Speaking.com, and Shawn Ellis of The Speakers Group.

Thank you to my speaker buddies at the National Speakers Association who were interviewed for this book, especially Patricia Fripp, whose generosity of spirit shines in everything she does.

Special gratitude to speaker and friend Mimi Donaldson, for contributing all your hard-earned wisdom to this book and my life.

Thank you to the talented Dawn Williams for the nights you stayed up transcribing my sometimes incoherent ramblings as well as making me laugh.

Much gratitude to everyone at Manus Literary and my agent, Penny Nelson, whose talents as a writer, editor, and negotiator made it possible for this book to be in my readers' hands.

Thank you, Daniela Rapp, for your insightful advice, as well as seeing the possibility of this book and making it happen. And thank you, Chuck Adams, for discovering me and seeing that a girl who got a *D* in high school writing could become an author.

Much appreciation to my partner in life, Gina Rubinstein, who talks me off the ledge and protects me from my evil thoughts.

To all my students who fought off fear, dug deep, and got their message out—you inspire me with your courage.

And finally, this book could not have been written without the über talented SJ Hodges. I can't thank you enough for your contribution to this book. You were my strict cheerleader every step of the way, asking the right questions, editing what I wrote, and "midwifing" this book at the same time you were having your own baby. Cecilia, Clayton, and you are a glorious message of love.

INTRODUCTION

This book started off as a traditional speaker's book. You know the kind—how to stand and project your voice, how to memorize a speech, what to do with those nervous hands of yours. But in the process of writing this book and working with my students to fine-tune the exercises, it became something bigger—less about the speaking industry and more about defining the Core Promise of a speech and, even greater, how to find The Message of You.

My Speaking Workshop was formed of an eclectic group of mothers, stand-up comics, nurses, lawyers, and business owners. There were thirty students in all and they plunged in, headfirst, to uncover their Message.

On showcase night I sat and watched as, one by one, each student courageously stood up and told his or her individual truth. Their messages, the Messages of Them, were a powerful wake-up call for the audience. They were *inspired* to respect themselves; to take responsibility for their actions and lives; to believe in themselves; to find courage. They were *taught* how to get rid of clutter, lighten up, and find their own style. And they were *entertained* immensely, from laughter to tears.

But that showcase night didn't just shake the earth underneath the audience; it also rattled the souls of the students. One of them, Naomi Lopez, the mother of a child with behavioral issues, had never spoken in front of people before. Her Message was about her journey with her child, "From Burden to Blessing." She might not have been a "professional" speaker, but when she told her Heart Story there wasn't a dry eye in the house. Afterward, she wrote to me:

> I am proof that *anyone* can do this. I want to spread the message that we parents are not alone. I went from a person who *never* performed or wanted to be in the spotlight, to a person with a message I want to share with whoever will listen to me. Sometimes God has dreams for us that are bigger then we can dream for [ourselves]. This class has been life changing. Thank You.

Within a few days, Naomi booked her first speaking engagement.

Wow. That was my first indication of the life-transforming power of The Message of You. I became even more excited as other students wrote to me of the changes in their lives. Then my own Message shifted. It happened on my birthday—a very special one, because it marked the date that I became older than my mother was when she died early in my life. Living longer than her made me aware of how finite existence is, and how I was now in a "bonus round" that I didn't want to screw up like I had so many other stages of my life. I felt optimistic since I had fallen in love and gotten married a few years before. The security of finally finding a loving life partner freed me emotionally to give more to others. I recommitted my remaining years to making a difference in other people's lives.

I volunteered to give my speech "Laughing Your Way Out of Stress" for the newly wounded soldiers in the spinal injury unit at the VA hospital in Long Beach, California. My student Judy Oliverio is a nurse there and she told me, "The place is so depressing for both the patients and the staff. We all need to be inspired and to laugh." I felt honored to have the chance to speak to these heroes.

Driving to the gig, I panicked. It occurred to me that saying "Hey, just laugh it off!" to a twenty-two-year-old who had just learned he will never walk again might be a bit insensitive. My Message didn't fit and I didn't have another. There was no backup plan. These people were already in pain. I didn't want to make their lives more miserable by literally adding insult to injury.

When I got to the hospital, I saw they had decorated a large multipurpose room with the banner "Laughter is the Best Medicine with Judy Carter." The colorful party balloons strung throughout underscored the bleak mood. On one side of the room, people were sitting in chairs and staring blankly at the floor, looking depressed and tired—and that was the staff. On the other side of the large room, looking like members of a rival gang, were spinal cord injury patients, many of whom were attached to ventilators. They were mostly young men. There were also some burn victims, wrapped from head to toe in yellow Lady Gaga–like gowns.

I was introduced to Nick Mendes, a soldier who was paralyzed from the neck down in an IED explosion in Afghanistan. He whispered "Hi" as the machines pushed air in and out of his lungs. His father, Dave Mendes, who had moved into the hospital to be near his son, took me aside and said, "I'm glad you're here because Nick has stopped doing his physical therapy. He's falling into a depression. The nurses tell me that if he doesn't do his therapy, he could die." Nick was twenty-two years old.

My speech seemed more and more pathetic and anemic to me. My mind was scrambling to come up with an approach, a great joke, or a story, that would make them feel that I understood, but nothing came to mind. I was out of my league. How could I ever, ever understand their pain? What could I possible say to alleviate their fear? "Hey, lighten up!" wasn't going to cut it.

The VP of HR got up and read my introduction. It was too late to leave. I had to go on.

I walked to the center of the room with nothing in my head. I took a breath. It was quiet. All I could hear were the ventilators breathing for the soldiers who could no longer even breathe on their own. I opened my mouth to speak, and to my utter surprise a story I had never told came out of me. I didn't think; the words just came. It was as if I was taken over by a Message that I had never written, that I had never told, but it was a Message that I had lived and a Message that had been inside me, waiting to be expressed.

I told them that my older sister, Marsha, was a quadriplegic from birth. After my parents died, I found a six-person group home for

Marsha, where she had professional nursing care as well as classes and weekend outings. She lived there until she died a few years ago, in her late fifties. When I arrived at her funeral, I was shocked. I expected to see a few people, but there were over a hundred mourners. People I didn't even know—her teachers throughout the years, her nurses, her caretakers, her friends. Then, one attendee after the next spoke about how my sister gave meaning to their lives. Story after story was told about my sister's humor, her warmth, her love of dirty jokes. There were people there who spent their holidays with my sister rather than with their own families. I had no idea. My sister Marsha—who couldn't talk or walk, who was fed by a tube in her stomach and solely communicated with facial expressions and gestures—had the ability to turn strangers into friends. She had the ability to make a difference in other people's lives.

As I told this story, I felt the mood in the VA hospital change. Everyone was feeling the same pain, yet it was better because we were all feeling it together—both staff and patients. I went on to share my Eureka Moment about my sister. I realized that, even in her limited capacity, she gave more to others than many of us who are fully functional. Her life stood for the message of caring—giving others the gift to be a better person. To be their best self. Marsha gave other people meaning in their lives because she enabled them to become better than they had imagined possible.

Then my Message came out of my mouth. It was something I had never consciously thought of before, never had put into words until that moment. I walked over to Nick's bedside. I held his hand, put my face very close to his, and told him, "All our lives have purpose. We might not know what it is, but you must believe that you do have a purpose. You can inspire others. You can help others. That's why you must get well—your life has meaning." I realized that I was the vehicle, a transmitter for the Message, and the Message was bigger than me. I then started delivering my comedy material and, having developed trust, they started laughing. Or rather, laughter exploded out of them, as it does from people who haven't laughed in a long time.

I started my career as a stand-up comic because I wanted laughs, I wanted love, and I wanted attention. But through teaching others to find their message—the Message of You—I found how much better it feels not to be "wanting" but "giving." There is no greater feeling in the world than to know you've made a difference in someone else's life.

A year later, I wanted to check in and see how Nick was doing. He'd been discharged and was living on base at Fort MacArthur, San Pedro, with his father and a caretaker. He was breathing on his own. He was sitting up straight. He was wheeling around in his mouth-operated electric chair with plenty of attitude. As he worked with his therapist to regain movement in his arms, he was cracking colorful jokes. I'd repeat them here, but then this book would be banned from schools. As I laughed and blushed, Nick told me he realized from my speech that "if you're not laughing, then you're not living."

After one of his therapy sessions at the VA hospital, we spent some private time together and he told me, "When I was first injured, a doctor told me I would never walk, that I would never move, that I would never be able to do anything. He was an A-hole."

Then Nick told me that he wanted to write a book. I asked him what his Message was and he told me, "I never truly appreciated the power of family. Without my family, I would be lost." Then this very young man looked directly into my eyes and said with the wisdom of a sage, "See, Judy, you and your body can do more than you think, more than you can imagine. I've learned never to quit. Never give up." Nick is now devoted to his physical therapy, as he wants to regain use of his hands so he can give that doctor the finger. A noble goal. A succinct message. To have been a part of Nick's journey has been a humbling and inspiring honor for me.

I'm looking forward to being part of your journey as well. The Message of Me is helping you to find The Message of You and I know, together, we can make a difference.

Hopefully, it would have made my sister and mother proud.

PART ONE

DISCOVER THE MESSAGE OF YOU

CHAPTER ONE

YOU ARE THE MESSAGE

Okay, I'm going to say something shocking. Ready?

Your greatest speech has already been delivered in front of a live audience.

And that speech was delivered masterfully and powerfully by you.

You may be staring at this and wondering how you missed this great moment, or thinking I've lost my mind. Hold on one second and think about what I've just said:

Your greatest speech already exists, even though you don't know it.

It's in the advice you give to your friends; in the lessons you teach your children; in the stories you tell your family. You've given parts of your speech when you helped your sister build her Web site, or when you shared the story of your immigrant grandparents' journey to America. The Message of You speech has expressed itself in the volunteer work you do, the way you run your business, the way you just know which color suits you, and which doesn't. It's in the stories you share that inspire others to tell the truth, conquer their fears, and lead happier, healthier, and wealthier lives. Your greatest speech is in the stories you tell every day because at the core of those stories is The Message of You.

The Message of You is a distillation of all of your experiences, both personal and professional, that have formed the narrative or meaning of your life. The wrinkle is, The Message of You is usually not obvious. Most of the time, the meaning of our lives is invisible to us. We can't be objective about our own journey. We can't see how our life influences others. We are so busy living we don't take note of the steps we took to find success. Yet, these are the very things that make people want to listen and know more about us. The good news is, not only can you discover The Message of You, but you can also develop it to inspire audiences, enhance your current profession, and launch a successful money-making career as a professional speaker.

I can prove it.

Chastity Davis had a problem. It all started with a simple dinner in Vancouver, Canada. Chastity Davis, BC Hydro's marketing manager joined her boss for a quick meal after work to talk about their upcoming convention. After a second round of drinks had been ordered, Chastity relaxed and opened up, sharing stories from her childhood. Chastity was a member of the Tla'amin Nation, one of the indigenous tribes of Canada. As she spoke about her passion for healing the earth and the words of wisdom she'd inherited from her ancestors, her boss looked her straight in the eye and said, "This is exactly what our convention attendees need to get inspired—you! I want you to be our closing keynote speaker."

Chastity's first thought was, "Absolutely not!" After all, it was one thing to share the dramatic and highly personal tales of the abuses suffered by her parents over dinner with her boss. It was quite another thing to stand on stage in front of five hundred of her colleagues and share those same intimate details. Chastity shook her head no, but her boss was persistent. "Chastity, it's only thirty minutes and all you have to do is just tell your story. Your message is exactly what everyone needs to hear. You'll be great."

Maybe it was the feeling that she could really make a difference in the world, or maybe it was that second glass of wine, but Chastity said yes. Then she did what all speakers, professional and amateur, do: she procrastinated.

One week before she was scheduled to step on stage, she realized she'd better write something to say—and quick! She sat down with her laptop and started writing. She wrote about her life, her parents, and the history of her people. Hours passed and, exhausted, Chastity gave up. She now had twenty pages of single-spaced, disconnected anecdotes and passionate pleas that read more like a manifesto than a coherent speech. She absolutely could not get up on a stage and read from it. What was she going to do?

It sounded so simple when her boss said, "Just tell your story." But what did that mean, exactly? Which story should she tell? The horror story about her mother's childhood when she was forced to attend Government Residential Schools on a reservation? Her family's battle with alcoholism? Her work with the First Nation families? How about her turbulent dating life? Or should she just focus on the warm and fuzzy stories of living with her grandparents? Her boss had said, "You have a great message." What did that mean? What was the message that her boss heard in her stories? More important, why would anyone really care?

Making things even more difficult was the fact that her audience expected her to speak about environmental issues. Chastity was scheduled as the closing keynote speaker for BP Hydro's annual convention, the topic this year being "The Green Initiative." She would be speaking in front of an audience full of volunteers from various departments, just like herself, who had committed to making their company more sensitive to the environment and more sustainable. Chastity's boss was, in fact, one of the co-chairs of the volunteer program, which was suffering through rough times. Volunteers were overwhelmed with the day-to-day responsibilities of their jobs. They didn't have time to fulfill their volunteer commitment. Goals hadn't been reached and the initial exuberance had all but shriveled up and died. How could her personal life story inspire others, and what in the world did it have to do with sustainability?

Chastity suddenly felt the full weight of this burden on her shoulders. Somehow, she had to convince a room full of stressed, fatigued, and already overworked volunteers to add even *more* work—without pay—to their hectic schedules. Who was she to show such bravado? She'd never been on television. She wasn't a best-selling author. Her life was far from perfect. She wasn't at her goal weight, she'd dated a few wackos, and all of her clothes were from Ross Dress for Less. She didn't consider herself to be charismatic, funny, or gorgeous, and the vast majority of her colleagues in the audience came from very different backgrounds. Would they relate to her experience as a Native Canadian? Even if they did, how would it inspire them to strive for sustainability and give up their scarce free time to help the Earth? Chastity felt defeated. She had but one thought: "Get me out of this." Unfortunately, it was too late to find another keynote speaker for the convention. Chastity was stuck and freaking out. She hopped online, found my Web site, and a few days before her keynote address we sat down via Skype to craft her speech.

Chastity's stories were dramatic and interesting, but they had no frame or context and offered no solution to a problem. Her speech lacked a Core Promise, and Chastity was unclear about the larger message she wanted to convey, what I call The Message of You. She just needed a process, a structure, and a framework in which to discover and write these two important components. We weren't starting from scratch—Chastity already had her topic and she knew her audience personally. As we examined her life, her message took shape. Chastity spoke about the time her alcoholic mother threw her out of the house when she was only seven years old. Seven years old and left to fend on her own! Revealing that story, Chastity found her Message, one handed down from her ancestors and a legacy of familial abuse. It was a Message that declared: no matter who we are, no matter how frightened we are, no matter how small and weak we feel, we can *step into our power* and succeed against seemingly insurmountable obstacles. Chastity stood on that stage, looked the volunteers in the audience square in the eye, and said, "If I can do it at seven years old, we can do it now. For the sake of my mother, for our people, for our children."

The results? She got a standing ovation with people wiping their eyes. Her message hit home and revived the volunteer program. Three managers from other departments asked her to present to the other divisions of BC Hydro and within one month of her talk, Chastity was officially asked by BC Hydro to spearhead their diversity training. She was just named Vice President of the BC Aboriginal Women's Leadership Association and she is now paid to speak across Canada on the role of women in leadership. Chastity then started her own business, working with the native community on leadership and sustainability and inspiring Native Canadians to "Step into Their Own Power," to get healthy, get educated, and start businesses. Sometimes, she still freaks out, but knowing the importance of her message gets her over her fears.

That's the power of The Message of You.

I could relate to Chastity's journey because, just like Chastity, my career as a professional speaker also began as a fluke. I was a high school teacher and I was *terrible* at it. I was fired after my second year in the classroom. Apparently, being the class clown is no more acceptable for a teacher than it is for a student. But as they say, when one door closes another opens. Getting fired freed me to pursue my real dream. I had been doing magic shows since I was eight years old and had always wanted to be a professional magician. So, at twenty-four years old, I took my comedy magic act on the road.

Traveling was a huge pain. My magic act had a lot of heavy props. I was lugging around a Black & Decker saw to cut men in half plus a whole assortment of props to accomplish such feats as my death-defying escape from my grandmother's girdle. Hey, it's a living. I was successful, touring the country, but it all came to a grinding halt when United Airlines lost my luggage and I had to go on *without* my props. No props meant no magic tricks. I had to stand onstage, just me, and so I told jokes. Unbelievably, I was a hit. Thanks to United, from that night on, I became a comic—with a carry-on.

I continued my career as a comic, headlining at comedy clubs all across the country and playing Vegas and Atlantic City, opening for some really cool people like Prince. I did hundreds of television appearances and by any measure, my career in stand-up was a success. So why wasn't I happy? Well, it wasn't very glamorous—getting heckled by drunks, staying in cheap motels, and dealing with crooked club owners. Life on the road can be a lonely life. If I had known then what I know now about the speaking profession, I would have spared myself the trials and tribulations of being a road comic.

I can tell you the exact moment I decided to quit stand-up. I was in New York and Walter, my miniature schnauzer, had been mugged.

That's right. My *dog* had been mugged, not me, and I had to run the poor thing to an emergency clinic right before I was supposed to go on-stage in Long Island. I was in no mood to be funny and I was late. I got to the club and it became clear, instantly, that God had tilted the world on its side and all the scumbags had trickled into this particular corner of the universe. They were drunk. They were mean. And before I even stepped foot on the stage, they were heckling me. I hadn't even said a word yet. I pushed through part of my routine and I had a joke that started with the line, "I worry about getting old . . ." and some guy in the front row snorted sarcastically and yelled, "*Getting* old?!"—insinuating that I was already well past my prime. (I was in my early thirties, by the way.) I don't know what happened but something in me broke open at that moment. I stopped and stood perfectly still. It hit me so clearly. Here I was standing in front of a bunch of drunks trying to make them laugh, just as I did as a kid in my own family. It was a Eureka Moment where ha-ha turned into a-ha. I was totally done. I walked off stage, picked up my dog, and went home to figure out what I would do next.

I formed a company called Comedy Workshops, and started teaching standup comedy. I wrote two books, *Standup Comedy: The Book* and *The Comedy Bible* to help aspiring comics craft their material and take it on the road. Oprah Winfrey booked me for her show and I became known as the comedy guru, the go-to gal for launching the careers of America's top comics. I got so much press that thousands of students lined up to study with me via my Los Angeles workshops as well as via online classes, teleseminars, and international classes in Canada, Russia, Sweden, Australia, and Germany. Things were going well, and I was paying the bills . . . but I missed performing.

About that time, a friend asked me to speak at her company's annual conference, The Produce and Fruit Association—ah the prestige! But all of a sudden, for one gig, *one* gig, I was getting paid *ten* times as much as I'd made doing nine gigs a week in a comedy club. Here's the weird part: I didn't have to do my act. They paid me to talk about comedy as a topic. I didn't even know what that meant so I just made something up. I created kind of a mash-up from my experiences of teaching comedy and added a few bits from my act. It was very uneven and awkward, but the audience seemed to enjoy it. Even though I had to share the stage with a dancing avocado, nobody threw anything at my head and at the end of the talk they handed me a big check. After it was over, all I could think was, "Speaking for a living rocks! How do I do this full time?"

I started researching the speaking business and found there were a lot more speaking gigs available than comedy gigs. Every day, in every city, there are hundreds of meetings and they all need speakers. There were also a lot of perks. Speakers are paid more than comics, they have a full hour to perform in front of sober and appreciative audiences, and best of all, as a speaker I didn't have to be the "hot, new, up-and-coming young talent" forever. In fact, in the speaking profession, experience, age, and wisdom are actually considered assets and not liabilities.

I joined the National Speakers Association where I met speakers who were making six figures every year. Many of these successful speakers had never been on TV, had never been asked for an autograph, and weren't entertainers, but not only did they have vibrant careers they were really making a difference in people's lives. I wanted what they had. I became obsessed with finding out the secret to their success. It didn't take long to figure it out. Even though I had been on hundreds of TV shows and had been nominated for Atlantic City Entertainer of the Year, these speakers had something I didn't: a message.

Ask any professional speaker, "What do you speak about?" and they can summarize, in a concise two-sentence phrase, their brand, their Message of You, the message of their lives. Even the "survivor" speakers, the ones who rely heavily on incredible life-and-death stories, still have a message to impart to their audiences. The same was true for the more technical speakers who gave informational-type talks on taxes, finance, and computer programming. Even they included a motivational message along with their facts and figures. No matter the speaker or the topic, everyone had one thing in common: they all included a message that was designed to inspire an audience to make tomorrow a better day than today.

As a stand-up comic, message didn't matter. My act was a series of disconnected jokes about everything—dieting, pets, relationships, and politics, whatever was on my mind. I had tons of material but no message, and I had no idea how to find one. I read every book on public speaking and the speaking industry I could find. I learned a great deal about marketing and how to keep my hands from flailing about, but there was no book on how to find a message or even how to write a speech! I learned about BOR (back of room) sales, how to have a dazzling Web site, and how to negotiate a contract even if I was a dummy. Where was the book that could help me find my message?

It didn't exist.

I realized I was going to have to figure this out myself. Stumbling through self-doubt and fear, I took classes; I watched other speakers and I began to recognize a pattern. The professional speakers that were most successful were able to convey their message because they were considered experts in their field. From accountants to cancer survivors, salesmen to system analysts, athletes to astronauts, they had examined their own success (and failures) to develop their own step-by-step methodology that could help others be just as successful.

I asked myself, "How am I an expert?" and looked at my career as a magician, comic, and teacher. I examined my life story of growing up with a severely disabled sister in a family where Daddy getting angry was as scary as an L.A. earthquake. It took a lot of work, but I finally found the Message of Me. Underneath my stories was a larger message about the transformational power of humor. My Message of Me was right under my nose the whole time, but I was too close to see it. I had the ruby slippers all along. My Message of Me combined all the elements of my life. When I was a teacher, I used humor to help my students learn. With my disabled sister Marsha, making her laugh created many moments of happiness in her otherwise tragic life. At the dinner table, laughter could ease tense situations and diffuse conflict. Playing a comedy gig in Vegas, I could wake up a dead audience. Teaching standup comedy, I helped so many of my students overcome the tragedies in their lives by turning their problems into punch lines. I knew how to teach the principles of comedy to standup students but now I realized comedy wasn't just for showbiz types. I saw humor as a life-and-business tool that could be used to decrease stress, resolve conflict, and improve health in the workplace. I had my Message of Me! Woo-Hoo!

I honed my speech by speaking for free at charity events, Chambers of Commerce, hospitals, churches; basically, any organization within thirty miles of my house got a call. At first, I sucked (note to self: don't say "suck" at a corporate gig) and it took me years to figure out how to frame my message to truly motivate and transform others. I had to find stories that were not only funny and entertaining, but also revealing, and supported my message. After much trial and error, (note to self: do *not* mention "nipples" at a business meeting) I became an in-demand speaker, presenting for Fortune 500 companies, traveling the world, sharing the stage with President Clinton and other high-profile speakers, flying on private jets, and speaking in front of some of the most powerful movers and shakers in the world. Along the way, I learned how to market myself, get agents interested, find gigs, create BOR sales, and brand myself as an expert.

When Chastity called me for help, it made me realize that someone needed to write the book you are reading. As I crisscrossed the world for my speaking engagements, more and more people told me their stories: of dreams fulfilled, passions unearthed, and funny, dramatic, and even tragic parts of their lives. It was clear that all of them wanted to be heard, and that many of their stories were absolutely fascinating. (OK, a few of them.) But I tuned my ears to hear something underneath their stories—their messages. Messages that not only entertained but had the potential to make dramatic differences in other people's lives. By helping people stand up in front of others and transform their messages into well crafted speeches, I felt that I too might contribute, in some small way, to the betterment of our world. By helping Chastity write a genuinely moving speech to inspire hundreds of Canadian volunteers, I might actually be helping the environmental movement become more than just recycling!

It was an amazing thought, and it's the reason I wrote this book. I'm here to tell you that your life has meaning, your stories can inspire, and your message can heal. Your TED—Technology, Entertainment, and Design—talk (see chapter two for more information) is already inside of you.

Sound naive? Too idealistic? In my twenty-five years on the

speaking circuit and coaching other speakers, I've seen it happen over and over again. A person who feels they are "nobody" steps up, tells their story, and discovers that they truly are "somebody" in this world. I see the surprise on their face when people in the audience line up to hug them and tell them that their stories made a difference in their lives. Unfortunately, most people don't know where to begin. Amateur speakers usually will tell their story in chronological order, as a list of "this happened, then this happened, and then this happened." That is more of an exercise in narcissism than an effective speech.

Mind you, I didn't find my Message of Me when I was giving my first speech. After much trial and error, I branded myself as a stress-reduction speaker who showed corporate America how to use comedy skills to relieve stress. In order to find my Message of Me, I had to examine my own journey, identify my life lessons, my professional credentials, as well as what Bookable Topics corporate America would be interested in hearing about. The combination of those elements created The Message of Me. I then used that information to create the Core Promise for each of my speeches, to develop my methodology (my Action Steps), and to choose my Heart Story. This book will walk *you* through that identical process, saving you the painful trial and error of flopping in front of a live audience. . . .

WAIT, WHAT PROCESS EXACTLY?

So, now you're going to ask me . . .

> But Judy, how do I identify which of my stories is my Heart Story? What are Action Steps? How can I possibly boil down the experiences of my life into one message, one Core Promise? And what the heck is a Core Promise anyway? And what does all this have to do with the speech I have to give to a room full of nurses (or executives or socialites or new parents or drug addicts) next month? *HELP!*

Okay, take a breath and let's start at the beginning. Let me give you an overview of my process. I'm going to try not to throw too much at you at once. If you just go through the chapters one by one and do all the exercises, you will succeed in finding your message, creating your speech, getting bookings, and making a difference.

HOW TO USE THIS BOOK

Part One of this book will help you to identify The Message of You. This is the foundation of your speech, your marketing materials, and even all your Tweets. You'll find it by combining different components of your experience: your life lessons, your professional expertise with the Bookable Topics of the speaker marketplace. With explanations and exercises, I will lead you by the hand and assist you to clarify your speaking goals, mine your professional experiences for expert credentials, scan your personal life for the tragedies and triumphs that shaped your outlook on life, identify your own methodology for success, stop procrastinating, and discover a bookable, marketable Message of You. And hey, even if you have no interest in pursuing a career as a professional speaker, you can still benefit from incorporating your Message of You into your work presentations or even social situations like a toast at a wedding or speaking during your child's Career Day. If this is the case, I'd encourage you to focus solely on Part One and Part Two of this book. You can skip the business primer in Part Three.

Part Two of this book will walk you through my Six-Step Method to Create Your Speech, with a final chapter that will guide you through a Carter Comedy Pass that is sure to keep your audience laughing. You'll learn how to write a great opening that will make the audience love you within sixty seconds, keep an audience engaged by talking about their problems, brag about yourself without isolating your audience, inspire your audience to take concrete Action Steps, share your Heart Story to create meaning, and bring the audience to their feet with an interactive Call to Action.

Part Three will show you performing and memorizing techniques so you can avoid flop sweat and other disasters, as well as showing you how to gather together the materials you need to successfully market your talk, write and negotiate contracts, and turn free gigs into paying gigs. If your goal is to become a paid, professional speaker, then make sure you don't skip any of the exercises in Part Three.

WHAT YOU'LL NEED TO MASTER THIS PROCESS

A Support System

It's important to work with a Buddy who will act as your audience, supplying feedback, writing material, and giving you support when you want to quit. Don't underestimate how powerful fear is. If you are like most people, you will hit points where you are stuck, confused, and just stop the process. Having regularly scheduled meetings with a Buddy will help both of you navigate your way to a speaking career. Many speakers form "Master Mind Groups" that meet at least once a month to help them develop, hone, and market their speaking skills. Or ask a friend, someone you feel comfortable sharing your thoughts with, to act as your sounding board. The best Speaker Buddies are people who make you feel smart and funny when you're around them.

Don't make excuses. Hook up with a Speaker Buddy right now. Being in the same location is no longer necessary as working via Skype works just as well. Matter of fact, me being a Jewish yenta, let me fix you up with someone. Visit MySpeakerBuddy.com to hook up with someone who can be there for you.

A Recording Device

Ideas don't necessarily happen when you want them to. They happen in life—at a party, during a business meeting, in bed. Come on, you can have sex anytime, but ideas need to be recorded whenever they happen, otherwise they will vanish. I use my iPhone to forever preserve my ramblings but you can use a digital voice recorder, an old tape recorder, a notepad, or a cocktail napkin. If you are like me and can't stand listening to your voice, go to TheMessageOfYou.com/services, where you will find a list of inexpensive services that will transcribe your audio notes and e-mail them to you.

A Notebook

In order to find The Message of You, we are going to do a lot of writing. The journey to find The Message of You is not a direct route. It would be great if I just asked you a few questions and . . . jackpot! The three cherries line up and out comes your winning Message of You. It takes a lot of writing to find the kernels of truth that will develop into your speech. In writing this book, there are hundreds of trees that had to be cut down to supply all the pages that nobody will ever see. Every writer knows that writing is a hit-and-miss process, but it would be a good idea to have a place to store all your ideas as they come to you, either a physical one, or a folder on your computer.

A Commitment

I'm sure that there are many things in your life that you've tried and when it got hard, you stopped. I would like to help you commit to this process of finding and putting together your speech, and not be like me on my diet program—which I always start with enthusiastic intent that ends three days later with a plate of pasta primavera.

I have no doubt there will be times in this process where you will want to quit. I'll be asking you to remember a story, and perhaps you won't be able to think of a thing. Here's the thing: creativity doesn't always happen on our time schedule. If you commit to this journey, you might find your Message of You sneaks up on you. You may be frustrated with an exercise in this book but then two days later, the dry cleaner says something that shakes loose a memory and suddenly your whole speech comes together. It's about staying open to the process. Commit yourself to staying open. If you quit, you'll never find that a-ha moment. There's a reason you picked up this book in the first place. Honor that intention.

COMMITMENT PLEDGE

I commit to the following:

1. I will read the whole book by_____. (date)

2. I'll complete all the exercises in this book (*even if I don't do them well*) by _____. (date)

3. When I get scared or find myself procrastinating, I will call _____. (name of buddy)

4. I will not stop until I've _____. (name your ultimate goal)

e-mail to: commitment@TheMessageOfYou.com

In my stand-up and speaking classes it's not always the talented ones who end up with major careers, it's the ones who never gave up. I just hate it when people quit. I think that if they stayed in the process one more week, one more day, one more hour, they could have succeeded.

Sharing your commitment with someone will help you stay accountable, so commit to me. The Message of Me is me helping you find The Message of You. Shoot me an e-mail at commitment@TheMessageOfYou.com and let me know that you are committing to this process. Let me know what kind of speaker you are, or, what kind of speaker you would like to become. If you're not sure how to answer those questions, keep reading for some guidance. Set some dates for yourself. Pick a date when you will finish Part One of this book. Then set another date to finish Part Two. Do not spend longer than one month on each part or you will lose your momentum. Shoot me an e-mail when you discover your Core Promise. Shoot me another when you give your first speech. I will follow your journey and send you encouragement throughout our process. Hey, some call it codependency. I choose to call it helpful.

Remember, Chastity had one week to write her speech! Just imagine what you can do with a lot more time to do the work. Are you going to have to get personal? Yes. Are you going to have to dig a bit to get to the juicy stuff? You better believe it. But don't worry. The Message of You is more than a book, it's a community and a movement. Come take this journey with me. Speak your message and change lives—including your own.

CHAPTER ONE CHECKLIST:

☐ Got a buddy (MySpeakerBuddy.com).

☐ Gathered my supplies (notebook or laptop and recorder).

☐ E-mailed Judy my commitment pledge.
(commitment@TheMessageOfYou.com)

☐ Set a date to finish Part One.

☐ Set a date to finish Part Two.

CHAPTER TWO

COMMIT TO THE BASICS

Congrats! You've just committed to being a part of a great industry called the professional speaking business. Welcome! If you're just starting out, you might not know anything about the business of speaking. After all, becoming a professional speaker wasn't exactly a choice on Career Day at my high school. As a matter of fact, when I tell people I speak for a living, they look at me in astonishment and ask, "You actually get paid to do that?"

Getting paid to share The Message of You takes a basic understanding of the industry itself and where you might fit. No worries. You won't have to learn a totally different language of acronyms, or master any technical procedures, or sign up for drug testing. You just need to establish your speaking goal and have a working grasp of some basic terms to get started.

YOUR SPEAKING GOALS

Each person reading this book has a different agenda. Some of you already have a speech and you want to make it funnier. Some of you are funny and you're looking for the message behind your jokes. Some of you make your living as an actor or a singer and you're looking for new performance opportunities. Some of you have an urgent message you want to share with the world. Some of you are absolutely terrified to step onstage.

It's important to me that every person reading this book is successful, because if I can help you to inspire others; if I can help you write a funnier speech; if I can help you make a living doing something you love doing, then I've made the world a little bit funnier, a little less boring, and a little more hopeful. Not that I hold myself to impossible standards or anything . . .

Read through these descriptions of speaker categories and figure out where you fit. Then, I'm going to ask you to evaluate your current speaking goals and, most important, to make a commitment to finish your speech and to present it in front of a live audience. You can do this. No sweat. Sooooooo . . . here we go.

The Pros

If you fall into this category, you probably already have a working speech that you use and that serves you well. But even established pros are anxious to take their careers to the next level. Your challenge will be to try something different, such as adding more humor, more personal stories, or uncovering a new message and writing a speech on a completely different topic.

THE PROS

The National Speakers' Association has 5,000 members across thirty-six local chapters.

The demographic of professional speakers is relatively gender-neutral with men at 53 percent and women at 47 percent and the majority between the ages of forty-six and fifty-five.

On the whole, they are an educated bunch with 35 percent holding Masters Degrees and another 14 percent with doctorates.

In the next ten years, the NSA expects their membership to increase by 20 percent, meaning that for aspiring Pros out there, the speaking circuit is expanding to include you!

One of the biggest problems Pro speakers have is that they ride the coattails of a speech they wrote fifteen years ago. Can you say, *stale!* "Hey, Neil Armstrong! It's been a long time since you walked on the moon. How about a couple of different stories?" All right, that *was* a big deal and we all want to hear that story, but if you're still relating anecdotes about meeting Nixon, it's time to update your material. In these times, it's not enough to have one speech. If you want to be rebooked for the same company or next year's convention, you've got to have a new speech every year!

I've worked with past presidents of the National Speakers' Association to help them write their new speeches and it doesn't matter how many times they've stepped onstage, the minute they see that blank page in front of them, they are reduced to a puddle of fear and anxiety. Actually, I have found that the more successful a speaker is, the harder it is to try something new. It doesn't matter if you've been at it for years, when you're working on a brand-new speech, you feel like a Novice. You have no idea where to start and you often find yourself in those well-worn ruts you've used to travel all this time. To get out of those ruts, I suggest you focus on chapter three, where I show you how to "CSI" your life lessons for the message of your new speech. (For you overseas readers: "CSI" is an acronym made popular from a TV show where Crime Scene Investigators look at the small details of an event to find its meaning. I've taken artistic license and I'm using it as a verb.)

Even if you don't want to write a new speech, examining your current speech with a fresh eye can turn a good speech into a great one, and make the difference between charging $1,500 per appearance or $25,000 just to show up. The main component you might be lacking? *Funny.* You need to add a heaping dose of funny to your material and you need to make sure the humor is consistently present throughout your speech. I've seen speakers open with a funny story but once they get to content, things get serious and it's a long ride to the next laugh.

As a matter of fact, the funnier you are, the more effective your speech will be. Studies have shown that when material is presented with humor, it raises the retention rates. It's no wonder that politicians, marketing executives, and copywriters all use comedy writers to "punch up" their material because humor makes audiences take notice and retain information. So follow along to uncover or maybe rediscover The Message of You and in Part Two, chapter fifteen, even if you are a tax attorney I will show you how to keep the audience laughing throughout your entire speech.

The Techies

There are a whole slew of Techie speakers who have extraordinarily specific and technical expertise in their fields. You are the beta-testers and the first adapters. In fact, if you are a Techie reading this book, you probably downloaded it in digital format. (If it's not a legal download, I'm coming with handcuffs, and, no, you won't enjoy it.)

BREAK OUT OF THE BREAKOUT SESSIONS!

Very often Techies get stuck as lower paid breakout session speakers.

"How to" breakout sessions are the workshops that are offered during a convention and attendance is optional. The audiences are smaller but usually more attentive and the pay is much, much lower than a general session with a keynoter, which is usually "mandatory" for the entire audience.

For Techies to become a keynoter, I recommend really paying attention in chapter three, where I will ask you to go beyond the "data" that you know, and travel to a distant universe where few Techies have gone—your emotions and passions, and revealing a little about your life.

And I'm not talking about the emotional experience of accidentally dropping your iPhone in the toilet.

You can be a financial adviser, a social media expert, a software engineer, or an actuary. You are what I call "pure content speakers" or Techies. Without stepping on your toes, some of your presentations, while important and much in demand, can also be absolutely painful to sit through. Come on! You know what I'm talking about. You've been trapped in a folding chair listening as your company sales director plodded through a humorless PowerPoint with two hours of slides filled with mind-numbing charts and graphs. Even if the topic was relevant to your job and informative, by the time all was said and done you'd turned into a zombie drained of your life force.

If you are currently working as a content speaker, or aspire to make your break in business and/or technical speaking, I don't mean to discourage you; in fact, I'm here to encourage you. Content doesn't have to be boring. It doesn't have to be pure facts and figures. Most content speakers usually focus 80 percent of their speech on their expertise instead of sharing the lessons learned from their personal life and relating those lessons back to the technical content.

MAKING YOUR MESSAGE STICK

"You can't just have a lot of mind-numbing numbers in your speech. If people don't remember what you say, you might as well not say it. By including personal stories, you can make your message stick."

—Brian Lord, speaker agent,
VP of Premiere Speakers Bureau

CASE STUDY
PHILIPPA GAMSE, SPEAKER AND AUTHOR OF
42 RULES FOR A WEB PRESENCE THAT WINS

"My area of expertise is Web and social media strategy, and I never expected to hear anyone say, 'You changed my life!'

"But it happened: people in my audiences have said that I've changed their lives because I've changed how they think about their approach to their online presence. They behave differently and see great results.

"This has led me to conclude that *all* speakers are motivational speakers. We're all hoping to influence our audiences to think, feel, or act differently in some regard."

Take, for example, my client, Becky Buckley, who is a Certified Financial Planner®. She came to see me because she wanted to grow her business by speaking to women's groups. Her presentations were full of all kinds of helpful numbers and lists, but they were easily dismissed as boring, "death by PowerPoint" financial talks. It wasn't until she dug into her own personal experiences that her speech really came to life. Becky had been deeply touched by working with one particular client, a newly widowed woman who didn't even know the passwords to her husband's bank accounts. The widow was on the verge of becoming homeless, and Becky had to become more than just her accountant. Becky became her lifeline, and through their friendship, her client prospered. More important, Becky realized that there was a real need among women to take better control of their finances. As I pushed her to tell me more, it became very clear that Becky didn't just want more clients; she wanted to make a difference in the lives of women. She had a mission, a message she wanted to impart. She wanted to empower women but she wasn't going to do it with charts and graphs. She had to dig deep, put herself out there, and tell her Heart Story: the story of how her unlikely friendship with the widow enriched both of their lives and launched her new career. It's a speech that not only gets her standing ovations, but now she's got more clients than she can handle. Becky is well on her way to becoming the next Suze Orman.

Just like Becky, each and every one of us has a gift to give: the story of our lives. Chapter thirteen will assist you to find that perfect personal story that drives home your message, turning facts and figures into memorable moments. Helping your audience connect to the facts and figures using personal stories, experiences and humor can turn a twice-a-year technical presentation into an in-demand hot topic for the speaking circuit, and bump a Techie up to a Pro.

The Entertainers

There is a major problem happening for performers and I call it the phenomena of "Bringer Shows" where a comic or singer or performer must not only produce their own show, but they have to guarantee a certain number of paying audience members before they are even allowed to perform. In two words, that sucks.

The speaking profession is a way for comics, actors, dancers, mimes, jugglers, singers, and storytellers to get off the couch, stop waiting for the phone to ring, and step in front of an appreciative audience for a full hour, in front of a sold-out house with no hecklers—and you don't have to produce the show! The only thing you have to bring is a great speech with an appealing message.

CASE STUDY
LOLA GILLEBAARD, SPEAKER AND HUMORIST

The entertainment industry might be notorious for ageism, but the speaking industry actually *wants* you to look, act, and be older!

Humorist Lola Gillebaard gets speaking gigs and she's in her eighties! When was the last time you saw an eighty-year-old female comic with her own special on Comedy Central? Ah...Never.

Mike Rayburn had a successful comedy guitar act, even playing Carnegie Hall, but he wanted to do more than make people laugh. He wanted to change people's lives. After years of trial and error, he found his message about showing people to not be stopped by their own limitations. In his speech he comes on with his guitar, but then his music and humor become the vehicle to communicate his message. He illustrates his points with his guitar.

"As a speaker, I wanted the audience to walk away laughing and loving the message." The results? In 2011, Mike was inaugurated into the National Speakers' Association's Hall of Fame and is one of America's top keynote speakers.

Many of you Entertainers have probably performed at corporate gigs, usually doing your act after an awards dinner, or emceeing a sales convention, or singing after a lunch. Actually, corporate gigs are where most celebrity comics make the bulk of their income. In Jerry Seinfeld's documentary, *Comedians*, Jay Leno makes a point to say that he doesn't spend a dime of his *Tonight Show* money, but lives nicely on his speaking engagements and live shows. Leno's current fee is $160,000 for a corporate event.

> ### CASE STUDY
> #### FROM STAND-UP TO SPEAKING
>
> "After I performed my speech for the first time, a woman from the audience hugged me and said, 'Thank you for your message.' I had touched her and that is way more gratifying than the free hot wings offered by most comedy clubs."—Jackie Fabulous, speaking student and pro comic, on moving from stand-up to speaking.

In other words, the real money is in speaking and here's the big secret about the industry: you don't have to be a celebrity to make that serious money. Yes, if you are the host of your own late night TV show, you will be getting speaking fees of $160,000 and more. But, since meeting planners are *desperate* for funny speakers there is room for those of us who have little or no media exposure to command high fees.

It is truly possible to make a decent living and still be creative, inventive, and original. It's not selling out. It's working with the bonus of getting paid, entertaining and making people laugh, and making a difference in people's lives. Yeah, you have to work clean and can't say George Carlin's "seven dirty words" and that's why, when I'm on the road, after a speech I will hop into a comedy club where I can say exactly what I want.

> ### CASE STUDY
> #### STEVE RIZZO, SPEAKER AND HUMORIST
>
> As a comic turned speaker, Steve Rizzo got successful fast, as he had what many speakers don't have—he's funny.
>
> In the eighties, Steve was a comic headlining comedy clubs and appearing on TV, but something was missing.
>
> "There's a teacher part of me that wasn't being used as a comic. That's when I discovered speaking."
>
> At the time he transitioned to speaking, Drew Carey was Steve's roommate and said, "You're not going to do this speaking crap, are you?"

There are two ways companies and organizations use Entertainers—as performers and as speakers. And what is the difference between an entertainer hired to give a show and an entertainer hired to give a keynote? Oh, around $20,000. I was hired by an insurance company to do a one-hour funny motivational speech on a week cruise in the Caribbean. The comics on board were hired by the ship. One of them had just done *Letterman* the week prior. They were housed in the bow of the ship, had to do four shows a week, and were paid $1,500 total. I was flown first class, allowed to travel with a friend, given a deluxe room, and had all expenses paid. On the last day, I gave a one-hour keynote address at 8 a.m. My fee for that was $25,000. There's the difference.

The challenge for you Entertainers to become higher paid speakers is to add The Message of You to your routine. Unlike Techies who have an overabundance of content with few laughs, Entertainers need to create content that has value for an audience. Being an entertainer is often about *getting*—getting laughs, applause, and acknowledgment. On the other hand, speaking is about *giving*—giving an audience empathy, solutions, and practical advice.

The goal for you Entertainers will be not only adding a sincere Message of You to your performance, but actually giving the audience solid Action Steps on how your advice can improve their lives. I highly suggest braving it through Part One, where you find your Core Promise as well as developing Action Steps that can bring an audience closer to their goals.

The Entrepreneurs

OFFLINE IS THE NEW ONLINE

Along with a strong Web presence, speaking is an essential tool for Entrepreneurs. Face-to-face is the new interface.

The vast majority of speakers stepping onstage or attempting to break into the market are Entrepreneurs, ambitious go-getters who pursue speaking opportunities to find new clients, to sell their products, and supplement their income. If you fit into this category you might work in sales, consulting and management for financial, government, and/or educational institutions, but you also might be self-published authors, freelancers, or small business owners. Or maybe you're an inventor who's figured out a method to lose weight using rubber bands in a whole new way.

PRODUCT PROMOTION

The late Steve Jobs, founder and former CEO of Apple, turned his speech of introducing new products into an art form. Dressed in jeans and a turtleneck, never standing in front of a podium but rather strolling on stage, he never let the fact that he was a Techie turn his speeches into a mechanical recitation of bytes of jargon. Rather he connected on a human level using stories about how Apple products change the lives of the people who use them. It may have looked like Jobs was talking off the cuff, but he admitted to spending a great deal of time memorizing and rehearsing his speeches. That's the brilliance of a great speaker—making a well-rehearsed speech look improvised. The result was massive sales. (Maybe not just because of his speech . . .)

A great speech is absolutely essential for anyone who wants to promote their products or services. I know when my speech hits home because there is a long, long line at the back of the room waiting to buy my books, CDs, and DVDs.

If you're an Entrepreneur, you already know that there is no substitute for personal relationships and name recognition. Speaking rather than Tweeting can be a way to attract new customers, especially now when we are all overwhelmed with impersonal Web relationships. "Offline is the new online"—meaning face-to-face human interaction is still the most powerful way to get new clients and to sell products and services. With that said, nobody wants to sit through a one-hour sales pitch—and believe me, audiences will have no patience if they sense you're a salesman using your speech just to move merchandise or drum up business.

At a book signing, authors can no longer just read from their books—they have to connect with their audiences, move them, and inspire them using a well-thought-out speech.

If your goal is to speak to get more clients or sell products, your challenge will be to create a keynote that has value in and of itself. It has to be informative, helpful, and motivational. Pay close attention to chapter three where you will discover the personal stories that will ultimately become your Heart Story. If you really connect to people with your speech, then after you speak, there will be a long line at the back of the room to buy your book, sign on to your time share, or even hire you for your next gig. Some Entrepreneurs will speak for free and come home with $20,000 in BOR (Back of the Room) sales.

The Survivors

"The Survivors" as I call them, are everyday people whose lives were rocked to the core by either a monumental event such as surviving a climb up Mount Everest, winning an Olympic medal, or writing this damn book. But seriously, some of you have survived tragedy, such as living through a plane crash or swimming through a tsunami or something much more intimate and personal like filing for divorce, losing your only son, or fighting drug addiction. You are the people actively seeking the meaning of your lives. You are the baby boomers, retirees, and cancer survivors who want to pass on your wisdom. You are the laid-off, underemployed workers who found a second chance and a second paycheck. You are the experts of your own lives. You have something to say and you want to help other people who may be struggling with similar issues. Your demographics cross every age, race, and gender divide. You currently work or have worked in every possible job imaginable. You want to make sense out of your struggles and you want to inspire, motivate, and be applauded for having made it to the other side. Perhaps, you want to heal yourself by helping to heal others.

FROM STORYTELLING TO SPEAKING

"You can't just depend on your survivor story to speak. To be a paid speaker, you have to figure out how people can apply what you've learned to their everyday life. To make the leap from storyteller to motivational speaker, you have to connect the dots, break down the steps for the audience on how they can make changes in their life. Find one thing that they can do today, rather than change their whole life."

—Brian Lord, speaker agent, VP of Premiere Speakers Bureau

CASE STUDY
W. MITCHELL

W. Mitchell was burned over 65 percent of his body when a laundry truck turned in front of the motorcycle he was riding in San Francisco. His face and hands were badly scarred and he lost most of each of his ten fingers. Then, just four years later, he crashed a small aircraft he was piloting and injured his spinal cord, leaving him paralyzed from the waist down.

W. Mitchell speaks on "It's Not What Happens To You, It's What You Do About It." He not only inspires his audience to shift their attitudes about living with paralysis and facing life's problems, he's improved the quality of his own life tremendously by opening up and telling his story. He has a thriving career and has become a millionaire with homes in Santa Barbara and Hawaii.

W. Mitchell didn't set out to become a millionaire and I am certain when his plane went down, he wasn't thinking "Hmmm, how can I profit from this moment?"

But W. Mitchell found a reason to live, found a reason to speak, and by speaking created an entirely new life.

Many survivor speakers start their careers by speaking for free to nonprofit organizations, schools, churches, any place they can reach others with their message. One of my speaking students, Art, was swamped with offers to speak at drug rehab clinics. Art had been a homeless drug addict who got off drugs, went back to school, and became a therapist. His story was compelling and helpful to other recovering addicts, but the rehabs couldn't pay him to speak. Art had to pick and choose which speaking engagements he could afford to do, take time off from work, and drive to the locations. His talks were always meaningful and met with appreciation, but he didn't feel he was making a big enough difference. He wasn't able to reach a larger audience with his message and it was actually costing him money to speak. He still wanted to be an activist for addicts but he had to find some way to fund his philanthropic efforts.

We worked together to expand his message to include a business angle. His Core Promise became "Getting Past Addictive Behaviors: Changing Habits and Committing to a Clear Vision of Your Dreams." It was a speech that remained true to his experience and message, but also one he could sell to a corporate audience. Art booked his first paying gigs and now uses the money he makes speaking on corporate stages to support the work he does gratis for drug rehabs.

In other words, to take your story of survival into the corporate speaking market, you need to have more than a great Heart Story. You have to bridge the gap between your personal experience of surviving a tiger attack and the experience of an administrative aide dealing with nasty clients all day long. If you have worked hard to overcome illness, poverty, or divorce, then sharing your strategies for success in the form of Action Steps, can not only assist others, but can become a full-time career. Some of you have more personal topics, including self-improvement, relationships, and women's issues. Probably 80 percent of your speech will focus on your Heart Story, the journey you took to survive lymphoma, to climb Kilimanjaro, to move from poor to rich.

Just be aware that Survivors must still qualify to speak by also having academic, professional, or business experience. This includes your college degree, your job, your accolades, the professional initials that follow your name, the book you wrote, your charity work, the plays you've been in, or the articles that ran about you in your local newspapers.

If you fit into this speaking category, focus intently on chapter three to find the message that runs underneath the story of your journey, as well as chapter four, where you qualify to speak by accentuating your credentials.

The Novices

Last but certainly not least are you Novices who might find yourself forced on stage. You are the speakers who must speak as part of your job, or like Chastity Davis from the last chapter, you got roped into a presentation after a couple of drinks. In rare instances, Novices will step onstage in the hopes that you can jump start a stalled career, grab that promotion, or lay the groundwork for a raise. Mostly, Novices are regular people with absolutely no experience who find themselves on stage, sweating, terrified, and miserable. You buy books to help learn presentation skills but you realize . . . you have no speech. That's when the fear kicks in hard.

I totally get it. Even though I work constantly, I have suffered through seventeen years of stage fright. It can be pure torture to see a speaking date circled on your calendar, looming over you, filling you with dread. It's like being in seventh grade, knowing you have to give an oral book report and you never read the book. You have no idea how you're going to fake it. You have no idea what to say.

As adults, our fears can intensify. But to be on the fast track to success and promotion, we all have to present our ideas to an audience. Learning how to be a better, more entertaining speaker, and thus getting positive results from speaking, will assist you in turning speaking into a positive experience, rather than one of humiliation. After all, if after you speak you have people coming up to you saying nice things, hugging you, and telling you what a difference you make ... well ... that might make going through the fear worth it. It can also improve your value in your current job.

Dave Orris worked as a corporate manager of a national supermarket chain. In addition to maintaining and managing a small office staff, most days would find him out in the field, supervising and training store employees and interfacing with the vendor community. As part of his job, each week he had to give a report in front of the staff—and each time he was filled with dread. After attending a seminar led by popular motivational speaker Ed Foreman, Dave thought, "If I could learn to inspire my teams as Ed inspired me and the other attendees, what lofty goals could my teams achieve?" He gave himself a challenge and joined Toastmasters International and began honing his presentation skills. As those skills grew, so did Dave's responsibilities and visibility within the company. More important, so did the effectiveness of Dave's teams as they set new, measurable standards of excellence.

The economic downturn took its toll on even the best managed companies. Layoffs were inevitable. The year 2010 was accompanied by a 90 percent reduction in Dave's department alone. As Dave was told, there was no doubt that his ability to effectively communicate, lead, and inspire others factored into the decision to retain his position within the company.

PROS IN TRAINING

Toastmasters International is a nonprofit organization that has 270,000 upwardly mobile members (including me) in 13,000 clubs. In California alone, there are 989 registered weekly Toastmasters meetings.

My fellow members are ambitious go-getters who pursue speaking opportunities to find new clients, to supplement their income, and for overall career advancement. They are actively working to improve their presentation skills.

One of our mottos is "Become the Speaker and Leader you want to Be."

It's natural to be frightened of speaking in front of others, but if you have a great message along with a well-thought-out and re-hearsed speech, that can go a long way to fighting fear. Pay special attention to the last chapter of Part One for a primer on how to deal with fear, and then focus on Part Two where I will guide you to write an entertaining speech with content *and* laughs. There I will show you how to use a Core Promise, a Heart Story, and Action Steps to build your speech. But like I mentioned before, it shouldn't be a daunting process.

While other types of speakers may use this book to punch up their content-heavy PowerPoint or try to rebrand themselves in a com-pletely new market, you're in the enviable position of having a blank slate. You can pursue any segment of the market you choose and you have the advantage of looking at your life with brand-new eyes. What you see will then become what you say . . . a super-cool way to dis-cover a whole new perspective on your life and your career. After all, having people hug you after a speech or asking for your autograph, hiring you for their conference, or just keeping your job can be a real self-esteem booster. Nothing like a lovefest to turn those Novice fears into "I Wanna Do It Again" excitement!

EXERCISE: YOUR SPEAKER PROFILE

You may think that answering the questions below before you've even written one word of your speech is putting the cart before the horse, but I beg to differ. Identifying the kind of speaker you currently are or aspire to be will help you to hone in on The Message of You and where you fit into the speaking business.

After reading the above descriptions you probably have an idea of which category you mostly fit into and some of you might fit into more than one. You might be a Pro who is also an Entertainer, or a Survivor who is also an Entrepreneur. Or a tap-dancing Techie who owns a T-shirt business and survived being hit by a train. Stranger things have happened.

You also might have a hint now of your speaking goals. In this exercise, write for twenty minutes without stopping and answer the questions below:

1. Am I speaking because it's part of my job? If so, how can being an inspiring speaker assist me with my job? How can speaking help me receive a promotion or keep my job if there are cutbacks?

2. Am I speaking because I have a message I want to share with the world? What would be the results of being able to truly motivate and inspire others?

3. Am I trying to broaden my client base? How would speaking help to increase the number of clients?

4. Am I already considered an expert? Are there companies or media outlets that hire experts in my field to speak? Which companies or shows?

5. What do I expect to get out of speaking—in other words, am I doing it for money, career advancement, or inspiration?

6. Is there an organization or a cause I want to represent or promote? What is it? How would speaking about my personal experiences help promote that organization?

7. What are my "entertaining" skills such as singing, juggling, comedy, magic, etc? Is there a message that I could add to my current act? What are the hidden talents I can add to my speech?

8. How can I activate the social media platform I already have in place via my Facebook page and my Twitter account or my blog? Could I create a speech that would appeal to my followers that would escalate me to celebrity status?

9. Am I trying to create a new revenue stream? How would speaking increase my current income?

CASE STUDY
THE PASSING ZONE

The Passing Zone is one of the most successful and sought-after keynote speaking teams working today. They are jugglers. That's right. Owen Morse and Jon Wee are a juggling duo with four Guinness World Records, eighteen Gold Medals from the International Jugglers' Association, and appearances on many national TV shows.

Jon and Owen illustrate to Corporate America the fundamentals of teamwork, by juggling chain saws. Their act is an example of the collaboration between two people who rely on each other's strengths, who communicate, trust, and have fun cooperating.

Looking over your answers, determine which category (or categories) you currently fall into?

☐ Pro

☐ Techie

☐ Entertainer

☐ Survivor

☐ Novice

Now, ask yourself, what is your biggest challenge as a Pro, Techie, Entertainer, Survivor, or Novice? Whether it's writing a second speech, adding a Heart Story, or getting over first-time speaking jitters, it will assist you in your process by setting yourself some goals.

Matter of fact, I'm here to help you. E-mail me your goals at commitment@TheMessageOf You.com and I will help keep you on track so you can make your goals a reality.

Becoming clear about your speaking goals will help to clarify The Message of You and save you valuable time as you begin to research speaking opportunities, because—and here's the great news—there are endless opportunities to launch your career as a speaker. Corporate

America is desperate for great speakers with a strong message sprinkled with laughs. Just look at the numbers:

- Eleven million meetings occur in the U.S. each and every day (source: Meetings in America).

- Thirty-seven percent of employee time is spent in meetings (source: National Statistics Council).

- $102.3 billion was spent on business meetings and events worldwide (source: Meetings in America).

- There are 57,000 meeting and convention planners currently employed (source: U.S. Department of Labor).

- The convention business is expected to grow 16 percent between 2008 and 2018, faster than the average for all other occupations (source: U.S. Department of Labor).

In other words, there are far more speaking opportunities than there are trained speakers. Meeting planners are desperate for well-prepared, inspiring speakers and are willing to pay them good money. The opportunities are not limited to the United States. Meeting Professionals International has over 20,000 active members and the professional speaking industry is an English-language based career. In fact, the Global Speakers Federation requires that English is either the first or second language of their members. Federation members include Australia, Canada, Malaysia, New Zealand, Singapore, South Africa, South Korea, the Netherlands, the United Kingdom, and the USA. How cool is it to be paid to vacation?

What do speakers speak about?

There are many hundreds of different topics that speakers cover, including personal development, business issues, diversity programs, leadership, sales, customer service, teamwork, organization, and motivation. The list is endless. That's why the focus of this book is helping you to determine what constitutes a Bookable Topic.

Simply put, these are the topics that audiences will pay to hear. Just because you're an expert on a certain topic doesn't mean you can get paid to talk about it. Now, for many speakers who have to speak at their job or who speak for charity, choosing a Bookable Topic is not an issue. You may even have an assigned topic and have no choice about it. But for those of you who would like to make a living as a speaker or are starting with a blank slate, you must take into account the topics considered "hot" by companies and organizations. Choosing a Bookable Topic is an important component when putting together a commercially viable Core Promise for your speech and developing your Message of You brand. In chapter four, I'll lead you through a few exercises to determine which Bookable Topic is right for you.

Where do speakers speak?

Speakers speak at conventions, expos, business meetings, women's groups, charity events, fund-raisers, hospital events, schools, churches, and TED talks. Basically anywhere people gather. I myself have spoken on large rock-and-roll style stages, as well as in hotel banquet halls, cruise ships, classrooms, auditoriums, parks, not to mention outside on the seventh hole of a golf course. (Note to self: do not wear spike heels when walking on a lawn.)

THE TED TALKS

TED started in 1984 as a conference bringing people together from three different worlds: Technology, Entertainment & Design.

The stated mission of the nonprofit is to build a clearinghouse that offers free knowledge and inspiration from the world's most inspired thinkers.

Since 2006, the talks have been offered for free viewing online with over 1,000 talks viewed nearly 500 million times among a growing global audience.

Speakers are given eighteen minutes to present their ideas.

Who knew eighteen minutes could change the world?

Why are speakers hired?

Speakers are hired as keynoters to motivate, inspire, or entertain. They are hired as trainers for breakout sessions to educate. They are hired as private consultants to improve a business; sometimes they are hired as emcees to host and lighten up the event. I've sometimes been hired to do all four for a conference. I'll do an early morning wake-them-up keynote, then an afternoon breakout session as a trainer, followed by emceeing their awards banquet, and continue the next day with private coaching for management on presentation skills.

SPEAKERS ON SALE

"If I have to pay for a keynoter to fly in I might as well get more value by having them also do a breakout session. This gives attendees an opportunity to dig deeper into the [keynote] topic with a hands-on, interactive, breakout session."

—Sandy Biback, CMP CMM, founder of Imagination⁺ Meeting Planners Inc.

Very often in large meetings, attendees will be divided into smaller groupings called breakout sessions. These sessions are usually forty-five to ninety minutes long and have specific skill-building topics. They're also more informal, with audience interaction and a speaker who usually provides a workbook. Breakout speakers don't get paid nearly as much as a keynoter, whose sessions can be anywhere from a few hours to all-day trainings to year-long training contracts. The most popular topics are sales, leadership, communication and presentation skills. Most speakers land these lucrative year-long consulting contracts because they used a keynote to promote their training business. This book is focused on developing a keynote speech for you. Keynoting is the Holy Grail of speaking, or as my Jewish grandmother would say, the keynoter is the "Big Macher!" It is the highest paid position. As with breakout sessions, a keynoter will usually speak between forty-five and ninety minutes and address the entire group. Keynoters are usually hired for a morning, after-lunch, or closing keynote. A keynote is the centerpiece of your speaking career and having a strong one will open doors to additional opportunities in training and consulting.

Who hires a speaker?

Very often companies will use speakers from within their company. Most of these internal speakers are not professionals and rarely get paid, although they get other things, such as appreciation, acknowledgment, and career advancement. For larger meetings, companies and organizations will hire an outside speaker, meaning someone not associated with their company to deliver a professional speech designed to motivate and entertain their group. They find these outside speakers via a speakers bureau.

A speakers bureau is an agent who books speakers for clients. Unlike Hollywood talent agents who have exclusive representation of their talent, speakers bureaus usually do not have exclusivity of their clients, and are able to book

HOW SPEAKER BUREAUS FIND A SPEAKER

"To find the right speaker for a client, we ask the meeting planner, 'What message do you want the audience to leave with?' This determines not only the type of speaker, but the speaker's positioning on their program.

"Not everyone can be a closing keynoter. A closing keynoter needs a rousing call-to-action to leave the audience with a powerful message."

—Kelly MacDonald-Hill, senior VP agent, Speakers' Spotlight

ELEVATOR PITCHES FROM THE PROS

"Too many leaders overcomplicate their jobs. In reality, a leader's success hinges on a few simple behaviors—behaviors that require remarkable levels of discipline. Based on the model in my first best-selling book, *The Five Temptations of a CEO,* I've captured the natural human tendencies that plague all leaders and often prevent them from fulfilling their potential."

—Patrick Lencioni, business visionary and thought leader

and take commissions from all speakers. Some speakers find themselves working with as many as thirty different bureaus. For bureaus, the company or association is the most important client, not the speaker. The bureaus work with meeting planners to assist them to find the perfect speaker. They take 25 percent to 50 percent of a speaker's salary for any job they book.

That's why most speakers prefer to deal directly with the client, since this is the person who is writing the check. The client can be a professional meeting planner, a committee, or the administrator who got stuck with the job of organizing an entire conference. With more and more speakers' YouTube videos on the Internet, many clients work directly with the speakers themselves rather than hiring via a bureau. It's also why you will need to develop a strong Web presence for your career.

> **"Working 24/7 and still can't get it all done? Most of us feel that the only way to manage the mounting chaos in our lives is to take control. If only we could get a handle on life! No wonder we have overwhelming to-do lists that leave us feeling exhausted and powerless. In a heartwarming and funny program you'll learn straightforward, innovative techniques for keeping your balance no matter what life throws your way."**
>
> —Mary LoVerde, speaker and life balance expert, author of *I Used to Have a Handle on Life But It Broke.*

You want to be able to attract **certified meeting planners** or CMPs. Large companies usually have a department of CMPs in charge of all aspects of meeting management, from establishing themes to hiring the speakers. For smaller events, sometimes the meeting planner is not a CMP, but rather, the unlucky and already overloaded company receptionist. For big events, very often committees are formed and their members search the Internet to find speakers. Then the committee as a whole decides on which one to hire.

You attract a CMP by having a great **elevator pitch**. An elevator pitch is a quick synopsis of your speech. Think of it as a way to tell people what you talk about in the time it takes to travel in an elevator from the parking level to the lobby. Elevator pitches are probably the most rehearsed two sentences of any speech, as many speakers are booked by tantalizing a meeting planner with a well-crafted haiku version of their message during a short conversation in an elevator, in line at a bathroom, or on an airport shuttle. It's usually said in terms of problem-solving such as "You know how hard it is these days for sales people to get new clients? I show them how they can double the number of new clients via the power of personal connections."

Big or small, paid or unpaid, every gig you book will require a **contract** that contains the terms of the engagement including fees, travel expenses, accommodations, requirements such as sound check, cancellation policy, and other event details. The **contract rider** usually has the audio/video requirements of the presentation including PowerPoint needs and type of microphone, as well as miscellaneous stuff such as audience seating and no green M & M's. Well, that's just for the rock stars of speaking.

You will also need to have a **fee schedule**, which is a fancy term for a speaker's pricing sheet. It usually lists a speaker's fees for keynotes, breakouts, and trainings, prices for educational materials, and discounts for local gigs and benefits.

BACK OF THE ROOM (BOR) SALES

Christine Cashen speaks on the fun factor in business and life. In her keynote she demonstrates the power of playing with props to relieve stress.

At the end of her keynote, people swarm to buy her bundles that include her book, *The Good Stuff,* as well as DVDs, clown noses, and flying frogs.

In Part Three of this book, I talk more about marketing materials and I also discuss **back of the room sales**. Many speakers make the bulk

of their money not from their speaking fee, but rather from selling sup-
plemental materials such as books, DVDs, CDs, T-shirts, consultations,
and other products and services *after* they speak.

You can check out these basic marketing tools on the Web site
MarketYourSpeech.com. There you can find a listing of fee schedules,
sample contracts, and additional resources to help support your new
career, or to serve as comparisons against your own current marketing materials.

Which speakers succeed?

That's probably the easiest question to answer. The speakers who succeed are the ones with a great speech that offers practical content and
is funny throughout. As they say in Hollywood, funny is money.

What makes a great speech?

There actually is a formula; add to the mix humor and inspiration and
you've got a great speech. I'll discuss that formula and how to inspire
and add humor in depth in Part Two, but for now, you need to know
the components you'll be creating.

1. Your Speaker Introduction
One of the most overlooked, yet important parts of a speech is the way
a speaker is introduced, as it sets up the Core Promise of the speech,
establishes a speaker's expertise, and sets the tone for the speech.

2. Your Proof of Expertise
To talk the talk, you have to have walked the walk. The Message of You
has to be backed up by your professional credentials. These include
traditional credits such as academic degrees, job experience, published
works, and media exposure. It also includes nontraditional ones such
as reality show appearances, a large number of social media follow-

ers, and others. These successes in life not only give you credibility but will also help to narrow down your choice of Bookable Topics, attract your audience, and define the Core Promise for each speech you write.

It should be noted that even if you are a Survivor, you must also qualify as an expert. You must be able to show that you've gone from victim to victor by creating or participating in an organization that helps other survivors, by speaking at charity events, by having a popular blog, winning awards, or some other credential. It's one thing to have a compelling story about what happened to you, but you must have found a way to use that story to help and inspire others.

3. Your Action Steps

These are a speaker's methodology. They are the specific, doable steps that audience members can use to solve the problem that your speech addresses. These Action Steps come from a speaker's personal and professional experiences, rather than a Google search. These steps are a part of The Message of You. Speeches can have one Action Step or many. Larry Winget, who is known as the "Pit Bull of Personal Development," puts his in the title of his book, *Shut Up, Stop Whining, and Get a Life*.

4. Your Support Stories

The Message of You is communicated via stories. As an artist uses paint, speakers use stories to communicate and enhance their message. A speaker will make a point, then tell a story that illustrates their point, and then make their point again. Speakers collect stories, not only from their lives but from other people's lives, and these become known as a speaker's Support Stories.

5. Your Heart Story

Usually toward the end of a speech, a speaker will tell a touching Heart Story. This shows how the speaker's Core Promise works in real-life situations. A Heart Story usually packs an emotional punch and takes the audience on a moving journey that can inspire change and transformation. Some are five minutes long, and some speakers base their entire speech around one long Heart Story. No matter the length, all heart stories include a Eureka Moment.

6. Your Call to Action

The Call to Action is used to wrap up a speech and to appeal to the audience to take action based on what they've learned from your message. It's usually a very simple action that they can do right away, such as vote, write an e-mail, volunteer, and so on.

7. Your Core Promise

A Core Promise is a succinct, one- or two-sentence statement that includes the problem your speech will address and the solution you will present to your audience. The Core Promise is the core *premise* of your speech. Get that? Your promise is your premise. **Each speech has its own Core Promise, but every speech you write and every Core Promise you develop should always relate to your brand—the larger Message of You.**

On the surface, a Core Promise seems so simple. But it often takes speakers pages and pages of writing and sometimes years of hit-and-miss attempts to find, boil down, and refine their Core Promise into a few easily understood sentences. It's my job to help you skip all those hit-and-miss years and help you hone in on your message much, much faster.

Essentially, your Core Promise must reference:

- Your topic.

- Your audience's problem.

- Your solutions and why you qualify to offer those solutions.

The Core Promise of each speech is very important. It is inextricably linked with The Message of You. That's why we're going to spend the vast majority of Part One of this book helping you to identify and write your Core Promise and the . . .

8. Message of You

The Message of You is your brand. It is what you stand for. It's what you are famous for or want to become famous for. It's your life work as well as the lessons you have already learned. It's what you'll be remembered for when you die. It's your legacy.

Think about any president's speech. There are the folksy and personal stories meant to humanize but underneath every story, behind every word is a driving point of view, an agenda, a message that must be driven home.

Obama got elected on a three-word Message of You: "Hope and Change." In order for him to discuss change, he had to qualify to speak on it by using personal and professional experiences. He had to present change as his Core Promise, a combination that showed that he held the solution to America's problems. He knew that people were losing their homes and having trouble paying bills, and he promised his policy would change that. Actually, the biggest disconnect between a politician and the public is the lack of implementing their message. As a speaker, we have to make good on what we promise.

Understanding The Message of You is not a step you can skip just because you're not the president, as it is absolutely essential to any speech you write. Not only is it the foundation upon which you will build your keynote but it is also necessary for all of your marketing materials including your Web site, handouts, PR, and press releases. Without The Message of You, you will be lost, your audience will be lost, and your Core Promise won't matter.

CORE PROMISES FROM WORKING PRO SPEAKERS

Let's look at a few examples from successful speakers who are already out there, bringing their messages to boardrooms, conference centers, living rooms, pulpits, and gatherings across the world. These are speakers earning large sums of money by providing solutions to real-life and business problems in an entertaining way. Their speeches actually transform audiences using humor, drama, stories, and personal revelations all wrapped around a singular message.

LISA FORD: WHY CUSTOMER SERVICE IS *NOT* ENOUGH

There is a reason today's customer service remains "mediocre" at best: lack of a committed strategy. In today's world, your company's customer service and customer experience must be decidedly different. You have the opportunity to make these things happen. When audiences listen to me, they walk away with a proven strategy for enhancing customer service and building customer loyalty. And with the enthusiasm to actually put these strategies to work immediately.

JOE CALLOWAY: THE CATEGORY OF ONE

Whether it's Apple, Southwest Airlines, Starbucks, or the great pizza place down the street, Category of One companies win because their cultures drive results. What does your culture drive? I do one thing—I help your company become a Category of One.

BEVERLY KIRKHART: HOW TO TURN SETBACKS INTO COMEBACKS

Every day thousands of people become victims of life-shattering events, like a cancer diagnosis. Instantly, they are faced with the challenge of how to thrive and persevere in the face of adversity. As a breast cancer survivor since 1993, I offer practical and proven ways professionals, caregivers, cancer patients, and others can turn their setbacks into comebacks and emerge as stronger, more positive people.

All professional speakers have found a simple but effective way to mash up their life lessons and their expertise into a message that encompasses the audience's problems and also suggests a solution. It's a simple formula.

Audience + Problem + Professional Experience + Personal Experience + Methodology = Results

"You know how . . . (insert your audience) your *new sales team, parents, doctors, admin staff, office staff, or volunteers.*" Once you are clear on The Message of You, then you will be able to identify who you are speaking to. If you are just starting out as a speaker, your audience will probably be the people you work with, the school your kid attends, or one of the organizations you already belong to.

". . . have this problem, they . . . (insert problem). *can't get work done at work because of too many meetings, are stressed and overwhelmed from working longer hours, facing emotional burnout working on the oncology ward, aren't attracting new clients, can't get customers to their Web site, have too much paperwork.*" Addressing the specific problems facing your audience will not only give you a connection to them, but be great fodder for getting laughs.

"From my experiences . . . (insert professional experience) *working fifteen years in HR, headlining comedy clubs, or working at JPL.*" This is where you tell the audience a story about how you've come to understand their problem. Along the way name drop and include your credentials.

"As well as, would you believe . . . (insert personal experiences) *fly fishing, surviving my own teenager, learning how to snowboard at fifty, getting ill with cancer and surviving against all odds.*" This part of the Core Promise will turn into your Heart Story, where you pull at their heart strings by telling a personal story about how you dealt with the problem and won.

"I show the audience how they can . . . (insert results or promise of speech) *increase sales, be better parents, increase efficiency, deal with change, have the home they dreamed of, increase their income by 30 percent.*" This is the specific result you will give your audience. Be careful about how much you promise. You've got one hour, probably not enough time to promise they will earn a million dollars, let go of all their stress, never have a difficult customer, or be able to bench-press a hundred pounds.

"By . . . (insert your methodology) *using their sense of humor, by connecting to clients, by appreciating what they have rather what they don't have.*" You are going to need to develop a method that will achieve what you promised. This is your methodology or your technique. You will find yours in chapter four by examining the steps you took to become successful.

Now, you don't have to be able to fill in those blanks just yet. In the next few chapters, I'm going to ask you to write a lot about yourself. Some of the exercises might not even make sense to you, or some might start you writing for hours wondering what this has to do with finding The Message of You. Trust me, all of these exercises are designed to help you find the right message for the right audience.

It would be great if there was a direct highway to find The Message of You. But, as in any fun trip, we are going to get off the main highway and examine all the country lanes, the different aspects of your life. It may seem that you are trying to put together a complicated jigsaw puzzle, where nothing seems to fit together, but hang in there and start with the first step of finding The Message of You in your life experiences—start with your death.

EXERCISE: WRITE YOUR EULOGY

The Message of You may be just as invisible to you as it was to Chastity Davis from chapter one. Now this might seem weird to you, but writing about what others will say about you when you're gone will give you a very quick idea about a possible Message of You.

Have you ever been to a funeral of someone you didn't know too well? If you did, you might have found that listening to the eulogy you got a pretty good idea of the message of their life. For some people that message is a personal one. The person was a loving mother or father, and the message that emerges is "Family First." Or maybe, at someone else's funeral, all the remembrances relate to career achievement and the message that emerges is "Leader and Innovator."

In this exercise, I want you to write two eulogies for yourself about you. One would be what you would imagine a coworker, boss, or client would say about you at your funeral. The second eulogy would be what you would imagine a loved one, family member, or friend would say about you.

In both of these eulogies include:

- What difference will they say you made in their lives?
- What skills will they say they learned from you?
- What stories will they tell about you?
- What will they say was the meaning of those stories?
- What will they want people to know about you?

Once you've finished writing both eulogies, call up your Buddy and make a date. Get together and read the eulogies aloud. Ask your Buddy the following questions:

- What themes did you hear?
- What did I teach others?
- What would you describe as my gift to others?
- What was the meaning of my life?
- Which stories seemed to sum me up?

OPPS?! NO BUDDY?

Most of the exercises in this book are designed to be done with a Buddy. If you don't have one, let me fix you up.

Go to MySpeakerBuddy.com to help you find the perfect person to work with. You don't even have to live in the same city, as online sessions work just as well as in person.

Don't worry if no Message of You leaps out yet. Perhaps you are reading this book so that when you do die, people will say that when they heard you speak, you made a dramatic difference in their life because you cared enough about others to share of yourself.

Wouldn't that be something?

CHAPTER TWO CHECKLIST:

☐ Selected which speaking categories I fit into.

☐ Identified my speaking challenges.

☐ E-mailed Judy my updated speaking goals.

☐ Wrote eulogy as a coworker.

☐ Wrote eulogy as a loved one.

☐ Met with my Buddy to share the eulogies.

☐ Brainstormed possible Message of You.

CHAPTER THREE

TURN YOUR MESS INTO A MESSAGE

In 2003, Aron Ralston's extraordinary human drama grabbed headlines around the world. A climber and avid outdoorsman, Ralston was hiking alone in a remote Utah canyon when an 800-pound boulder broke loose, crushing his right hand and pinning him against the canyon wall. After five days with no water or food and no way to escape, Ralston resigned himself to die. He shot a good-bye video for his family and documented the date of his death by carving it into the boulder. The next morning, he woke up. He was still alive. He made a life-or-death decision. He chose to cut off his arm in order to escape. After breaking his bone and sawing through his own flesh for two hours, he then had to rappel a sixty-five-foot cliff out of the canyon, and hike seven more miles before he was rescued. But he lived, and his miraculous survival was international news. Aron went on to write a book about his ordeal, which was then made into a feature film starring James Franco.

As an inspirational speaker, Aron Ralston has an unforgettable journey: an ordinary man pushed beyond his limits to confront fear and pain to accomplish the extraordinary. To survive in the face of certain death. But it's the message of his story that appeals to corporate America. Aron has fashioned his near tragedy into a triumphant speech entitled "127 Hours: Between a Rock and a Hard Place." Now, that's a title that resonates with anyone working in corporate America. It references a ticking clock deadline and, metaphorically speaking, we've all felt that we've been "up against the wall" in our lives. Aron presents his Core Promise and encourages his audiences to "step out of the grave and into your life again." It's no wonder that with his compelling story combined with his powerful corporate-relevant message that Ralston commands an honorarium of $25,000 per domestic speaking appearance and up to $37,000 for international speeches. He told me when we spoke at the same event together, "I never regret that this happened to me, because it's given my life a purpose." His story and message have not only created his legacy, but have made a difference in the lives of others.

Already, I can hear you protesting . . .

"Judy, I've never been in a life-or-death situation like that. I can't possibly compete in the speaking market if I'm expected to top Aron Ralston's story!"

Well, here's the good news: you don't have to top Aron Ralston to have a career as a professional speaker. The stories you tell do not have to be heroic stories of survival but they absolutely *must* have a message that is relevant to your audience. Each of us has had a journey where we had to overcome obstacles to have success. Each of us has found ourselves in a big mess. It's our goal to turn that mess into a message.

Your journey from having a *problem* (your mess) to finding a *solution* (your Action Steps) might have lasted longer than 127 hours. It might have been the twenty-five years it took you to go from maxed-out credit cards to owning your own house. It might have been your journey from sick to healthy, or like my journey, from drama queen to comedy queen. You were never trapped under a boulder, but perhaps you were nearly crushed by a financial avalanche; you weathered an abusive relationship; you managed to keep your home during an economic disaster; or, even scarier and more dangerous than a boulder, you survived your kid's teenage years.

Dr. Anthony Wolf did just that. As a clinical psychologist he has a practice of counseling teenagers and their parents. When his own kids reached that age he thought he knew all there was to know about being the parent of a teenager. But, as his own children rebelled, he found out that the great wisdom he was dispensing to his clients wasn't quite as wise as he thought it was. "It was a very humbling process as I learned that [there are] certain things you can't know about parenting a teenager unless you have been a parent of a teenager."

Dr. Wolf found what was missing in his practice—his sense of humor. When his daughter got to be a sassy teenager, he turned his own frustrations into cartoons about kids becoming teenagers. After a while he had a lot of cartoons so he gathered them in a book, *I'll Be Home Before Midnight and I Won't Get Pregnant*. To his surprise, it was published and he became a much-sought-after speaker. Dr. Wolf is now frequently quoted in the national media on issues of parenting and appears on national television programs including *The Today Show, Fox Morning News, CBS Morning News, The View,* and more.

WHAT DOES SNOWBOARDING HAVE TO DO WITH SALES?

Messages come in big and small packages. Sometimes, the most mundane incidents of our day hide a business message that can be of value to sales meetings.

For instance, I spent years learning how to snowboard. My big problem was getting off the chair lift. My head was filled with tons of tips and techniques on how to get off the lift, but somehow, I always fell. I even had the unique talent to bring down everyone else on the chair with me. Pathetic. No matter how many times I rode the lift, it was always the same process. In my mind, I repeated everything I learned. I'd play the loop in my head, "Breathe, point, look, lean forward, balance, and . . . go."

Then one day, I was distracted and all of a sudden, it was time to jump off the lift. I wasn't prepared and to make matters worse, a child on the chair in front of me fell, blocking my way. I had no time to think of my steps, no time to breathe, no time to recite my mantra. My body took over and miraculously, I swooped around the fallen girl and stayed on my own two feet. Someone even commented, "You are quick on that board." They assumed I was a Pro.

That day I learned overthinking gets in the way of our natural talents. We have to turn off the critical, plotting, safety mind and tap into our innate abilities. We can do more than we think we can. Can you see how a story with a message like that could be relatable to a business audience? To motivate a sales force to get out into the field and "jump off the chair" and trust that they will land on their feet? For instance, "You can recite sales formulas over and over again and that will bring you a certain level of success, but at a certain point, you've got to *ride* your own instincts."

This chapter will help you mine your life journey for compelling mess-to-success stories, whether they are heroic or intimate, ordinary or otherworldly, and I'll then ask you to CSI those stories for The Message of You that lies hidden in the details. Remember, the job of crime scene investigators is similar to your job in this chapter—to examine the smallest details of your life to discover the larger meaning of your existence. It will seem like a messy process. You'll end up with a collection of anecdotes, stories, and images that may feel unrelated at first, but trust the process. Finding The Message of You isn't a nicely groomed hiking trail through the woods, it's like hacking through the jungle with a machete. In the dark. Without a compass. You're going to feel lost. You may even feel pinned underneath a boulder and not be able to move for a few days. But just remember Aron Ralston had to cut off his arm to live. All you have to do is get out of bed and sit in front of your computer. So, let's get started.

Remember in the fourth grade when you had to do book reports and find the moral of the story? That's what we want to do with your life stories. Go beyond the plot of "what happened" to find the "message" of what happened—the life lessons that your story illustrates. The Message of You.

From listening to bedtime stories as a child to discussing the latest movie on a date, you have likely developed the skill to finding the messages behind the stories you hear. Very often, those life lessons are blatantly obvious. At the end of Dorothy's journey through Oz, she actually says the life lesson out loud, "There is no place like home." At the end of each irreverent *South Park* TV episode, there is a life lesson that the boys say, such as "Parents are retarded" or "Mutated heads growing from your chest make an excellent distraction."

All right, so some life lessons are more useful than others . . .

The following exercises are designed to uncover the underlying themes that reveal themselves in the day-to-day stories you tell as well as your journey from problem to solution. You don't have to make up these messages as they are already there. In order to understand the motivational messages that are running through your own life stories, you're going to need an "outside" eye, as it's hard to be able to truly see the meaning of your personal life journey. Sometimes you need someone who can listen to your stories as an audience would to discern their underlying meaning. That person is your Speaker Buddy. As I suggested earlier, don't go through this process without one.

Remember that recorder I asked you to buy back in chapter one? Now's the time to whip it out. Stories with The Message of You are happening around you and to you all the time, so always carry your recorder and don't hesitate to use it when you find yourself telling a great story—no matter where you are. When golden ideas happen, a Pro knows better than to let the nuggets go. It may be awkward to stop in the middle of your date and talk into your iPhone but that's what it takes to develop a talent for spotting the significant moments of your life. Actors already do this. They can be in the middle of a fight with their lover, and as they pass a mirror they make sure to notice what an angry person looks like so they can summon up that facial expression the next time they play an angry character. You must learn to live *and* observe at the same time.

Here's one way to develop that power of observation.

EXERCISE: BAD DAY, GOOD DAY, SAME DAY

Before we tackle the Message of You contained in the larger story of your life journey, it might be helpful to practice finding the Message of You in what happened on a day that started off bad but ended up being a good day for you. Stories don't have to be huge and dramatic to be effective. In my speech, I tell a story about a cancelled flight at the airport and how dealing with the ticketing agent changed my attitude in a profound way. In terms of my life, it's a small moment but the story is a huge part of my speech and the message of that moment resonates with those who hear it.

In other words, a story can be about anything and everything. From the moment you wake up to the moment you're reading this, there are countless stories and they all have one thing in common— they contain an underlying Message of You.

Try this exercise. Write about a day that started off bad. Tell the story of how you transformed the day from challenging to awesome. Your journey can be from cranky to happy, from lonely to hooking up, from depressed to excited. If you can't remember a day when this happened, then write about what's wrong with your day right now and determine how you are going to change this day from crappy to spectacular.

If you've only been up for ten minutes, you may think it's impossible to find a story. But if you focus on the details of your thoughts, your actions, and your environment, you'll find there's more wrong with your morning than you think.

Here's an example using one of my mornings on the road:

I wake up in the Comfort Inn in New Jersey with the alarm blaring at 6 a.m. I didn't set the alarm. It must have been the last person who stayed in this room. Maybe this alarm has been going off by itself for the past month with nobody in the room. I try to turn the alarm off and I can't. Why do they make alarm clocks so complicated? This alarm clock has black writing on black buttons so there is no way I can even see where the off button is. I yank the cord out of the wall and it finally stops. There's no going back to sleep so I get up. I'm not in a good mood and I wonder how in hell I'm going to speak in four hours and be funny. I figure this is a good time to check my Facebook page. There are about twelve people posting how much they like my book, *The Comedy Bible,* but there is one person posting a very disturbing message—a sort of rant about me being a selfish bitch. I start obsessing: Who is this guy? Did I sleep with him? Did I not answer something he sent? Am I selfish? Should I defend myself or delete him? I decide to delete him, but Facebook has changed their format once again, and just like with the alarm clock I can't figure out how to ban this person. Oh, I'm getting depressed. I want to call home, but it's 3 a.m. in LA. Too early to wake someone up to complain. Complaining is something to do in the afternoon because by then, everyone is depressed or upset, but nobody likes to hear crankiness first thing in the morning.

Now you try it. Set your writing alarm to write for fifteen minutes. Write the first ten minutes of your day today. Get into the details. Write about your thoughts, what happened, any conversation you had. If you have a hard time writing, then try this: cover your computer monitor. Sometimes not reading what you write while you write can help you be less critical monitor. Sometimes not reading what you write while you write it can help you be less critical.

WHAT DOES DELIVERING A BABY HAVE TO DO WITH A BUSINESS CONFERENCE?

Canadian speaker Palmo Carpino discusses "Connectivity Equals Productivity: Getting Your Message Across Effectively." One of his Support Stories is how he delivered his third son in the back of his car en route to the hospital.

"What people connect with is the emotions of that story. After all, everyone in business has had a time when they had to improvise. By telling a personal story to a business audience, I connect on an emotional level, which stays with an audience a lot longer than facts and figures."

Once you've written about the mess of the morning, find something that made your day a little, or a lot, better.

During my New Jersey adventure, I called my best friend to complain and we had a good laugh about that stranger and his ranting. Laughing made me feel better, so much so that I called my buddy, Ben, and we worked out some comedy material about overly complicated alarm clock controls. I performed the new material in my speech and it killed. I turned my mess into material!

Once you have written about your morning, don't read what you wrote immediately. Get away from your computer for a while and put some distance between you and what you wrote. Tomorrow or sometime later this week, I want you to meet up with your creative Buddy and read what you wrote. Then I want you to both make a list of the life lessons contained within this story.

What do I mean by "life lesson"?

Let's use my morning at the Comfort Inn as an example. When I CSI that story, I can see that the very things that annoyed me, the clock and the stranger, turned out to be the same things that brought me laughs with my friends and laughs from the audience. I realized that, when I was by myself I focused on the negative. On everything that went wrong. After all, on my Facebook page I have countless friends who say many wonderful things about my books and how my workshops have changed their lives. But, what did I focus on? The one bad thing a stranger said. And I was in New Jersey to give a speech about "lightening up your life with laughter." The irony.

There seem to be several "life lessons" hidden in the first ten minutes of my day.

1. The annoying things that happen to us every day can be funny.

2. If you focus on the negative, you are certain to feel unhappy.

3. When you laugh at a problem, it decreases in size.

Okay, your turn. Work with your Buddy to uncover three or four life lessons from your story. Start by asking yourself these questions. If you have trouble answering the questions, have your Buddy answer them for you.

1. Where did you start and where did you end?

2. What was the moment when everything changed?

3. What do you want in your story?

4. What obstacles got in the way of you getting what you want?

5. What did you need to learn how to do?

6. What are the life lessons you gleaned from your story?

7. What are three steps that you could take, or that you have taken that could help someone overcome obstacles such as these? (Later on I will be referring to these steps as your Action

Steps. Your methodology. It would be good practice to start noticing how you go from problems to solutions, even in the little stuff.) Most of our life lessons contain irony, as speakers usually speak about what they need to learn. By writing about my stay at the hotel, I notice that I am often overwhelmed by the stresses of everyday life, and yet I speak about using a sense of humor to combat stress. I am speaking about that which I need to learn. It's a message, it's *my* message and one I must remind myself to live authentically.

How about you? Any larger message jumping out at you? If so, along with your "story" file create a document called "My Speech Message" and start compiling a list of the life lessons and messages you discovered. Don't worry right now if they sound stupid, dull, or confusing. We will add a lot more information to that document by the end of this chapter.

And feel free to use this exercise over and over again. Choose ten minutes from any part of your day and write away!

Remember: the purpose of this exercise is to assist you in discovering the life lessons in the smaller stories of your life. Later, when you look back at these stories, you might find a theme emerging that could be The Message of You. It is also a useful speaking skill to be able to glean life lessons from stories. When you write your speech, before each story you tell, you will state the life lesson learned—the point of the story. It may seem like spoon-feeding the audience but trust me, it works.

Now that you've focused on the minutiae of your morning, and practiced identifying life lessons in the small moments, let's look at the larger stories in your life. On your voyage from mess to success, let's see what big boulders you've had to push out of your way.

EXERCISE: FROM MESS TO SUCCESS

What's that saying? "Into each life, a little rain must fall." Well, some of us might feel like we've been trying to swim through a flash flood!

Fortunately, what was challenging in the moment can make great fodder for a motivational speech. This exercise will search your personal life for your ups and the downs, your tragedies and the triumphs. How did you move from mess to success? What were the moments that shaped your outlook on life? What is your life journey? What is The Autobiography of Your Life?

Take a moment now and create a chronological time line of your personal life. Don't spend hours on this. I want you to write very, very fast. Set an alarm for thirty minutes and make notations about the major personal moments in your life. Don't worry right now about your professional experiences like jobs or awards, just focus on your relationships and the more touchy-feely stuff. Start with the day you were born and move quickly through the years to this moment, right now, when you are holding this book in your hands.

Here is an example from one of my students:

1971: Born in South Carolina to a single mom. Grandma moves in with Mom.

1973: Mom remarries. Pregnant with my sister.

1976: Enrolled in kindergarten. Able to read naptime stories to kids.

1983: Grandma dies. Devastated. Mom loses it. Mess!

1985: Mom divorces. We have to move to Minnesota. Awful. Hate winters. Mess!

1987: Elected student body president. Popular. Happy. Success!

1989: First member of family to go to college. Full scholarship. Proud. Success!

1992: Move to Houston, Texas to live with my boyfriend. Disaster. Mess!

1996: Left boyfriend for last time. Launched my business in my garage. Success!

You get the idea. Once you have a full outline of your years, I want you to CSI the list for the larger journey of your life. Ask yourself these questions:

1. Which of these moments were successes? Take a moment to fill in even more of your successes, writing down even the ones you take for granted—your marriage of ten years, owning your own home, organizing a neighborhood watch, convincing the assessor's office to lower your property taxes, the after-dinner conversation when your kids actually enjoyed talking to you. Ask a close friend to add anything you've missed.

2. Which of these moments felt like failures or defeats? Which of these moments can be identified as "mess" moments? For example, when you bounced a check on a good friend, the day you were served your second divorce papers, the Thanksgiving when you worked rather than celebrated with your family, and so on. It might hurt to reveal the "negative" aspects of your life, but for the sake of this exercise open up and write it all out. You never have to show anyone if you don't want to share it.

3. Examine the list of messes and success. How did you get from one of the messes to one of the successes?

4. Ask yourself: "Do these moments reflect a larger journey?" In other words, do all of these moments have something in common with each other? Have they been leading you in a specific direction? Have they been part of a lifelong struggle? Were there obstacles that led up to a big Eureka Moment?

5. Circle two of your major successes and two of your messes.

6. Are these moments reflective of your major life battle? What is the battle you wage? It could be a battle for your health, for your family, for your wealth, against injustice, etc.

7. Write out one Eureka Moment in detail where your life changed. Write it out in glorious detail down to remembering the color of your shoes.

Put yourself in that moment and feel the event as it unfolds, focusing on your feelings and thoughts during that time. This exercise doesn't work well unless the stories you've chosen include a Eureka Moment, as opposed to general overview statements such as "I was a workaholic," "I overcame a hearing impairment," "I felt lonely and left out."

8. Make sure to include descriptions of everyone who was involved. Was there someone involved who learned a lesson from watching or participating in your journey? Did you act as a teacher in some way?

This is an important point. Speaking is a more entertaining way to teach. (At least, it's supposed to be more entertaining—more on that later on in my Comedy Pass chapter.) And teaching is something we all do every day of our lives, especially if we want to make a difference in the world. You share your Message of You when you tutor a student in your field of expertise, but you also teach when you give pep talks to your kids; when you train a new employee; when you give fashion tips to a friend or dating advice; or you share a recipe in an online chat room. And here's the thing: we are always teaching exactly what we ourselves need to learn. We are always teaching the Message of Our Lives. Even if we can't recognize it. That's why the next exercise is about reaching out to friends and family to borrow their more objective points of view.

EXERCISE: INTERVIEW YOUR TRIBE

In this exercise, I want you to ask your closest friends, your family members, and your coworkers two questions: "What have you learned from me?" and "What are the stories I tell over and over again?"

CASE STUDY
PAULA FAUST

Speaking student Paula Faust asked her family and coworkers, "What have you learned from me?"

Her eighteen-year-old daughter told her that she learned the importance of finding "the funny" in life. Her high school friend told her that she learned that "having a big mouth can work in your favor." Her best friend told her that she taught her, "Never go to bed with a stranger." OK, some of the life lessons are more insightful than others.

But her big surprise came when she learned the impact she had on the people she worked with on her job as a transit manager. Her coworker shared, "You've shown me how having a sense of humor can help me deal with difficult people by not taking things so seriously."

Paula then used this information to build her speech entitled, "Using Humor to Charm and Disarm Your Customers."

What have you learned from me?

You're going to be very surprised by the responses you get when you ask the people in your life this question. The answers will range wildly from "how to use an iPhone" to "how to get a second date." Whatever they are, write them down and keep them with your collection of stories. Can you remember any stories that illustrate these teaching moments? Write those down, too. How did you teach your seventy-year-old grandma to use an iPhone? How did you convince your sister to laugh when her basement flooded? How did you talk your best friend into that second date with her now husband? Don't worry if the stories are the same as the ones you've unearthed in the last exercise. In fact, that's even better.

What stories do I tell over and over again?

Support Stories are stories that you tell at parties, among friends, or when meeting a stranger. These stories can cover two seconds that changed your life forever or cover twenty years of your life. They can include a peak moment such as meeting a celebrity, having fifteen minutes of fame, or winning the lottery, or they can be about the tough times such as a family death, your plunge into depression, or a horrible car accident. The one thing these stories have in common is they are entertaining. You are probably used to getting a reaction from people who hear it or else you wouldn't be telling the story over and over again. These are your go-to stories you tell when someone needs a laugh or motivation to work on their marriage, or the courage to face a tough job interview, or just to get out of a funk.

As you read this, many stories will come to mind. Don't judge if they are good enough, funny, dramatic, or interesting. In this initial investigation, *all* the stories that come to mind are relevant. Create a file called "Support Stories." Start jotting down your stories ASAP. If you can't think of any at the moment, that's normal. That's my case. I have no memory-on-demand of stories, but then I'll be at a party and a great story comes out of me and that's when I remember, "Oh yeah, that's an entertaining story." This means that you will need to carry the recorder we talked about earlier so you can *record the stories as you actually tell them.* You might think that you will remember them, but you probably won't. You need to mine your life for your stories *as they happen.*

Once you've maxed out your memory bank, call your friends, family, and coworkers and ask them which stories you tell over and over again. Believe, me, they will know. They've heard them more than once.

Gather your list of stories and *pick three stories*: your funniest story, your most dramatic story, and a story you never get tired of telling. Write them out in detail.

By now, it should be clear that in order to become a professional speaker and to tell a great story with a profound message, you have to have lived it. Fortunately, living isn't a choice. You have to do that every day and if you are like most people, you weren't born rich, smart, or successful—you've had to work your way to achieve the success you've had.

Author Liz Murray's memoir, *Breaking Night,* is not only a best-selling book (as well as the basis for the Lifetime Television movie, *Homeless to Harvard*), but Ms. Murray is a big deal on the speaking circuit. When she was fifteen, she found herself living on the streets after her mentally ill, drug-addicted parents failed to keep their family together. Although troubled and desperate, instead of crumbling Murray had hope and determination, and worked her way up and out of homelessness all the way to Harvard University. The underlying message of her speech became the name of her company, her business, and her workshops—Manifest Living. It is her Message of You and it is her brand. According to her Web site, she describes her business as "a company that provides workshops that empower adults to create the extraordinary things in their lives." It is the message of her personal life journey that allows her to speak at Fortune 500 companies as well as at TED conferences.

Rags-to-riches stories never get old. Audiences love stories that travel from despair to hope. In fact, not sharing a story where you were a "loser" might cast you as an arrogant know-it-all. Highlighting the challenges you've had to overcome gives you credibility and compassion.

Using the exercises above is how I found my Message of You. My lists looked something like this:

My successes are:

> Having four books published by a major press.
>
> Having Oprah recommend my book on her show.
>
> Being a headlining comic.
>
> Building my dream house.
>
> Losing forty pounds in Weight Watchers.

My messes were:

> A battle with depression.
>
> My mother dying suddenly.
>
> Growing up with an alcoholic father.
>
> Having a sister who was born quadriplegic with CP.
>
> Getting fired as a high school teacher.

At first, I didn't see a journey but then I noticed that through it all, I was always funny even though I didn't live a "funny" life. In fact, I had a rather difficult childhood but I used comedy to deal with life's difficulties and ultimately, it became my career and my biggest success. I actually taught my stand-up students how to "Turn Problems into Punch Lines." That was my brand. Once I realized turning problems into punch lines was actually reflective of the journey of my life, I used that message for my speaking career. That's why I can now say, thank God for my troubled childhood, tumultuous love relationships, and all the difficult people in my life! Woo-Hoo!

Now, what about you?

Is there one story that seems to keep jumping out at you? Is there one story that everyone remembers as your "best" story? One particular story that contains the journey of your life? Does that story suggest a life lesson, a message that could be inspiring to an audience? A lesson that could help others to be healthier, wealthier, and happier? This may be your Heart Story. Let's test it out.

EXERCISE: CHOOSING A HEART STORY

Throughout your speech you will be using many personal stories to illustrate problems, solutions, and Action Steps. These stories will be your Support Stories. Toward the end of your speech you will present your Heart Story. Your Heart Story differs from your Support Stories in that it *must* communicate your Message of You and the Core Promise of your speech. The stories you explore in this section may not turn out to be the Heart Story you choose for your speech since we haven't yet determined your Message of You or talked about your Bookable Topic.

But, for now, we are in brainstorming mode. We're collecting lots of options so when you are ready to write your speech and solidify your Message of You, you'll have plenty of material to use. Besides, speakers have numerous Heart Stories upon which they rely. Changing the Heart Story of your speech is one way you can "customize" your talk for a certain client. But we'll talk about customization later in Part Two.

The secret to picking a Heart Story is to first find the Eureka Moment when you realized something about your life had changed. A Heart Story is not a chronological time line of your life events, but rather a moment in time that is explored with laser-like focus. It's the specific moment where you learned the secret of becoming richer, happier, or healthier. It's the moment when you decided to change or were forced to change your ways. Within this moment, perhaps you learned something that could be a valuable life lesson to others.

Make a date with your Buddy. From all the work you did above, pick three of your stories and tell them to each other. As you both are listening to each other, jot down the life lessons you hear in each story and be able to answer these questions:

- Which story has a real a-ha moment?

- What does the character learn in that story?

- What life lessons do you, the listener, get from that story?

- What do all three stories have in common?

- What are the messages contained in these three stories?

- Which message has the most power to help an audience learn how to be healthier, happier, or wealthier?

That last question may confuse you. What do I mean by a powerful message? It's one you have lived. It's a message that your life experiences qualify you to talk about. It's a message that entertains. It's a message that is inspiring. You might find that one of your stories has more power than the others. You're getting closer to your Heart Story.

Focus on that story and ask even more questions. If you don't have the answers to these questions, maybe your Buddy can help you find them.

- When the story begins, what is your situation?

- What does the hero of the story (meaning you) want?

- What were the obstacles you encountered in the story?

- Did the obstacles escalate in intensity?

- Where did you end up?

- How did you end up there?

- What was the moment where everything changed?

- What changed in that moment—what was the "before" and "after" of that moment?

- What steps did you take to solve your problems?

- What did you learn from your journey?

- What is the larger message this story conveys?

- What can an audience learn from the story?

- How can an audience apply the story to their own problems right now?

FINDING YOUR DOWN MOMENT

Journeys don't have to be dramatic. Your fall from grace can be just five feet.

Speaker Barbara May talks to companies about how to improve performance. Her Heart Story is about falling off the balance beam during her first gymnastics competition. She really pumps up the humor and humiliation of falling off, not once, but five times.

She explains, "My coach encouraged me to get back up and as a result I learned the importance of getting back up after a fall. This is an important message that applies to the business world. Let's face it, everyone makes mistakes and the important thing is to get back up."

Once you're both satisfied that the story you've chosen work as potential Heart Story, summarize it into the beginnings of your Core Promise:

1. In my life I went from (insert mess) to (insert success).

2. From my journey I learned (insert life lesson).

3. Because of my life journey, I can teach people (insert possible goals an audience can achieve).

Using Liz Murray's story as an example, she might have filled out those three questions in this way: "In my life I have gone from homelessness to Harvard. From my journey I learned how malleable life can be—stable one moment and homeless the next, and that there isn't any one clear-cut answer, but that change is a process. What I teach people is that no matter what happens to them, through hard work and faith, they can succeed."

Congratulations. You have almost completed the first step out of three to find and hone The Message of You. Let's check to see if you're ready to move on to chapter four. Can you easily fill in these blanks?

I have gone from (mess) _____ to (success) _____, and I want to teach others how they can _____ so they can achieve _____. To do this, I will tell the story about _____ _____. The life lesson contained within that story is _____ and the larger message is _____ _____. This message can be of value to people who want to know how to _____.

Story Checklist:

☐ Collected at least three stories.

☐ Identified life lessons in those three stories.

☐ Identified the mess and success of each story.

☐ Examined my journey from problem to solution.

☐ Figured out the steps I took to overcome and achieve.

☐ Narrowed down my choices to one potential Heart Story.

You've done it! You've uncovered the life lessons hidden within your personal journey as you moved from low point to your success, problem to solution, and you are well on your way to finding the Core Promise of your speech. Hopefully, you now have notebooks full of usable messages and stories that can be incorporated into The Message of You. I know that this chapter was tough, especially for you Techies and Novices. It's difficult to have a bird's eye view of our own life, and some of the memories can be painful. But now that you've done the heavy lifting of sifting through your personal life, you can switch off the mushy, touchy-feely part of your brain and focus instead on establishing your professional credentials. I can almost hear your sigh of relief.

Now it's time to CSI your professional success as well. In the next chapter, we're going to search through your professional experiences to determine which will qualify you to appear at paid speaking gigs, and which topics are relevant to your credentials. Just because we're moving on to more "cerebral" elements of our search doesn't mean your stories will go forgotten. Your life journey from problem to solution is the reason audiences will love you. But first, you have to get past the gatekeepers at the door.

The meeting planners.

CHAPTER THREE CHECKLIST:

☐ Wrote the first ten minutes of my day.

☐ Uncovered three or four life lessons from that story.

☐ Created a chronological time line of my personal life.

☐ Examined the time line for my larger journey of life.

☐ Interviewed my tribe.

☐ Identified my Support Stories.

☐ Chose a Heart Story.

☐ Created the beginnings of my Core Promise.

CHAPTER FOUR

TURNING YOUR EXPERTISE INTO A BOOKABLE TOPIC

The first thing a meeting planner will do when searching for a speaker is Google the topic/issue of their convention or meeting to identify the speakers who specialize in that particular issue. That means you need to craft your speech with an awareness of a Bookable Topic.

The next thing a meeting planner will do is check out your credentials to make sure that they are hiring an expert. Why? Because when you speak, there are questions in the minds of everyone in the audience: "Why should I listen to you?" "What have you done in your life that qualifies you to speak to me?"

Don't let those questions scare you!

Oh, I can already hear you fretting more as I write this . . .

"But Judy, I never graduated from college, I haven't published a book, and the only celebrity I know is a guy I dated in high school who is now on a reality show called Rehab Dropouts. *I don't think anyone is going to consider me an expert."*

Don't worry if you are just starting out and feel a like a fake when referring to yourself as an expert. Many of my speaking students feel fraudulent for calling themselves experts. Here's a secret: most of my peers who have been on TV and are the authors of highly successful books also feel queasy about calling themselves experts. We *all* suffer at some time or another from self-doubt, and for good reason: many speakers haven't graduated from a fancy college or haven't published books, nor do they hang with important people. Patricia Fripp, one of the pioneer women of professional speaking, never graduated from college and yet she is hired to speak at Fortune 500 companies and she became the first female president of the National Speakers' Association as well as an inductee into the Speakers Hall of Fame. So, what qualifies her to be a world-renowned expert on sales and marketing? It was her business experiences as a hair stylist.

Yes, you read me right—a hair stylist.

As Patricia says, "When I was first asked to speak at a Salon conference, it was a shock to me to realize just how much I knew from cutting hair. At first, I had no idea of what to talk about. But, upon examination, I realized I had developed considerable expertise in my journey from hair stylist to running my own salon. After all, I knew how to get referrals, repeat business, keep customers, train staff to deliver, and price my services. What I learned was more than a haircut; it was a motivational experience that qualified me as an expert on the topic of getting and keeping clients."

Certainly since Ms. Fripp started speaking, she gained many more established signs of being an expert, including media appearances, published books, and a long list of important clients. So, as she now says, "Maybe I didn't go to Stanford, but now I speak there."

See? It doesn't matter if you haven't graduated from an Ivy League school or if you never even attended college. You don't need to have a big-shot job title or even a multimillion-dollar estate to prove your worth. There are many ways to qualify as an expert besides academic degrees, a hefty bank account, or a fancy job title. What you

QUALIFYING TO SPEAK YOUR MESSAGE

"A speaker needs to be credible before they can speak in front of people. I don't want someone talking about microeconomics if their day job is a clown for children's birthday parties."

—Sandy Biback, CMP CMM, founder, Imagination⁺ Meeting Planners Inc.

need to prove is that someone besides you and your mother has acknowledged your expertise.

The audience wants proof that you are a living example of the success of your message. They need to know that because you have walked your talk, you have accomplished something and that you've been recognized by others as well. You can't talk about generational conflict in the workplace just because you fight regularly with your parents. Professional credentials will establish your expertise and get you past the meeting planner.

Now, I'm not ignoring all the work you did in the last chapter. Your personal stories are still important. They connect you to the audience and convey your Message of You. We will be using them for sure. But really, would you take advice from a financial adviser who had some great stories but wasn't certified as a financial planner and had never held a job? I didn't think so.

Let's start looking at the professional side of your life story. What you find there might surprise you.

What does it mean to be an expert?

In most countries becoming an expert consists of completing specific educational curriculums, acquiring professional job titles, and working for years in established professions. However, there are many other nontraditional routes of establishing expert credentials. In the United States, sometimes becoming an expert means that you found yourself on a reality show called *The Biggest Loser*. Poof! You're a now a diet expert and "Hello, speaking gigs!" Celebrity status goes a long way.

CASE STUDY
PETE THOMAS, LOSER TO WINNER

Most reality TV stars make the bulk of their money from speaking. Pete Thomas is the season two winner of NBC's *The Biggest Loser*. He turned his weight-loss success into a full-time career as a motivational speaker. Pete's keynote spreads his "Winning Principles" to organizations worldwide.

As Pete says, "I help others understand, that in life there are many things that try to weigh us down. For 60 percent of Americans, physical weight is one of them. But once we come to understand the principles for achieving true success in life—no matter what your weight is, physical or otherwise—you can overcome. You can succeed and you can win!"

Whether your credentials are the traditional academic sort, or you have been crowned an expert by *Project Runway,* you need to gather up proof that you're an expert. Your proof can be a diploma, a job, a degree, an award, or a TV show you were on. Or, sometimes you can get the credibility of being an expert because another acknowledged expert gave you a testimonial.

When Oprah held up my book, *Stand-Up Comedy: The Book,* on her TV show and said, "Judy Carter can show you how to make your sense of humor pay off," at that moment, I was crowned an expert, and speaking engagements poured in. However, I got that show from already branding myself as an expert by writing a book, and I got the book deal because I convinced a publisher I was an expert from my professional experiences, which included:

- Running my own company—Comedy Workshops.

- Years of teaching comedy.

- Years of experience headlining comedy clubs.

- Playing Vegas and opening for famous people.

- Numerous reviews in the press and other media exposure.

So what is your area of expertise?

I was coaching WWE pro female champion wrestler Melina Perez, who wanted to get out of wrestling and into speaking. Melina had tons of professional experience in her field of expertise, wrestling, including wins, titles, and TV and media appearances. She qualified as an expert in women's sports, as well as succeeding as a woman in a male-dominated business. Many people have more than one expertise and that can lead to having more than one speech. There was one credential that Melina downplayed, and it was the very thing that served as proof that she was a role model for girls and women alike. The toy company Mattel had turned Melina into an action figure doll. Now, there are tons of PhDs out there in the speaking circuit, but how many of them can say they have their own action figure! Melina's journey from a poor Hispanic family to action figure became the title of her speech: "From Ordinary to Extraordinary: Wrestling with Hope."

OK, so nobody has turned you into an action figure, but don't skip too quickly through this exercise. Your qualification might be a non-traditional, offbeat one that never made it to your résumé. Entrepreneurs, Techies, and Professionals will have no problem looking through this list and finding their credentials. Novices may have to rely heavily on our second exercise—teaching them how to bump up their credits—while Survivors may just complain:

"But Judy, I just want to tell people my story of surviving cancer. I don't have a degree; I just have a compelling, inspiring story."

Again, I'm not downplaying your story but you've got to turn that story into a credential by relating it to your professional experience. After surviving cancer, did you volunteer to work with health-care providers? Did you found a cancer self-help group? Did you write articles that were published about your story? Did you write a book about it?

How are you walking your talk?

EXERCISE: YOUR JOURNEY TO SUCCESS

Use the questions and prompts below to identify your credentials. Don't give up if you don't see right away how you qualify as an expert.

You have to start someplace and some of your nontraditional credentials might not be so obvious to you.

Education and Academic Degrees

What degrees do you have? Did you go to an impressive college? A trade school? Any letters after your name? PhD? MD? Any certificate programs? Master classes with an artist? Any fellowship programs, residency abroad, language courses, an apprenticeship?

Again, think about nontraditional education such as culinary training, circus school, or receiving a black belt in karate.

Job Experience

Whether you've been a working stand-up comic, COO of an upstart Internet company, or a lawyer, your employment past and present means that someone else recognized and paid for your expertise. Make a chronological list of every job you've ever held from that first job at McDonalds as a burger flipper to the job you currently hold as you read this book.

CASE STUDY
MICHAEL SOON LEE

Michael was a marketing director for the State of California, a professor of marketing at universities, as well as a black belt in karate. He combines his credentials to present "Black Belt Negotiating," a speech on becoming a masterful negotiator using lessons from the martial arts, where he also includes personal stories of his journey from being picked on as a kid to becoming a confident champion.

Distinguished Colleagues

My speaking fee soared after I shared the stage with former president Bill Clinton. Whom have you worked with, studied with, partied with, hung with, lived beside, slept with, shared a meal with, etc.? Make a list of all the famous faces and well-known names in your life. The bigger the name, the better. Don't be ashamed to name-drop. It's a helpful way to bypass the gatekeepers and get to your audience.

NAME-DROPPING

Victoria Labalme speaks on improving communication and was inducted into the National Speakers Association's Hall of Fame. Her educational credits include studying with the mime artist Marcel Marceau. Yes, even studying with a famous mime can qualify you to speak.

Awards and Accomplishments

Don't leave anything out, including the first-place ribbon your dog won in obedience training. There are a lot of animal organizations that hire speakers. If you can't remember all of your accolades, break out the scrapbooks and old calendars, dig through those drawers and clean out the attic. You're certain to stumble onto a trophy, a ribbon, a certificate—something that will jog your memory. Winning an Olympic medal ain't such a bad credit, either.

Bonnie St. John is a survivor. Her life journey gives her a compelling story of overcoming her disability of having only one leg, as well as poverty, divorce, and struggles related to gender and race. Her message is a powerful one: "to stay positive and live joyfully no matter what life dishes out." Great message, but it is her credentials that give her message credibility. Bonnie was the first African American to win Olympic medals in ski racing; she graduated with honors from Harvard University and won a Rhodes Scholarship to Oxford; she was appointed to the White House National Economic Council; she has been featured on

The Today Show, Montel Williams, CNN, *Good Morning America,* as well as in *People* magazine, *The New York Times, Essence,* and many others publications. She has been critically acclaimed as an author. She is no slacker.

All of her awards and accomplishments back up her message of "falling down and getting up—in life, at an Olympic ski race, or in business." Currently she is one of the most highly sought after keynote speakers in the country. As she says in her own words, "If a one-legged, African-American girl with no money from San Diego, where there's no snow, can go to the Olympics as a ski racer . . . people think to themselves, 'Surely I can follow my dream and find the joy in my life.'"

WHO DO BUREAUS BOOK?

"I only book speakers who have credentials. In other words, a speaker has to be a celebrity or have excelled in running their own business, running a marathon, or running a TV show before they get paid for running off their mouth."
—Jonathan Wygant, owner and CEO of BigSpeak Motivational Speakers Bureau

Well, maybe after just reading about Bonnie, you wannabe speakers can comb your life for your own accomplishments.

Media Exposure and Platform

If a newspaper says you are an expert then you are, even if that newspaper is the *Tuscaloosa Times.* If you've been on the news, in magazines, on TV, have written books or have a radio show, that validates you as an expert.

If you have a blog that is followed by thousands or a massive Twitter following or a maxed-out Facebook page, these are good, good things. People are already listening to you and interested in what you have to say. Matter of fact, the day I'm reading this, I just got a call from a corporate client who learned about me from reading my blog. She liked my message and is booking me to speak at her convention.

But no one starts out with a thousand blog readers. The way to develop your credibility is by consistently writing each week.

Here are some tips for writing a blog.

Keep your blog consistent with The Message of You. Put all other commentary about personal matters that don't have to do with your message in a personal, invite-only place. When a client is searching for a speaker for leadership, you don't want your "How to Select a Great Vibrator" blog post to come up in a Google search.

- Always include a valuable tip for your reader.

- Invite other experts to contribute to your blog.

- Place your blog on other Web sites.

- Make sure you have an easy way for your readers to register for your blog.

- Have a place for people to comment. Know that most people who read your blog won't comment, but that doesn't mean that they aren't reading.

Once you've finished collecting all the information about your professional credentials, answer these questions:

- What are you known for among your friends?

- What are you known for in the world?

- Where did you start out professionally and where are you now?

- What are you most proud of?

- What kind of difference have you made for others?

- What causes are you involved in?

LET A STRANGER DETERMINE YOUR EXPERTISE

Take note of the questions strangers ask you. Comic and speaker Stephen O'Keefe is often asked what life is like for a deaf person.

"People are surprised that I've created a great life for my family. Until people asked me, I didn't realize the extent of my competence. I realized that I had skills that were shareable beyond my sense of humor."

If you're at a loss as to how to answer those questions, ask your friends directly. Then make a date with your Speaker Buddy and read your answers aloud to each other. Be able to defend your answers with information from this chapter and the prior chapters.

Here's an example from one of my students:

"In the world, I am most known for my skills as an interior designer. I can prove this by my credential of having high-profile clients such as Adam Sandler, and for my monthly column in Dwell magazine. My personal life journey from hoarder to host also qualifies me to talk about redesigning a life by redesigning your space."

Defend each answer with a short paragraph like the one above. Once you're done, read them over again and see if there are any larger themes that seem to repeat. This very well may be either your Core Promise (as it pertains to your speech) or your Message of You (as it pertains to your brand). We'll look at that more closely in the next chapter. For now, let's keep working on establishing your expertise.

You may have discovered by doing the above exercises that your credentials are looking a bit murky—as in your top credential is the Friendliness award you won in fifth grade. You need to ask yourself if you have achieved the level of success you want to have achieved in order to speak. Do you qualify? Have you walked your talk? Not everyone has.

I had a wannabe speaker approach me for coaching. He was struggling to find his topic. His life experiences had an underlying theme of "Losses." He had lost his father at an early age, lost his marriage, and was a successful stock trader until he lost all his money. When I first spoke to him, I suggested the topic of "reinvention"—a hot topic among baby boomers. However, when trying to find his message, I discovered that he was still single, broke, and mourning his father's death, which happened forty years earlier. He had never really rebounded from his losses. He needed to achieve some level of success before he could be a speaker. Speaking is not separate from your life—it *is* your life. You can't be talking about winning when you're a loser. And you have to have proof about your successes. Fortunately, there are ways to get that proof.

EXERCISE: BUMP UP YOUR CREDITS

Now, if you don't have diplomas, haven't been published, or been quoted on CNN, there are still many other ways to establish your expertise. Perhaps you are a member of an acclaimed association, or you blog on your topic and have a lot of fans. How about that mention in the Huffington Post? Or the time you donated as a mentor? Maybe you shared the stage with someone famous? Even if none of these are true, don't get discouraged if you don't have any impressive credentials. Take these suggestions and apply them *now* before you even begin writing your speech.

1. Submit articles.
Become a published writer by submitting articles to newspapers, magazines, your company newsletter, blogs, and trade newsletters. Go to MarketYourSpeech.com/articles for a list of ways to submit your work and get published. Every profession has trade magazines. Determine which ones your target audience reads and write a piece for them. If you're not sure who your "target audience" might be, read chapter eight, where I help you find your tribe.

GETTING PUBLISHED: INDUSTRY MAGAZINES

Pam Lontos, speaker and marketing consultant, promotes writing articles for association and business magazines as one of the best ways a speaker can get noticed by the people who will hire them.

"People read their industry magazines cover to cover, so write an article based on your topic that solves the readers' problems and addresses their needs. You only need one to two pages of useful information with your name, speaker topic, and contact information at the end."

Pam suggests that articles bring speakers three distinct benefits:

1. Every time your name appears in a magazine, you gain the same status as other authors in that issue. Often these are industry leaders or famous experts.

2. Whereas an advertisement is expensive and less credible, an article costs you nothing and people take the information seriously.

3. You are getting an implied endorsement from each of the magazines that publish your article.

CASE STUDY

RANDYE KAYE (voice talent, speaker, author of
Ben Behind His Voices: One Family's Journey from the Chaos of Schizophrenia to Hope)

"I wrote a memoir about the effects of my son's schizophrenia on my family but I couldn't find a publisher. So I started writing a blog, posted some videos of keynotes on YouTube (not even very slick—I am using a *flip chart* in one!), and sent a newsletter out via Constant Contact. I also started writing articles for the Best Ever You, Network Technorati, my voice-over blog ("Life on the Voiceover List"), and anyone else who asked.

The results were amazing.

First, someone read my blog, suggested I send my book to their agent, and as a result I got my new literary agent. Then, the articles and blog posts I wrote helped convince Rowman & Littlefield to accept the book for publication—partially because they saw that I could be a great partner in promotion. Next, an article I wrote, "Ten Reasons to Love Your Library"—first on Technorati—went viral within those circles and was picked up by the American Library Association for publication in their newsletter—the same week my book was released for sale to libraries! In addition, a pharmaceutical company has sponsored me as a nonbranded spokesperson/speaker for messages such as the need to include families in mental illness treatment plans.

Through that association, I have spoken at APA (American Psychiatric Association), APNA (American Psychiatric Nurses Association), US Psych Congress, and pharmaceutical sales meetings, and my articles about this message and my presentations have been placed on nurses.com, *SZ* (Schizophrenia) *Magazine,* and more. Additionally, they sponsored an RMT (radio media tour) and SMT (satellite media tour), where I appeared on venues like Fox News and Lifetime. This collaboration was a direct result of their having found me through my blogs, and that YouTube video with the flip chart!"

2. Self-publish.

There are people who have a compelling message and interesting life experiences, but no credentials. I always encourage these people to self-publish a book. I refer them to professionals who can distill their message, find their Action Steps, hone their Heart Story, and organize it into a book. These books don't have to be long, but rather can be short booklets of less than 100 pages. Then, not only are you a published author but you have gained clarity on The Message of You. Speakers give a lot of thought to developing their message, their brand, and their audience, but sometimes they forget to develop their writing voice. That's where a ghostwriter can come in. A good ghostwriter can mimic a speaker's diction, tone, cadence, and—if they're really good—sense of humor. When an audience member buys the book, it's because they want to hear the voice of that speaker over and over again. They want to share that voice with their friends or their family. A speaker's voice *must* come across on the page. For information on services to assist you in writing your book, or to have someone to write it for you, go to MarketYourSpeech.com/publishing.

3. Produce your own podcasts.

You don't even have to wait to get on the radio anymore. You can create your own radio station! Go to MarketYourSpeech.com /podcasts to learn how to record a basic podcast. A podcast is helpful because it will assist you not only in honing The Message of You, but will also build your audience and followers, establishing you as an expert.

4. Become a regular guest on the radio.

National Public Radio is an excellent way to start, as anyone with a smartphone can record a piece and submit it. I created several pieces on my message of "Humor," which keeps the phone ringing.

HOW DOES NATIONAL PUBLIC RADIO FIND THEIR EXPERTS?

"NPR uses experts on practically every one of our programs," says Art Silverman, senior producer at NPR's *All Things Considered.* "We go online looking at book titles, blogs, Tweets, as well as to see who has been quoted on other shows.

"We use online services, such as profnet.com to do a search if we are looking for specific experts.

"I depend on referrals, and the 'human Rolodex' of our staff here is very influential. Very often I'll find an expert because someone on our staff has gone to school with someone, had a great professor, just read a book, a Tweet, or a blog of someone smart and interesting.

"I'll follow trends on Twitter as well as use Facebook to find stories and experts.

"I also read hundreds of e-mails as well as NPR comments. I scan the subject and see if it's an expert on a topic that is newsworthy."

SILVERMAN'S TIPS FOR GETTING ON THE AIR AT NPR

1. Listen to what we put on the air. Understand what we do. Search our database (NPR.org) to see if we've done it before.

2. Shape your pitch to relate to a current event. For instance, if you are a weight-loss expert, then pitch a piece relating your health expertise with an upcoming election and how people vote for skinny people. Or, if you are participating in a newsworthy event, you can invite an NPR reporter to go along with you, as you're essentially giving us access to a newsworthy adventure.

3. E-mail us your pitch. Keep it short. Have your contact information in it and put keywords in the subject line. If you already have recorded some audio, you can attach it. Lots of people on staff look through e-mail every day. If it looks novel or smart and is also well written, you might get on the air.

4. Don't send it to every show. If you don't hear back, then you can take it to another one of our programs.

Kandee G is the host of the *Nothing But Good News Radio Show* on an all-business radio network in Miami. She got the gig by calling in weekly to a radio show reporting on good news. The segment was so successful that a radio station in Orlando, Florida, contacted her and her career began with her own radio show. As she says, "Now, my listeners call asking me to speak at their events."

Being a radio host has sharpened her speaking skills. "Radio has taught me how to think in the moment, react to changes, and speak in a clear, concise way."

Tips for anyone getting their own radio show:

- Teleconference/Webinar on a topic of your expertise. There are countless services, even free ones where you can have thousands of listeners hearing you give advice as well as interview guests while you're in front of your computer in your PJs.

- Broker time to get your own radio show. There are certain stations that will sell blocks of time and you can find stations that are in your niche market. There are health and wellness, wealth building, personal development networks.

- Record and submit short radio pieces on your message to public radio stations.

- Blog Talk Radio Online. Anyone can have a Blog Talk Radio show for very little money. It's a great way to exercise that muscle to become someone who can become an on-air personality.

(Go to MarketYourSpeech/radio for links and resources for getting on air.)

BECOME AN EXPERT ON A REALITY SHOW

Gina Rubinstein is an Emmy Award–winning producer of many reality TV shows. Where does she find her on-camera experts? From Hollywood agents?

No, from Google.

"In TV, I find experts from looking at Web sites and YouTube videos. We use experts in so many different areas, including real estate, comedy, mold removal, politics, paranormal, scientists, you name it."

---

5. Produce, direct, star, and distribute your own videos on YouTube.
The first thing a meeting planner will do is click on your YouTube videos. Rather than posting the video of your baby moon-walking like Michael Jackson, you might want to post videos of you speaking, teaching, or doing your act. Whatever your talent, catch it on film.

Award-winning speaker and humorist Jeanne Robertson found fame and fortune in an unexpected and, at first, unwelcome place. Without Jeanne's permission, an audience member had uploaded one of her best stories to YouTube. At first Jeanne was furious: she felt violated that someone gave away her signature story that took her years to develop. Then something amazing happened. Jeanne's video went viral. Over six million baby boomers e-mailed it to each other. Here's the thing about YouTube: you can track what city your hits are coming from. Jeanne then turned her hilarious motivational speech into a one-person show and took it to those cities. The results? Jeanne played to sold-out houses where people actually begged her to tell the YouTube story. Go to MarketYourSpeech.com/videos to see Jeanne's clip. If you get a great live clip from your speech, where the audience goes crazy, don't hesitate to upload it to YouTube. It can give you professional credibility overnight.

6. Volunteer.
I met Scott Pixley at the Houston chapter of the National Speakers' Association. He's the president of NSA Houston. What is the difference between being a member of an NSA chapter and its president? Oh, let's see . . . one meeting! Over dinner, Scott, who speaks on "The Power of Connection," told me that he takes a leadership role in most of the organizations that he joins. Over the years he has served as:

- Chair, Young Professionals of Tulsa

- President, Young Guns (Oklahoma State)

- Advisory Board Member, Boys & Girls Clubs of Green Country (Tulsa)

- Board Member and Chief Fundraising Emcee for Oklahoma State University Alumni Association Tulsa Chapter

- Adult Programs Committee, Leadership Tulsa

- Board Member, Tulsa Foundation for Architecture

All of this involvement in leadership roles creates credentials. The results? Scott has been invited to speak at many of the organizations where he volunteers and many of them have led to paying gigs.

7. Speak!

Yes, the best way to develop credentials as a speaker is to speak. When I first went into speaking, I wasn't branded as the Goddess of Comedy. Matter of fact, I didn't have a lot of credentials that would be of interest to a business. My credentials made me an expert in the field of comedy but they didn't necessarily translate to a Fortune 500 setting. I began building my brand by volunteering to speak for cancer survivors at the Wellness Center. The title of my talk was "Healing with Humor." After speaking for free at many events, I was introduced to a *Wall Street Journal* reporter who thought my speech and my approach to combating illness with humor was newsworthy. The article ran and suddenly, I was an expert. Once the *Wall Street Journal* says you are an expert— you are an expert! My phone started ringing off the hook. The moral of that story is: luck happens to those who are already taking action.

I know it seems like a catch-22 situation, much like trying to break into the Screen Actors Guild—you want to act but you have to have a SAG card to work, but to get a card you have to already have an acting job. It makes no sense. Fortunately, with speaking it's easier than landing that juicy role in HBO's next hit series. In chapter seven, I even teach you how to book your first gig. By the time you finish this book, you'll have a speaking engagement on your calendar.

Right now, however, it's time to pick your Bookable Topic.

YOUR BOOKABLE TOPIC

I was recently hired to coach Laura Tenenbaum, who worked at the Jet Propulsion Laboratory here in California. As if that wasn't impressive enough, she was a professor of oceanography at a major university. I was excited to meet her. Working at JPL certainly established her as an expert in her field, and she'd expressed a burning desire to speak. I couldn't wait to get started.

Imagine my shock when we sat down for our first consultation and she announced that she wanted to speak about the yoga and circus training classes she'd been taking. My jaw hit the floor. I couldn't contain myself. I yelled at her, "You work at the Jet Propulsion Laboratory! You are an expert on climate change—that's your Bookable Topic!"

But my new client wasn't interested in speaking about her field of expertise. In fact, she was completely frustrated by the recycling movement and was quite opinionated about it. She told me, "Climate change is boring. Everyone is talking about that. I want to do something different. I want to be more personal. I want to be unique. I want to do a TED speech."

It took a heated (no pun intended) conversation but eventually I convinced my client that if she wanted to be hired as a professional (and paid) speaker, she had to qualify as an expert and she had to speak about a topic that was in-demand on the speaking circuit. Her expertise was climate change, and the fact that "everyone was talking about it" was a great thing. That meant there were audiences who not only wanted to hear about it but were willing to pay to hear about it! That meant there was a market niche she could fulfill, which meant she would work as a speaker. And wasn't that the goal?

I explained to my client that within the topic of her expertise, climate change, she could incorporate stories and experiences from her yoga and circus training. Once we worked out her Core Promise, we added her personal stories to make her point of view on climate change totally unique. I explained, "It's not *what* you talk about, it's *how* you

FRESH, HOT BOOKABLE TOPICS

"Hot topics are determined by larger forces. When the economy crashed, clients wanted speakers who spoke on Innovation and Change. In general, clients hire speakers who speak on leadership, motivation, customer fulfillment, and satisfaction, as well as health care and women's issues."

—Jonathan Wygant, owner and CEO of BigSpeak Motivational Speakers Bureau

talk about it. Your professional experience forms that foundation on which you build your Message of You."

In other words, your professional qualifications are your biggest clue in finding your bookable topic and your paying audience. Your Bookable Topic needs to be based on your credentials. Credentials give you credibility. What you qualify to talk about from your professional experience might, at first, seem boring to you. After all, being a CPA discussing private wealth management, a director of HR speaking about employee retention, or a scientist speaking about climate change might not sound like hot, sexy topics, but once you realize those speakers are making upwards of $10,000 per keynote address, those topics get *way* sexier!

But to reach out to these eager audiences, you have to be speaking about a Bookable Topic. Here's the thing: a meeting planner isn't going to say, "Find me a speaker who is funny with great stories." Rather, they will be looking for an entertaining speaker who talks on a specific topic that fits into the theme of their meeting such as "Dealing with Change," "Leadership," or "Entrepreneurship." They will Google the topic, not the speaker. So, you've got to merge The Message of You with a Bookable Topic that you are qualified to speak about.

After selecting your audience and knowing the problem you are going to address, finding your Bookable Topic is the third consideration you must make in finding your Core Promise. The marketability of what you talk about is important. You might be an expert in marine biology and have some great fish stories, but how many ichthyology conventions exist? Outside of the annual Sierra Club convention, there aren't many gigs where you'd get paid to explain the breeding habits of Siamese fighting fish. You've got to think bookable.

One of my students, Travis Taft, just spoke at an origami convention. Yes, even people who fold paper into birds have conventions that hire speakers. Travis has a compelling Heart Story. At seventeen years of age, he had a

FINDING YOUR NICHE-NESS

"You have to find your unique niche. Even if you are a CEO of a Fortune 500 company that means that there are 499 people just like you. If a speakers bureau already has ten people in your niche, then you have to find a way to be different by finding your uniqueness."

—Brian Lord, speaker agent,
VP of Premiere Speakers Bureau

body-surfing accident that left him with a devastating spinal cord injury. The doctors said he would be a quadriplegic, unable to move or feel sensation in both his upper and lower body. But Travis was determined to heal. I was there, by his hospital bed, the day his finger moved. Travis believes it was his unrelenting desire to become an origami master that gave him the will to move his hands again. Through hard work and against all odds, not only did Travis regain the use of his hands, but he can now even walk. His story can inspire others to rise above their own personal challenges if he can find a way to make origami a Bookable Topic. I'm now coaching Travis to broaden the scope of his speech to include his Heart Story, and to develop his Message of You to reflect the awesome journey of his life. His skill with origami can then be presented as a stress reduction technique, or a team-building technique, as well as an instrument of personal development for a corporate audience. With this new approach, he can reach out to a larger, better paying audience and he can have a career as a speaker that supports his passion for origami.

Not everyone has the kind of Heart Story that can turn origami into a Bookable Topic. Many amateur speakers think it's a good idea to choose an obscure topic nobody else speaks on because they don't want competition. That is a mistake. There is a reason nobody speaks on it—it's because there isn't an audience.

Listed in this chapter are the speaking topics that bureaus and meeting planners most often try to fill. Look over this list and determine which are related to your professional or personal qualifications. Can you claim to be an expert about any of them? Check all that apply but remember the name of this game is not checking a lot of boxes, but only the ones that you are highly qualified to speak about.

Shawn Ellis, owner of The Speakers Group bureau says, "When I see that a speaker talks on a lot of topics, I sense that they aren't very good, as you can't be an expert on everything." With that said, pay particular attention to the larger subject headings that encapsulate many smaller topics. The bigger your topic, the broader your audience base.

I'm a perfect example of this. Since I speak on reducing stress, this qualifies me to speak . . . um . . . everywhere. Everyone wants to experience less stress in their lives. Everyone wants to laugh as they learn. I have been hired to speak at all sorts of business meetings, conventions, expos, spinal cord injury wards at the VA, award banquets, cruise ships, schools, colleges, animal shelters, cancer survivor events, 10K races, medical events, vendor events, homeowner associations, and even the navy, the army, and the air force. I've also been hired by numerous governmental agencies including the FAA, the FICA, the Federal Reserve Board, and even the IRS. Yes, it's so weird getting a good call from the IRS wanting to give *me* money!

The combination of my Bookable Topic, Stress Reduction, with Humor as my Message of You has resulted in numerous speeches with Core Promises such as "Laugh Your Way Through Stress" for a business audience, "Laughter Is the Best Medicine" for a health-care audience, or "When Things Get Dire, Inspire" for the management crowd.

As you look at the list below, think about topics that are reflective of your journey and mesh with your credentials, but are also broad enough to be inclusive of many audiences. Some of the topics can be combined in the same speech. For instance, you can have a humor speech about travel issues for people with disabilities.

BOOKABLE TOPICS FOR SPEAKERS

Advertising

Branding

Communication Skills

Consumer Trends

Creativity / Ideation

Customer Service

Disability Issues

Diversity

Economic Future

Energy Issues

Environmental Issues

Generation X & Beyond

Hospitality

Innovation

Law

Management Skills

Negotiation Techniques

Organizational Skills

Overcoming Adversity

Parenting

Personal Development

Politics / World Affairs

Product Development

Recruitment/Retention

Retail

Risk Management

Science

Small Business

Aging

Change

Conflict Resolution

Corporate Culture

Crisis Management

Cyber Security

Disaster Preparedness

E-Commerces

Emerging Markets

Entrepreneurial Skills

Ethics / Values

Health Care / Wellness

Identity Theft

Investing

Leadership

Mergers & Acquisitions

Networking

Outsourcing

Overcoming Obstacles

Peak Performance

Personal Finance

Presentation Skills

Real Estate

Relationships

Retirement

Sales / Marketing

Security / Fraud

Social Media

Spirituality   Sports Life Lessons

Spouse Programs   Strategic Planning

Stress Management   Substance Abuse

Success   Team Building

Technology   Time Management

Travel   Volunteerism

Women's Issues   Work / Life Balance

Workforce Issues

Note: For up-to-date information related to Bookable Topics go to MarketYourSpeech.com/topic.

The following exercises will assist you in bolstering your confidence as well as familiarizing you with other speakers who speak on similar topics. Don't worry if they have the same topic as you do. There is room for everyone. It's not the topic that makes you a successful speaker, but what you do with it. A hundred speakers can speak on the same topic, but no one has your stories, your solutions, or your message.

EXERCISE: THE OFF-THE-CUFF CONFIDENCE BUILDER

Set an in-person meeting with your Speaker Buddy. Using the boxes you checked off from the list above, write the topics on pieces of paper, and put them in a bowl or a bag. Include your topics and your Buddy's topics in the same bag. Next, take turns picking out a topic and talking nonstop for three minutes as if you are the foremost expert on that topic by following this format:

1. "You people have a problem about (insert topic)." Talk for thirty seconds about what you would imagine the problem your audience has.

2. "Today I want to show you how you can (insert results)." Talk about the results that they are going to get from this speech for thirty seconds.

3. "I am qualified to talk to you about some solutions because I . . ." Make up a thirty-second story about how you became an expert on this topic and mention your professional experiences. Again, if you don't have any, make it up as you go as this exercise is just to give you the feel of giving a speech.

4. "I really understand what you are going through because on a personal level when I . . ." Tell a personal thirty-second story about something that happened to you that makes you truly understand The Problem the audience has with this topic. Again, make up a story if you don't have one. Just keep talking.

5. "Today I'm going to show you how to solve your problem by . . ." Now, end your three-minute speech by talking about how you are going to solve an aspect of their problem. Again, you may not know anything about the subject, so just fake it. Don't stop talking for three minutes. Make up words if you have to. The point is to sound like an expert and build your confidence as a speaker, as well as get a feel of the structure of a speech. Who knows, you might be surprised to find you actually are an expert!

EXERCISE: SUSS OUT YOUR COMPETITION

Using the topics you chose from the list above, do a Google or other Internet search to find out who the leading speakers are on that topic. Use the search phrase "[Topic] Speaker" or peruse the speaker bureau Web sites to find their client lists. If there are numerous speakers that are speaking on your topic, consider that topic commercial and viable. If you aren't using one of the above topics and you can't find anyone covering your chosen topic, it's time to rethink your choice. Note the purpose of this exercise is not to steal another speaker's approach to a topic, but for you to familiarize yourself with the marketability of your subject matter. You also need to know what sort of solutions other speakers offer. You must handle the topic in a different kind of way, *but* you need to know what's out there.

Narrow down your topics by asking yourself:

- Do I have both personal *and* professional experiences with this topic?

- Will my credentials qualify me as an expert in this topic?

Although other speakers are speaking on this topic, is there something new that I can bring to this topic? For instance, there are many men speaking on leadership, but not many women.

Get your list down to no more than three topics.

CHAPTER FOUR CHECKLIST:

☐ Created a list of my credentials.

☐ Picked a few topics that I qualify to talk about.

☐ Researched my topic on the Internet.

☐ Bumped up my credits if I needed to.

☐ Chose Bookable Topics that I qualify to speak about.

☐ Met with my Speaker Buddy and improvised a speech.

☐ Researched my competition.

☐ Narrowed myself to three topics or less.

CHAPTER FIVE

THEIR PROBLEM, YOUR SOLUTION

Tony Alessandra is an award-winning speaker whose keynote speech "How to Get and Keep Customers for Life" helps companies develop customer loyalty and adaptability in their sales team. At the beginning of his speech, Tony doesn't instantly offer his Action Steps or solutions, but rather hits them hard with their problems—problems that have negative consequences for their pocketbooks.

Now, you might think . . .

Judy, problems are unpleasant. Why would he remind them of just how messed up their life is? Aren't we supposed to be there to inspire and make the audience feel good?

Have you noticed that people don't usually go to a doctor until they're in pain? People ignore the dentist until their gums are bleeding or a tooth is loose. People toss out bills they can't pay, or avoid collection calls until they've lost their house or their credit ratings have tanked.

Most of us adapt to living in chaos, being broke, or feeling powerless. It's a speaker's job to make an audience not only aware that they have a problem, but *why* it's a problem and to make them understand that they no longer have to tolerate their situation. Denial is a powerful, powerful force. It keeps people stuck. As a speaker, it's your job to get them unstuck!

The reason speakers get paid a lot of money is because they provide their audiences with more than just an engaging, funny, or dramatic experience. Taking the audience on a journey from problem to solution they leave their audience with real tools—what I call Action Steps—that are meant to spur and inspire change. Most likely you'll be hired to speak to a company because they already have a specific problem they want to solve. If The Problem is profits are down, meeting planners will book a speaker to motivate their sales force. If the staff is facing burnout and stress, the meeting planner will book a speaker to boost spirits. If there's been a recent merger, a meeting planner will book a speaker who provides solutions for coping with change. Often, meeting planners will take The Problem or "challenge" that their employees are facing and use it as the theme of the meeting or even the entire conference. Some examples of themes include: higher sales, keeping pace with change, increasing communication, improving morale, and so on. Meeting planners will then select speakers who fit the chosen theme—in other words, the speaker who can offer effective solutions for The Problems facing the audience will land the job.

WHAT DO MEETING PLANNERS WANT?

"When I'm looking for a speaker, I don't want a canned presentation. I want a speaker who takes the time to find out about the audience and the challenges that the audience is facing. I appreciate speakers who do the research in advance of the presentation as well as those who arrive at the event early and attended the meetings so they work in what happened in a meeting. I want someone who becomes emotionally involved so it's not just a job."

—Bonnie Wallsh, MA, CMP, CMM, chief strategist, Bonnie Wallsh Associates

Whatever their problem, a speaker's job is to understand the specifics of that problem and to provide solutions. That means that your Core Promise must show an understanding of the "challenge" (that's business speak for "nightmares") facing the company and that your Action Steps must present viable, doable solutions. Later in your Heart Story, you'll show that you are living proof of the solution. And yes, you will have to tinker with your speech before each engagement to further personalize the material but your Core Promise shouldn't fluctuate greatly.

No one actually expects a one-hour speech to fix all the company problems, but meeting planners and companies do expect a speaker to provide some actionable suggestions—Action Steps—that can shift employee attitudes in a positive direction. When everyone is back in the office on Monday, meeting planners want to hear how much everyone enjoyed and learned from the speaker. Bosses want to see smiles on faces. It's your job to provide just a little ray of sunshine, inspiration, or know-how that employees can take back to their desk, to their family, and to their lives. If you can do that, you will be worth a lot of money in the speaking biz.

Finding the problem/solution aspect of your speech is the final piece of the Core Promise—it is the act of combining The Message of You with the message of the meeting. But how do you find those Action Steps, and how do you even know what problem needs to be solved?

There are really only three big problems that will motivate your audience to change. No matter what Bookable Topics you selected in the previous chapter, you will have to find a way to connect your audience's specific problems to one or all of the big three:

Big Problem One: Wealth

Everyone needs more money, wants to make more money, has bills to pay, mouths to feed, is worried about job security, or is hoping to improve their career. Everyone has concerns about their wealth.

Big Problem Two: Health

Mental, physical, spiritual, emotional, everyone needs healthy bodies and healthy minds in order to live. When that health is threatened by disease, stress, environmental factors, you'd better believe people will want to hear new solutions!

Big Problem Three: Relationships

Whether it's sidestepping office politics in the boardroom, whispering sweet nothings in the bedroom, or sweating in front of twenty-five bored teenagers in the classroom, everyone is constantly negotiating and renegotiating their relationships with family, friends, and even enemies. Love, sex, hatred. People will pay attention if your solutions will help them better relate to others.

Tap into one or more of the big three and you will put the audience in touch with their pain. Once they are desperate for change they will be open to the cure and you will give it to them. Presenting your solution in this way will have the audience hanging on your every word.

This is why Tony's speech is so effective. He's able to convince the audience that their problems are standing in the way of them making more money and is preventing long-lasting relationships with their clients.

To better understand this process, let's look closely at this section of Tony's speech. Tony believes that there are four distinct customer personalities: the Director, the Thinker, the Relater, and the Socializer. He introduces the *problems* associated with each personality by explaining:

". . . Relaters seek harmony and close, personal one-to-one relationships. They are loyal team players, good listeners, and the glue that holds the team together, but they don't like conflict or rocking the boat. It's easy to hurt their feelings, but you won't know it until they get out of your sight. They will pull out a little book, write your name on it, and put a check mark by it . . ."

After outlining the three other personality types, Tony explains the *consequences* of ignoring the personalities of customers.

"If a client won't buy what you are selling, you blame the client. But the problem is that you, the salesperson, described the product in terms of how it moved and motivated you rather than how it can move and motivate them, the client."

Tony doesn't stop there. He even goes after the CEO.

"The way your company categorizes its customers is outdated. You define clients in Clint Eastwood terms of the good [client], the bad [client], and the ugly [client]. The bad customers—the ones who aren't making you money—you try to change them and when that doesn't work, you just cut them out and focus solely on the profitable clients."

Tony can do this because he's done his homework. He knows his audience. That's why he can do the same speech for all his engagements because his message is relatable to most companies. When you truly understand The Problem of a large group of people, your mythology can become a speech that resonates for thousands of audiences. Tony is successful because he knows his audience's problems and he fully understands the complexity and severity of the consequences if those problems go unchecked.

The question is . . . do you?

EXERCISE: EXPLORING THE PROBLEM OF YOUR TOPIC

You may have chosen many Bookable Topics in the last chapter, but for now focus on one topic. It should be a topic where you've had hands-on experience working in that field or you qualify to talk about it because of your life experiences. Even if you think you know everything there is to know about your topic, in this exercise I'm going to ask you to interview others who

IT'S NOT ABOUT YOU!

"We look for speakers who are able to be effectively focused on the client's problem. Narcissism can get in the way of a speaker being effective and able to transform others."

—Jonathan Wygant, BigSpeak Motivational Speakers Bureau

work in that field. Don't pick someone who is a speaker, but rather someone who would likely be an audience member.

For instance, if your topic is "Entrepreneurship," find a friend who owns their own business. If you picked "Effective Management" as your topic, choose a manager you worked with at a past job or a friend who manages a company or a team of people. If your topic is "Time Management," then track down someone who is raising a family as well as having a career. Got it? Find someone who could benefit from listening to your expertise.

This person can be a friend, a coworker, anyone related to your topic. Even if you feel you are a master at this topic, don't skip this exercise. We always have more to learn and there is always room for surprise.

When I first started, my Message of Me pointed to the Bookable Topics of Humor and Stress Reduction. When I did this exercise, I had to think of someone who could really benefit from my message of using humor to decrease stress. My first thought was everyone, but that was too general and wouldn't help me write my speech. So I picked people dealing with cancer. I was sure they, of all people, could use a laugh. I looked up organizations and contacted Gilda's Club, an organization formed by the late comedy legend, Gilda Radner, to assist people going through cancer treatment. Several members, including their president, were more than happy to be interviewed by me.

From interviewing several cancer survivors, as well as staff who worked with them, I not only identified the stresses facing cancer survivors, but the president asked me to speak at her organization. Woo-Hoo! So, before I even *had* my speech, I had my first real gig.

Here are some sample questions you can ask a mock audience member:

1. What is a bad day for people dealing with this topic?

2. What are three problems that everyone in this industry (or topic) has in common?

3. What are some of the bad consequences of these problems? For instance, someone who speaks on organizational skills might list "living in chaos" as a problem. The consequences of that

could be "being late to work because you're always looking for your keys," "spending money to replace items you've lost." And so on.

4. What would be a few beneficial results of speech on (insert your topic)?

When I interviewed cancer survivors about what was stressing them, what emerged were the stresses of:

- "A bad day is when I have to deal with doctors and insurance people in the same day. They don't listen. They treat me like I'm a machine and there is too much paperwork."

- "One of the problems of having a life-threatening illness has to be helping friends deal with *their* grief over my illness. I don't have enough energy to take care of myself and now I have to take care of my friends."

- "The result of all these problems is that I'm depressed from having cancer, anxious about seeing the doctor, exhausted from taking care of my friend's feelings, and pissed at the insurance companies."

Desired benefits of my speech were:

1. Laughter can improve the immune system.

2. A sense of humor can transform you from "just another patient" into a real person in the eyes of the insurance companies and the doctors.

3. Sharing laughs with friends takes the focus of illness and puts it back on the friendship.

Okay, your turn.

After interviewing a few people, determine ten big problems that face your target audience.

Looking over that list, which of these problems can be connected to the big three: wealth, health, or relationships? How? Make a list of the possible beneficial results of your speech.

SOLVING THE AUDIENCE'S PROBLEM

Speakers have to offer hope. Remember my client who didn't want to talk about climate change? When I asked her for a solution, her first reaction was to throw her hands up and say, "It's hopeless. There is nothing one person can do." Well, nobody in their right mind would book that speech. "Hey, I'm here to talk about hopelessness. Kool-Aid anybody?"

Working with my climate change professor, I made a few suggestions about solutions that might be better received, such as: "Enjoy the beauty of the planet now," "Renew your commitment to recycling," or "The power of one person."

Meeting planners want to know how people will feel at the end of your speech and this part of The Message of You is where you express just that: "You are going to learn how to . . . ," "You are going to leave knowing . . ."

Later on, when you write your speech in Part Two, this formula will be broken down into specific Action Steps that you will present to the audience. For now, you need to identify a few gifts you are giving to your audience and how it will solve their problem.

EXERCISE: YOUR SOLUTIONS FOR SUCCESS

Let's start with examining the steps you took when you zigzagged your way from failure to success in your own life. Remember those stories you collected in chapter three? The ones about your journey from failure to success? There, I asked you to pay attention to the life lessons you learned. Those lessons and stories will come in handy now.

So many of the ways we solve our problems are intuitive, subconscious. Most of us are so busy living we never stop to examine how we got to where we are now. Most successful people can't tell you what steps they took to become successful. Football coaches can't always explain how they won the championship game. In the moment, they were acting on talent and intuition.

This is where you come in. If you can discern your own methodology of problem solving, then you can use what you learned from your own life to teach others. This is your challenge in this chapter. Here I will lead you to research the problems surrounding the topic you chose in the last chapter, and examine your own steps to success, both personally and professionally; you will create the final piece of The Message of You.

FINDING SOLUTIONS IN YOUR OWN PROBLEMS

"I suffered from terrible stage fright, but I found a way to help myself and developed a method to help other people feel comfortable in front of groups; so, they too can share their ideas, insights, and expertise to make a difference in the world."

—Sandra Zimmer, speaker and author of *It's Your Time to Shine: How to Overcome Fear of Public Speaking, Develop Authentic Presence and Speak From Your Heart*

We all have learned something in our lives. In your journey to success some things worked and got you to a new place, while some things may have set you back a few steps. In order to speak, you need to be able to succinctly tell an audience the step-by-step directions you took from problem to solution.

I'm asking you to take a helicopter view of your life journey. Here are a few ways to do it:

1. Looking at the story of your life journey (chapter three), write out all the steps you took to solve your problems.

2. What were five steps you took that led you to a specific success?

3. What were the long-term results of those actions or circumstances?

4. How can those steps solve a problem that your speech will address?

When I transitioned from performing stand-up comedy to teaching, I was overwhelmed with fear. How could I teach someone how to be funny? But at my first class, when students were having trouble memorizing their act, coming up with punch lines, or even trying to get over stage fright, I was amazed at how much I knew. All those years playing clubs, and all those pages of writing comedy material gave me the expertise to know exactly what advice to give my students. That's when I wrote my first book, *Standup Comedy: The Book,* which became the compilation of those solutions and Action Steps I developed on the fly for comics.

You know a lot. More than you think. From living your life, from doing your job, you've become an expert and you are capable of passing that knowledge on to others. Remember, you are not expected to solve all problems. There's no need to make outrageous promises you can't deliver. No person can be a master of everything. The solutions you will teach *have* to be the ones that you've used in your own life and they have to work. This is where you walk your talk.

It is only *after* outlining The Problem(s) that Tony Alessandra introduces the audience to his solution in three Action Steps. He tells them:

"In order to exceed a customer's expectations you need to do three things: identify, manage, and monitor. Identify the customer's expectations and become client-centered in understanding their needs and goals. Second, we have to manage the client's expectations so they aren't too high. Third, we have to monitor them and inspect what the customer expects. Follow these three Action Steps and you have a good chance of exceeding your customer's expectations and even generating new customers."

Tony has branded his solutions, his Action Steps, and created a trademarked Core Promise called The Platinum Rule™. Before you start registering your own trademark, it's best to investigate the solutions you hope to offer.

EXERCISE: PUTTING *YOUR* FIX ON *THEIR* PROBLEM

If you completed the exercises in the previous chapters, you should be able to answer these questions:

1. Who is your audience? (Women, baby boomers, health-care workers, cancer patients, administrative aides, technical support, etc.)

2. Write for twenty minutes on the three biggest problems facing your audience, based on what you learned from interviewing your contact.

3. From your expertise and personal experiences, write for thirty minutes on what you learned from your own life experiences that could be offered as solutions to your audience's problems.

4. Looking at what you wrote, brainstorm five to ten possible actions that could be taken to achieve these solutions such as "remove clutter" or "express your appreciation." Don't go into detail. Write these ideas in two or three word statements.

5. What would be the result of enacting those five to ten possible steps? Less negativity? Better sales? Healthier eating habits? Ultimately, what is the goal and how does it relate to The Big Three?

You may be asking yourself, "What is my goal?" as you sift through the reams of material you've created to get to this page. It may seem as if you have a gobbledygook of essays, stories, and messages, but look again. All the work you put in is finally going to pay off. Now you have enough information to turn The Message of You into the Core Promise of your speech.

CHAPTER FIVE CHECKLIST:

☐ Researched "The Problem" by interviewing someone in the field that I will be speaking to.

☐ Created a list of the possible problems facing my audience.

☐ Found how the consequences of The Problem relates to a person's health, wealth, or relationships.

☐ Examined my life journey for my solutions to The Problems.

☐ Ended up with a gobbledygook of essays, stories, and messages.

CHAPTER SIX

PUTTING THE PIECES TOGETHER:
THE CORE PROMISE FORMULA

When Laura Tenenbaum called me, she was confused and over-whelmed. Her head was spinning with literally hundreds of stories and possible messages. Laura had an enviable problem—she was an expert in too many topics. She had too many interests. She'd found her passion in life during a college science class, when she learned about sea slugs. Yes, you heard me right—sea slugs. They fascinated her enough that she changed her major at the University of California Santa Cruz to marine science. She then spent a number of years overseas teaching scuba diving before landing a job as an adjunct professor at Glendale Community College, then went on to become a Communication and Education Specialist at NASA's Jet Propulsion Laboratory in their Earth and Climate Communication division. Laura was frozen in place, unable to focus and formulate a Core Promise. She had assumed that writing her Core Promise would be just as straightforward a process as putting together a résumé.

It wasn't.

Now, Laura had a major problem and she wanted a solution. (A-ha! See how I snuck that in there!) Laura wanted a fill-in-the-blank formula.

Fortunately, I had developed just that formula.

THE CORE PROMISE FORMULA

"You know how . . ." **(insert your audience)**

"Your new sales team, parents, doctors, women, volunteers, employees, or even just "people."

". . . have this problem, they are . . ." **(insert problem)**

". . . stressed and overwhelmed from working longer hours, facing emotional burnout working on the oncology ward, aren't attracting new clients, can't get customers to their Web site, have too much paperwork, don't have a retirement plan and are going to end up broke . . ."

"From my experiences . . ." **(insert professional experience)**

"Working fifteen years in HR, flying to the moon, headlining comedy clubs, working at the IRS . . ."

"As well as what I learned from . . ." **(insert personal experiences)**

"Surviving my own teenager, surviving third degree burns over 80 percent of my body, struggling with dyslexia, successfully changing careers at fifty years old . . ."

"I show the audience how they can also . . ." **(insert the expected results)**

This is the promise of your speech. For example, "lead funnier and happier lives, create new business, increase their sales, learn how to get out of depression, increase sales, be better parents, increase efficiency, deal with change, have the home they dreamed of, increase their income by 30 percent."

"By . . ." **(insert your solution or methodology)**

"Adding just ten minutes to each workday, using their sense of humor to dissolve conflict, having fewer meetings, initiating a four-day work week, focusing on appreciating what they have rather than wanting what they don't have."

Laura was thrilled to be given the formula. After months of wading through her hobbies and stories and experiences working in the male-dominated world of science, she finally had a way to contain, communicate and understand her speech.

It only took her ten minutes to fill in the blanks:

"*You know how many ordinary people, non-scientists, think about climate change and other environmental issues as kind of depressing and overwhelming? Even when you feel like you can do something, it just feels like whatever you do is too small. Besides, green solutions can cost a lot, and people have other things competing for their attention, such as women's right, gay rights, and Angry Birds. From my experiences as a college professor and part of the earth science communication team at NASA, as well as what I learned from my own views from looking at Earth from space as well as from the bottom of the ocean as a scuba diver, I show audiences how to reacquaint themselves with the thrill of science and feel that they can make a difference, by rekindling their love affair with Planet Earth and appreciating the wonder that is right here under our feet at all times.*"

Okay, your turn.

The Core Promise of your speech should, in brief, reflect the logical step-by-step outline of your entire speech. If any of the six components are missing, your speech won't work.

Let's review the steps of your Core Promise to make sure that each is structurally sound before you begin writing your speech.

Ask yourself these questions about each section:

Audience

- Do you qualify to speak to your audience?

- Will your credentials mean something to your chosen audience?

- Do you already have a personal connection to a group or audience because you work for the organization?

- Is there an association you belong to?

- Do you understand the needs of your audience?

- Can your audience relate to you?

- Can you identify your audience?

Problems

- Are The Problems you're tackling authentic and relevant to the organization?

- Are they backed up by interviews that you've done?

- Are they timely?

- Are they dire?

- Do they relate to the Big Three—health, wealth, and relationships?

Your Credentials

Do you have relevant professional credentials that qualify you to solve the specific problems you've stated? If not, start the process over again to find the audience and The Problems you qualify to solve.

Your Personal Experience

- Have you personally had to deal with The Problems you've stated?

- Have you overcome them?

- Have you learned a life lesson that can be imparted?

- Do you have Support Stories and a Heart Story to illustrate that lesson? If not, go back and rework chapter five.

Your Promise/Results

Your promise and your results *must solve the problem*. Don't begin your speech outlining the specific problems of time management and then have the results be about leadership skills. The promise of your speech must directly relate to the problems you outlined.

Your Methodology

Your Action Steps must address *the stated problem*. If your steps do not address The Problem, then start over again and set up a problem that your methodology can address.

In my workshops at KeynoteU.com, we usually spend two weeks on just the Core Promise, making sure each piece of the puzzle fits perfectly. Making sure that one step leads to the next step. Making sure that the solution fits The Problem. This might seem like a lot of mind-numbing work, but it does pay off big time. The students who rush and don't take the time to make sure their Core Promise makes logical sense end up with a speech that doesn't make sense. That disconnect then extends to the audience as well as their confusing marketing materials.

If you've ever watched a house being built, you will see that there are months spent laying the foundation. If the foundation is faulty, no matter how much time and energy goes into building the rest of the house, it will not be sound. Your Core Promise is the foundation of your speech. It has to be rock solid in its foundation.

Writing all this out, you may find that you have a real mouthful of a message. While you may have plenty of room on your Web site to announce your Core Promise, when you call up a meeting planner, you'll have about fifteen seconds to knock 'em dead. That's why you'll now need to create the Elevator Pitch version of your Core Promise.

ELEVATOR PITCH

The Elevator Pitch is the condensed mini-version of the above formula.

Their Problem + Your Expertise + The Message of You = Elevator Pitch

For example, let's look at speaking student Tracy Suttles's Elevator Pitch:

Their problem: *Do you ever lose a sale and you don't know why?*

Your expertise: *From my fifteen years experience in sales training where I've improved sales as much as 85 percent.*

The Message of You: *I'm going to show you how to navigate beyond your sales script to personalize your sales approach through the art of conversation.*

Now you try it.

From this point on, I want you to practice saying your Elevator Pitch out loud over and over again. Say it when you wake up in the morning. Say it in the shower and say it in your car on the drive to work. As you say it to people it will evolve, as you will need to change any part that feels awkward. It's okay to get away from the exact wording, as it needs to sound natural for you to say it. It needs to become authentically yours. Once it is, condense it even further by squeezing your Elevator Pitch into the title of your speech.

TITLES THAT TITILLATE

Now that you've written all the components of your speech, it's time to find the perfect title. A title is the first thing meeting planners see. It's the first thing audience members read in their programs, and it determines whether meeting planners will book you or move on to your competitor. It also determines how many audience members will show up for your keynote!

CREATE YOUR OWN LANGUAGE

"The best way to corner a niche is to create your own word and use it in your title. When you do that, (i.e., Tongue Fu!®, SerenDestiny®, Freakonomics), you can trademark that word.

"Now, you don't just have a clever book or speech title, you have a business empire because you can monetize and merchandize in perpetuity."

—Sam Horn, speaker and author of *POP! Create the Perfect Pitch, Title, and Tagline for Anything*

1. Write all the words associated with the problem that you plan on addressing in your speech. (For example, suppose you lost two hundred pounds, and you now talk about how to lose weight even if you hate to diet, hate to exercise, and have a slow metabolism. Among the words you would write down would be lose, weight, hate, diet, exercise, slow, and metabolism.)

2. Now, write all the words associated with your solution.

3. Expand your list of words by using a thesaurus to find even more words with the same or similar meaning (synonyms). For example, if I look up the word "diet" I get watch your weight, reduce, starve yourself, fast, etc.

4. Add your new words (plus variations, like starving or starve).

5. Now, try arranging words into snappy titles using one of more of these title tips:

- Modify familiar catch phrases and expressions so that they are relevant to your topic in the title, i.e., "The Cure for the Common Brand" (from "the cure for the common cold") or "How to Use Poker Strategy to Have a Winning Hand in Life" (from "a winning hand").

- Use "from" (problem) and "to" (solution) so that it illustrates the change your speech will make (i.e., "From Confrontation to Communication").

- Mention your qualifications to speak on your topic in the title. ("From Homeless to Harvard" is written by a woman who did exactly what the title implies.)

- Use numbers or steps in your title (i.e., "Four Easy Steps to Sell Your Writing"). Doing so makes a difficult problem seem more manageable.

- Identify your target market in your presentation title (i.e., "Management Strategies for Real Estate Agents"—this title makes your speech more appealing to Realtors than a general management speech or anyone and everyone). When starting out, it's a good idea to narrow your focus to an audience that you have access to. Then, as you grow in popularity, you can make your title more general.

Look to magazine covers to find good titles that have sizzle.

7. Rhyming words can make a memorable title. If any of the words in your description of the problem or solution rhyme, you might want to use them in the title. For example, "Lose Weight Without the Hate: Five Steps to a Perfect Body Without Dieting or Exercise."

8. Name a technique after yourself, as in "Carter's Comedy Technique for Breaking the Ice with New Customers." (The advantage to this technique is that, if your method becomes famous, so do you.)

SURVEY SAYS . . .

Take a break from *Words With Friends* and put your Facebook friends to good use by involving them in your speech research. Use a Facebook or Twitter survey to get instant feedback on the possible titles of your speech. Consider it a good title when a friend comments, "Great title! Perfect for my company. Let me see if you can speak at our next meeting."

Once you have a few ideas for titles, Google the best ones to make sure that nobody else is using the same titles.

Find five people who resemble your target audience in terms of demographics and other characteristics. For example, if your speech is called "Retire in Style: Five Steps to Stop Working and Start Living," then your fifty-year-old uncle can give you a much more valuable opinion than your teenage skateboarder cousin. Have them rank the titles you're considering from best to worst.

Choose your title, and write it in your notes.

CHAPTER SIX CHECKLIST:

☐ Condensed The Message of You into the Core Promise Formula.

☐ Practiced my Elevator Pitch.

☐ Got a title for my speech.

In the end, it's so simple isn't it? It all boils down to a few powerful sentences that somehow manage to convey all the writing you did about yourself, your audience, and your expertise. Don't hate me for making you write pages and pages of material. You're going to use all of it again in Part Two, as we now expand these powerful sentences into your keynote speech.

That's right, it's time to jump in there and write your speech.

CHAPTER SEVEN

JUDY'S SUREFIRE ANTIPROCRASTINATION PLAN

Hey, wait! Didn't I just say it was time to write your speech?

Yes, I did.

But if you're anything like me, just hearing that declaration caused you to put this book down, start cleaning out the fridge, organizing your sock drawer, or suddenly decide to take up scrapbooking. You, my friend, are in the grips of the Procrastination Monster.

But, wait, it gets even scarier.

You are going to book your first speaking gig now—before you've written your speech.

You might now be wondering if I'm writing while inebriated. I am not. At least not today . . . but with that said, drunk or not, I know for certain that you will *not* complete writing your speech unless you have a speaking gig waiting for you on your calendar. How do I know this? Because speaking is scary, and most people (i.e., anyone with a brain) avoid things that scare them. A survey taken by *USA Today* found that the number one fear people share is public speaking. The number two fear is the fear of dying. This means people would rather their parachute not open than have to speak in front of a group of people. To quote Jerry Seinfeld, "That means that at a funeral, people would prefer to be the guy in the box than the guy giving the sermon."

NEED HELP?

Go to KeynoteU.com for your own personal speaking tutor.

Then there are the people, such as, oh, let me think—everyone, who find writing even scarier than speaking! Most of my new coaching clients are speakers who have a gig scheduled within a few days and they are, like Chastity from chapter one of this book, in a state of panic. They have put off writing their speech until the very last moment, and they call me begging for help to avoid the humiliation of failure.

Fear itself isn't the problem. It's the way you deal with it—or don't deal with it—that is the problem. You might not even be aware how often actions and decisions are solely based on fear. For instance, you might not go to a party because you're frightened to go alone, but you tell yourself, "I'm too tired, I have a big day tomorrow." Probably just the same way you skipped the harder exercises in this book thinking you'd get back to them. If you are like most wannabe creative types, your storage area is filled with unfinished screenplays, slides, and photos that you will someday scan and organize, and journals filled with "great ideas." Maybe you excitedly start a project but when it takes too much time, too much energy, you bail. You want the immediate rewards, whether it is money or applause. You want some sort of appreciation for the hard work. Your inner critic kicks in: "You're not really good at this. What makes you think you can tell others what to do with their life? You don't really know what to do with yours!" This is when 90 percent of people give up. Starting is easy. Finishing is hard. Most of us are all good starters, but there are fewer of us at the finish line. We are sprinters, rather than marathon runners.

Here's the thing. Successful people finish stuff.

Some of my students ask me if I think that they have enough talent to make it as a speaker or a comic. The problem is that it's not talent that makes a speaker successful. I've watched so many amazingly talented performers who never let go of their day jobs. Meanwhile, I've seen less talented people go on to fame and fortune. (You can make your own list on that one.) So, what do those people have that is more important than talent? They have persistence—the will to keep going when fear tells them to stop. There are a lot of people who want to be successful, but fewer who are willing to do what it takes. They make the time to work on their speeches even if their lives are busy and stressed. They don't close the computer when their inner critic tells them to stop.

This type of unexpressed fear could be slowing your career advancement. You might be avoiding expressing your ideas—both in speeches and in general—because you feel uncomfortable about the possibility of failure. But instead of facing that fear, you tell yourself, "I can just send this out in a memo" or "I'll keep this to myself—why rock the boat?" or "I'll write my speech later; I've got to check Facebook..." When you experience fear, remember that seemingly brave people are *not actually brave*! They are just as nervous and just as freaked out as you! What distinguishes the seemingly brave from the clearly fearful is that the brave ones act *despite* their fear. They don't allow fear to stop them and neither should you.

Writing your speech might seem like a daunting job. But if you break it down into smaller portions, it is manageable. It's like gardening. I wanted to grow a vegetable garden, so I planted a bunch of seeds. When they all started to grow I got overwhelmed, and a friend told me to break the garden down into small squares. Just plant a few of the squares. All of a sudden it got manageable. The same goes for your speech. If you break down writing your speech into six segments, it becomes easier to handle. That's why in Part Two, we take it section by section.

Now, the reason people plant a garden is because they want and/or need to eat what they've grown. Hunger is pretty good motivation. You need an equally compelling reason to finish writing your speech. Booking your first gig will be that motivation. It will be the ticking clock in the back of your brain as you obsessively update your Facebook page or clean the bathtub for the fifteenth time. Procrastination is a drug that manifests in many forms: futzing, eating, drinking, catching up on that *CSI: Miami* marathon, or even actual drugs. When I'm supposed to write, I find so many excuses to delay my process: I will obsessively look for ideas in the refrigerator, eat tons of snacks, have a glass of wine, and by 8 p.m., I'm thirty-eight Weight Watcher points over goal with no pages to show for it. So I swear to you, there is no better way to ensure you will finish your speech than by having a speaking gig looming on your calendar. Consider it motivation for the motivator you are supposed to be.

The first gig you'll book will be a freebie. Even though there are thousands of companies who want to hire and pay outside speakers to educate, inspire, and motivate their audience with a keynote you need practice. If you're just starting your career, it's better to speak for free at your workplace or for a charity group or nonprofit while you hone your speech. Plus, you probably don't yet have what is necessary to land a paying gig. And I don't mean that in talent terms. You may be very talented, but to book a paying gig you need some basic marketing materials such as a killer video demo, a cool Web site, and "Happy Letters" from past clients. I discuss these further in Part Three.

Even if you are a Pro, you may want to try out your new speech in a less stressful situation. Free gigs may not give you money but they will give you experience, help you further develop content, and, if all goes well, provide you with video clips and referral letters so you can go from free to fee.

As I mentioned before, one of my first gigs was speaking for cancer survivors. At the time of my call with the president of that group, I hadn't written my speech. All I had was a title, "Using Humor to Heal." She was thrilled and set a time for me to speak, a month away. That date kicked my butt into gear. The gig went well—so well that one of the audience members, a sociologist from UCLA, approached me after the keynote and said the magic words, "How much would you charge to speak to my group?" I made up a number like $750 and he said fine! My career was off and running.

The point is I never would have written my speech without that first gig on my calendar. You've got to book it to do it!

EXERCISE: GET YOUR SH*T TOGETHER

Even though you're pursuing a freebie, there is still one marketing item you will need to line up a gig. It's called an EPK (electronic press kit).

Your EPK includes:

- ☐ Your speech title
- ☐ Your speech in brief
- ☐ A brief bio
- ☐ A professional picture

Your Speech Title

Just use that baby you created in chapter six. Done!

Your Speech in Brief

You've already got that! It's your Elevator Pitch. Done!

A Brief Bio

Condense your bio to no longer than fifty words. The shorter the better. Start with your most impressive credentials and reference how it relates to the title of your speech.

A Professional Picture

Make it a recent photo. There is nothing worse than showing up at a gig and the client can't recognize you from the high school prom picture you sent them. And no, you can't crop out your wife or your best Buddy from the photo and just hope they ignore the arm around your shoulder. That's creepy. Invest in a photo session or if you're broke, have a friend use your digital camera. Brush your hair, check your teeth for lipstick smears, stand in front of a plain background, and smile.

How much is this going to cost you to put together? Nothing. I've created a Web site where you can create and send out your EPKs for free and you don't need any graphic design skill to do it. I told you I'm committed to you being a success. So, go to SpeakerDemo.com, where you can create your EPK.

Now, as for booking your gig . . .

Practically all speakers get their start from someone they know, or an organization that they belong to. Right now, there is probably one degree of separation between you and your audience. Look in your wallet—there are speaking opportunities right there. Your credit card company, insurance company, your school, the associations you belong to, and even the public library has meetings that use speakers.

SPEAKING OPPS WITHIN YOUR PROFESSION

One of my speaking students is a nurse and found plenty of opportunities associated with her profession. Nurses can speak at nursing association meetings, nurse local association chapter meetings, nursing schools, drug rep dinners, vendor expos, health fairs, hospitals, clinics, CEU Education Days, National Nurses Week, and staff orientations at hospitals, annual conventions, staff health programs, and more.

Very often your workplace is a bonanza of speaking opportunities. One of the biggest complaints you have is there are too many meetings. Just flip that, and it means that there are plenty of opportunities for you to speak. At smaller meetings, companies use in-house speakers.

That means that Mary from HR will be enlisted to give a presentation on the company's "Go Green Program."

The person who signs your paychecks is a great person to talk to about booking your first gig. One of my students worked as a greeter at Banana Republic. She put together a five-minute comedy routine about her job and showed it to her boss, who asked her to do it at their next meeting. Next thing you know, she was invited to give a thirty-minute speech at the Banana Republic national meeting on the topic of "The Power of a First Impression."

If you work for a company, volunteering to speak at these meetings is an excellent way to hone your speaking abilities and get some time onstage, or what I like to call "ring time." If it goes well, speaking can put you on the fast track to promotion. No matter where you are on the corporate speaking totem pole, there are speaking opportunities for you. Here are ways to track them down.

EXERCISE: FIND YOUR TRIBE

1. Make a list of all the nonprofit organizations in your neighborhood that might welcome speakers: the military, a rotary club, Girl Scouts, PTA, and so on. Do you have any personal connections to these organizations? Do you know anyone who does?

2. Look back over chapter four, where you made an exhaustive list of your past professional experiences. Could you approach any of those companies or organizations and offer your services? Do you know anyone who still works there?

3. Make a list of your close friends and family. Do they belong to any groups who would welcome a speaker? Name-dropping is worth its weight in gold.

4. Remember that list of topics you brainstormed in chapter four? Google your Bookable Topics and make a list of organizations that pop up in your search.

5. Research your Facebook friends. Look under their Likes section to see if they are affiliated with any nonprofits. Look at their profession/career ticker and take notes on who works where.

MAKE THE CALL

I find that making calls on my behalf is harder than giving the speech. This is where everyone wishes they had a manager who could do it for them. Well, guess what? You do have a manager—your Speaker Buddy. It's a lot easier to yak about how great someone else is. When I'm coaching my students, I get them a free gig and they can do a test run of their speech. It's so much easier to call up a school, or a business, and tout the benefits of my student's speech rather than bragging about myself. Actually, early in my stand-up career I didn't have an agent, so I created a character called Pam Keller and I made calls pretending to be her. This worked for a while until a comedy club owner wanted to meet up with her and it got awkward!

Don't worry. Neither you nor your Buddy needs to be a shark to book these gigs. You just have to know what to do and say to sound like a Pro. You have to know how to cold-call a client.

How to Cold-Call a Client

1. First target the organizations where you have a personal connection or referral.

2. Look up the organization on the Internet and make sure they have meetings scheduled. Find out when their next meeting may be.

3. Identify the person who books meetings. This is sometimes the hardest part. Don't waste your spiel on the operator. When you call, ask, "Do you know who books speakers for your meetings?" Sometimes you will be connected to someone who will connect you to someone else and so on, until you find the right person.

4. Let the meeting planner know who referred you or how you are associated with their group. "Such and such suggested that you use speakers and I might be a good match." Or, "My son went to your school, and I'm grateful and I wanted to give back." Next, ask them "Do you have any events coming up that you could use a speaker who speaks on (insert your topic here)."

5. If they don't, then ask them if they can refer you to someone else.

6. If they do have an event, then ask if you can send your electronic press package to give them a better idea of your approach to the topic.

7. Finally, ask them if they prefer communication via the phone or e-mail, and get a time to speak with them again. Be specific. "Can I call you again Friday at 3:30 p.m.?"

You may be surprised at how appreciative people are that you want to give freely of your time and expertise. Make the calls! This may turn out to be easier than it seems right now.

And now you have a date on your calendar!!!!

CHAPTER SEVEN CHECKLIST:

☐ Created my EPK.

☐ Tracked down potential places to speak.

☐ Called a potential client.

☐ Put a date on my calendar.

Now . . . let's write your speech!

PART TWO

JUDY'S SEVEN-STEP METHOD
FOR WRITING A
HILARIOUS AND INSPIRING SPEECH

CHAPTER EIGHT

IT'S ABOUT THEM

If you followed the steps in Part One, you have all the materials you need to tackle writing your speech. Don't worry if your stories seem vague or messy, or if your Core Promise doesn't yet seem right or perfect. In this section, Part Two, I will take you through a series of exercises that will transform your Heart Story and Core Promise into a fully realized speech that inspires your audience and, hopefully, results in a big check, big laughs, and a standing ovation for you. You just need to know one thing . . .

If Part One of this book was all about You, then consider Part Two to be all about Them.

See, here's the thing . . . even if your Heart Story is so amazing that Hollywood has optioned the movie version, a major star has attached to play you, and the industry is already buzzing about its Oscar potential, it's simply not enough to step onto a stage and talk. Your Heart Story and your Core Promise have to be framed, set up, and structured in such a way that they will instantly grab the attention of a room full of strangers. You can't assume that just because you were able to secure a speaking engagement, you're wearing an expensive suit and all your friends think you're brilliant, that complete strangers will listen attentively or even care about you.

NEED HELP

Got to KeynoteU.com. Some people work better with guided instruction. Go to KeynoteU.com, and register for a teacher to guide you through each chapter, of a course that best suits you.

One of the biggest mistakes my students make is assuming that their audience cares about them. Teaching stand-up comedy to fledgling comics in Hollywood, land of profound narcissism, this notion that "nobody cares about you" comes as a complete shock. After all, most wannabe entertainers dream of standing in a spotlight, getting the attention they never got as a child. They envision their act as one huge me fest with the audience laughing at hilarious stories about their childhood, their dating life, their disappointments. Go to any amateur comedy night and you will hear unemployed comics open with the worst possible setup: "Let me tell you a little bit about *myself.*"

Maybe twenty years ago that line could grab an audience's attention, but now, in our speedy, A.D.D., double latte, multitasking, Tweeting-while-talking culture, anyone who stands in front of a room full of worldwide Web-surfers with handheld instant access to small screen entertainment better find a way to truly connect. Your audience is full of people carrying iPhones and iPads. They are, to steal a line from *Seinfeld,* "masters of their own domain," instantly able to manipulate what they hear and see to cater to their whims. Apple had it right when they put the "I" in front of their products. They get it. It's all about "I."

Authenticity is your only weapon because, let's face it, as a speaker you probably aren't going to have cinematic 3-D special effects or Brad Pitt joining you at the podium, and you won't be delivering your speech while wrestling a Bengal tiger. Even if you did, the audience might still check their e-mail while your head is in the tiger's jaws or, better yet, Tweet pictures of themselves with Brad Pitt and not you!

Speaking is a low-tech connection. It is old fashioned, one-on-one communication, a face-to-face connection. Speaking is just you, standing onstage with a lavalier microphone and maybe a PowerPoint presentation, trying to transform a hotel multipurpose room into a platform for inspiration and change. Your audiences will be stone-cold sober (or worse, hungover from the night before) and they are usually there not by choice, but because their job requires them to attend. Standing up to simply tell your Heart Story without first crafting a killer opening, adding a few laughs, clarifying your Action Steps, and leaving them with a strong Call to Action is a sure way of flopping like a wet fish on dry land.

Terrified yet?

The good news is there is only one simple secret you need to know to win over your audience. Ready for this?

YOUR SPEECH IS ABOUT THE AUDIENCE AND NOT ABOUT YOU

Think about it. If you're on a first date and the person across from you talks incessantly about themselves, you're probably going to fake an emergency phone call and there certainly won't be a second date. A great date is a conversation between two interested parties, just like a great speech is a conversation between the speaker and the audience. A great speech gets a second booking.

It's this simple secret that turns good speakers into great speakers, speakers who understand the fundamental truth. Audiences care about only one thing constantly and passionately: they are obsessed with themselves. People are often overwhelmed and consumed by their own lives. Knowing this, you can become very successful by approaching everything you create, everything you market, and everything you say with an "It's All About Them" attitude.

Connie Podesta is a master of this.

Now you may never have heard of Connie Podesta, but there are two million people out there who have. Connie is a world-renowned motivational speaker who is hired by thousands of companies to speak on leadership, change, dealing with difficult people, and other issues. Her goal is to motivate businesses to achieve "Fearless Success" and in the process, she's written seven books.

"I keep a list of all of my stories and examples and after my initial conference call with a client, I sort through my stories to find the ones that will address their specific needs. Fifty percent of the time, I have to write a new story that illustrates the point that I understand their pain and I've had the same problem." Connie goes on to explain, "The goal of my story is to rave about the company that hired me while still being authentic and true to my own experience. I tell a story that makes my audience proud to be a part of their company and proud that I've been affected by them. I want my story to communicate how proud I am to be in their presence."

WHY DON'T YOU CALL?

"The simplest way to customize your speech is to phone members of the audience in advance and ask them what they expect from your session and why they expect it. Then use their quotes throughout your presentation."

—Allan Pease, Australian motivational speaker and author of *The Definitive Book of Body Language*

For example, when Connie was hired to speak for McDonald's, she wanted to emphasize the personal relationship she'd had with their company since childhood. "I started with a story about my dad bringing hamburgers home from the very first McDonald's on the South Side of Chicago, then I talked about how when I was broke, McDonald's helped me live through the tough times, and finally it all came full circle when my own kids were little and I could buy them a hamburger like my dad had done for me. It was a big deal for my kids to go through the drive-through. I finished by saying that I was honored to speak for McDonald's because they'd been with me for most of my life."

Connie reaches out with an "It's All About Them" attitude. And it's this singular focus on her audience that allows her to command speaking fees of $18,000 to $30,000 a keynote. In other words, caring enough to research your audience, tailoring your speech to their problems and their concerns, and developing merchandise that supports their desires will ensure that you become a successful speaker. Understand this one rule and Part Two of this book will be a cakewalk.

Remember chapter five, where I had you brainstorm the problems and solution possibly facing your potential audience? Well, now that you have a real gig on the books, it's time to get much more specific about your research.

I mean, you do have a gig on the books . . . right?

Please tell me you didn't skip that part!

If you did, I want you to go back and line up your first gig. Volunteer to speak somewhere, anywhere, even if it's a presentation at your Cactus Club. Without the fear of having to show up and speak, procrastination will take over and writing your speech will take a backseat to playing *Angry Birds* on your iPhone. If you are a Novice, then this first gig is critical. Without a client, you can't get specific and if you're not specific, your speech will turn into an amorphous blob of clichés. Just like Connie, you've got to tailor your stories and your Core Promise to the specific needs of your current client. For example, if everyone is losing their pensions in order to keep their jobs, or if heavy layoffs have dampened people's spirits, that's information you need to know before you step onstage.

When you travel, you probably read up on local customs to avoid embarrassing yourself. Before traveling to Africa, I learned that public displays of affection were highly frowned upon. Not that I was planning a makeout session on a bus, but it was good to know that even holding hands in public could be problematic. In Israel, I learned that driving through some orthodox neighborhoods on their Sabbath could get your car stoned.

Speaking engagements are similar to traveling in a foreign country. Each industry or organization has its own customs, its own unspoken social rules, and, in some cases—especially in a government agency—they actually have their own language relying on acronyms instead of words. You are the outsider coming in to address this crowd and all eyes will be upon you. Doesn't it just make sense to research your audience in advance?

I have shared the platform with many celebrity speakers including Deepak Chopra and even former president Bill Clinton and I assure you, most of them have an advance team that does extensive research to make sure their speeches are personalized, relevant, and hit home. Matter of fact, when any U.S. president speaks he has an advance team round up local stories and the names of local dignitaries to refer to in his speech. Of course, the more famous you are, the less you have to work the crowd because you come with a preapproval rating. Nevertheless, everyone who wants to have a successful experience as a speaker researches the environment, politics, and culture of where they are. This is why you have to act as your own advance team.

EXERCISE: THE PREP TALKS

One month prior to your gig, call the meeting planner to ask them basic logistical information about the gig, including: time, place, length of speech, size of the audience, placement on program, sound check, etc. I've included a list of these questions located in the sidebar. They will give you the basic lay of the land, but there are other questions you can ask that will assist you customizing your speech.

QUESTION THE BASICS

How many people will be in the audience?

What is my placement on the program?

What is the age and gender demographic of my audience?

How will they be seated?

What is the stage setup?

What is the required attire for the audience?

When is the sound check?

Who will be introducing me and what do they do in the company?

What speaker did you hire at your last event and what did you like and dislike about him or her?

How long do you want me to speak?

What are the challenges facing your organization?

Question One: "What happens before I go on?"

Knowing what your audience has been doing will help you with your opening. When I was hired to perform an 8 a.m. breakfast speech, it was extremely helpful to learn that my audience had a Casino Night scheduled for the night before. They would be out until midnight and then have to be up for an 8 a.m. morning keynote.

Standing in front of a blurry-eyed audience I got a laugh within the first fifteen seconds by saying, "This is different for me because as a comic, I usually perform for people who are drunk—not people who are hungover."

WHAT THE "HECK?"

"Coming from comedy clubs to the corporate market, I learned how to work clean. Free speech is one thing, common sense is another. Usually the objection comes from your choice of one or two words. Change them. That's what the thesaurus is for."

—Dale Irvin, veteran comedian and a member of the Professional Speakers Hall of Fame.

Question Two: "Who spoke at your last meeting and what didn't you like about them?"

With one question, you can avoid making the mistakes of your predecessor. When I asked a client this question, they complained, "He did a lot of audience participation, 'Stand up and shake someone's hand.' We got a lot of complaints from our employees." That was good information to have. No audience participation for that particular client.

On another gig, a client complained about their last speaker, saying, "She talked about her Jewish grandmother. We're all Catholic here. No one could relate." That was a gig saver for me. I had planned to include a story about my Jewish grandmother. Cut!

Question Three: "What is the culture of this audience?"

You need to know, well in advance, the politics, religion, and values of your audience. You need to know if they're a "What the *hell*" audience or a "What the *heck*" audience. You need to know because one "crap" or even a "jeez!" can alienate an entire audience.

I was hired to speak at a women's event in a rural town in North Dakota. On the plane ride to my gig, it became clear everyone else knew each other. "Hey, Bob, will we see you in church this Sunday?" "Margaret, how's it going at the library?" I felt suspicious eyes on me. No one knew who I was or why I was on that plane. I started up a conversation with the librarian on what I thought was a safe topic—the weather. The librarian told me, "It gets down to thirty degrees below zero in the winter." "Oh jeez!" I replied. That's when the woman behind me unbuckled her seat belt, stood up, and wagged her finger, reprimanding me. "We do *not* use that kind of language here," she said. Though it was embarrassing to be called out on a plane, you better believe that was good information to have before I stepped onstage. When I got to my gig, I asked the promoter if I could rehearse my speech in front of the most conservative person attending the keynote. I asked her to make a buzzing sound if I said anything that seemed off-color, or inappropriate. What an eye-opener. Buzz! Buzz! Buzz!

Question Four: "Can you give me the contact info of three people who will be in the audience and might likely be critical of my speech?"

That's right. I actually ask to speak to the troublemakers *before* I get to the venue. Why? Because with one phone call or one e-mail, I've transformed a tough cookie into a fan. Now, when I use part of our conversation in my speech, the troublemaker will nudge the person sitting next to him and claim, "That was my line!"

These advance calls also give me great insider information to identify the concerns and issues of the company. Since I speak on using humor to deal with stress, when I call these three people I ask them, "What is a bad day at the office?" You better believe I get an earful. As a result, I can be super-specific with the customization of my speech. I may end my speech with *my* story but I start it with *their* stories. Even if you're addressing a large convention comprised of employees from every different department, you can still make those phone calls. Just identify the subgroups that will be represented—administrative, IT, management, etc. Then speak to one employee from each of these divisions. What if you're not speaking to a company, but rather to a social function where nobody knows each other? The same rule applies— find a few people to yak to prior to the gig.

Never assume that your audience has the same problems as you. Unless you work at the Psychic Network, you won't know until you ask and if you don't ask, the results can be a miserable mistake creating a palpable disconnect with the audience. I came close to making that mistake when I was hired to speak to a group of fifty-year-old Michigan women, many of them farm owners. Since I am a woman near their age, I assumed my stresses were their stresses. At the last minute, I changed my mind and made a few phone calls. Doing research, I found I really knew nothing about their lives. We may have been the same age and gender but our lives couldn't have been further apart:

- They were dealing with empty-nest syndrome, or even worse, grown children *not*-leaving-the-nest syndrome. I didn't have kids. I just had dogs that needed baths and anti-flea pills once a month.

- They lived in Michigan where temperatures could drop to forty-five degrees below zero. I live in Los Angeles where if it dips below seventy degrees, I have to put on a cardigan.

- When I'm hungry in LA, I pick up the phone and order delivery from the hundreds of restaurants that surround me. When these ladies are hungry in Michigan, their husbands go hunting and bring home an elk that they then have to gut, carve, cook, and serve in time for dinner. For real.

I knew I had to change my opening. I won the ladies over when, right at the top, I announced that not only do they clean the house, take care of the children, gut, carve, and cook the wildlife for dinner all while keeping a full-time job, but it was their butt on the John Deere tractor and not their husbands' every weekend. They loved that I took the time to learn about their lives and they welcomed this stranger from La-La Land with their laughter.

Don't assume that you know their problems.

You don't.

EXERCISE: INTERVIEW THE AUDIENCE

Some of these questions will look familiar since you've already done a mini-version of this exercise in Part One, chapter five. This time, however, you're not asking for generalities or hypothetical situations, you're asking the audience members for specific information about their company.

Now that you have the contact information for three of your audience members, call them up and use the following questions, or write questions of your own to get people talking about the problems your speech addresses. Write down everything they say. You never know which parts of their responses will come in handy, and you can use the material to build on later.

1. What is your day like?

2. What happens on a bad day?

3. What happens on a good day?

4. What are the problems around your office? You can tailor this question to be even more specific. If you've been hired to speak about "Keeping Your Employees" ask what specific problems are contributing to their employee retention issues.

5. What solutions have been attempted to correct The Problem (your topic) and how have they succeeded or failed? You don't

want to suggest an improvement to them only to have the entire audience thinking, "Yeah, we tried that last year and it didn't work."

6. Why do *you* think they failed or succeeded?

7. Is there an elephant in the room? In other words, is there something everyone is complaining about behind the backs of management? What's the big blind spot? Later, in the comedy punch-up chapter, you will find formulas for these complaints that will get a guaranteed laugh.

8. What did you like or not like about last year's speaker? Repeat what some of the other people you interviewed have said about them. Just because one person says something doesn't mean that it's true for everyone. Check it out.

9. What's your favorite event during this (conference, meeting, trade show) and why?

10. If you could change one thing about your company, what would you change?

You can download a template of questions to ask at www.TheMessageOfYou.com.

Once you've interviewed your three audience members, call up your speaker Buddy and schedule a time to meet. Without overthinking it, I want each of you to present a three-minute version of your possible speech to each other. That's right. Just like I asked you to jump in head-first and secure a speaking gig without having a written speech, now I'm asking you to give a version of your speech before you've even written it!

Just use this formula as a launching pad:

> How many of you (INSERT A PROBLEM THE AUDIENCE HAS)?
>
> Today, I'm going to show you (INSERT YOUR CORE PROMISE).

I learned this when I (INSERT YOUR EXPERTISE).

One thing you can do is (INSERT AN ACTION STEP).

I know this to be true because (INSERT A HEART STORY).

So, how many of you are going to (INSERT A SMALL ACTION PEOPLE CAN TAKE RIGHT AWAY).

Set a timer for three minutes and ready, set . . . go!

Not so hard, right? In three minutes, you have essentially outlined your speech. The rest of Part Two is here to help you take those three minutes and transform them into a thirty-minute or one-hour keynote. You're going to use my Seven-Step Method to:

- Open with their Problem

- Promise them what they will learn

- Prove to them you're an expert

- Show them the way with Action Steps

- Reveal how your Heart Story speaks to them

- Give them a Call to Action

THE FORMULA WORKS!

"I couldn't get my speech together, but using this formula made it all come together. It was like erecting the frame of your dream house. Just like in construction, at this point there is still a lot of work to do, but you have a clear idea of what the finished product will look like."

—speaking student David Schmidt, "Improve Retention; Remove the Tension"

Then, you're going to go over your entire speech with the final chapter of Part Two, "The Funny is Money Comedy Pass."

Hit all the above steps with authenticity, great content, and a lot of laughs and you've got yourself a winning speech that people will pay a lot of money to hear you present.

Now, you might be thinking:

"But Judy, if everyone uses these same steps, won't we all sound alike?"

Absolutely not. Every movie uses the same three-act structure with results as diverse as *Gone with the Wind, The Hangover,* and *Saw.* As audiences, we are trained to expect structure. We expect movies to have three acts, jokes to have a setup and then a payoff, stories to have a beginning, middle, and an end. Honoring that expectation, I developed a seven-step process that creates a structure that has been road-tested in front of worldwide audiences and taught to thousands of students of every age, ethnicity, and profession. I know this method works because I use it myself.

YOUR UNIQUE MESSAGE

"You could have a hundred speakers speaking about leadership—each following the same general presentation structure— and as long as each person is being true to him- or herself, you'll have a hundred different messages. That's because everyone has a different personality, a different perspective, a different point of emphasis. You're the only one who can say what you have to say.

—Shawn Ellis, speaker agent, president, The Speakers Group

Personalizing your speech comes down to how you execute each step. Some speakers share a forty-minute Heart Story and then just frame it with twenty minutes spread among the other five steps. Some Techies drill home their Action Steps and only use their Heart Story as an anecdote. It truly depends on your personal style and the expectations of your audience. If you are hired to provide a speech entitled "How to Tweet," your audience will expect to receive Action Steps and educational content no matter how hilarious that forty-five-minute story about your grandma Tweeting might be. On the other hand, nobody pays to hear Aron Ralston speak about hiking techniques. Aaron's audience wants to hear a story about survival. They want to hear his Heart Story.

Basically, there are no hard-and-fast rules about how much time you should allot for each step within your speech. At the end of each chapter, I'll provide you with possible time constraints and you should consider them suggestions instead of rules. Know that, with practice and with audience feedback, you will find your own timing, and just trust that your material will create its own rhythm. With that said, you'll still need to cover all six steps whether you're giving a one-hour keynote address or a shorter half-hour breakout session and you should not, I repeat, *should not,* overstay your welcome onstage. If you've been hired to do one hour, do the full one hour but don't push it to one fifteen. Meeting planners have scheduled their events tightly and if you throw off their whole day, you'll have a hard time landing a second job from that planner.

Here's one more word of advice and this is the big moneymaker secret tip, so listen up: Your speech has to be funny!

YOUR SPEECH HAS TO BE FUNNY

Like I said before, funny is money. That's why I've dedicated an entire chapter in Part Two to my seventh step, polishing your speech with a comedy pass. But that's jumping the gun a bit. First, your speech has to work on its own terms, then you'll add the humor. Before you decide to break the rules you might want to understand them first, so on to Step One: The First-Minute Moment.

CHAPTER NINE

STEP ONE: YOU'VE GOT SIXTY SECONDS
TO MAKE THEM LOVE YOU

Whether you're writing a one-hour keynote, a half-hour presentation, or even a ten-minute sales pitch, the first sixty seconds of your speech—that's right, I said *the first sixty seconds*—are absolutely the most important. I can't stress this enough. It's a point I'm going to make over and over throughout this chapter. You've got exactly one minute to win over your audience, otherwise you'll be spending the next twenty-nine or fifty-nine minutes in a flop sweat, frantically tap-dancing your way through the awkward and painful silence of a hostile room. Believe me, I've been there.

Yes, it's true. I, Judy Carter, Goddess of Speaking and Learned Author of this book, have completely bombed during the opening of an important speech. Okay, maybe more than just one opening of maybe more than one important speech. Like the time I had to run from an angry mob of mothers in a rural Kenyan village. True story. If only I had read the local paper, I would have known about the witch who was turning children into snakes, and I probably wouldn't have opened with a magic trick. Now *that's* a rough opener!

Fortunately, not every opening is met with the instantaneous and physical feedback they provided in Kenya. In West Virginia, my audience didn't chase me out of the room, but they sure made it clear they didn't like me. It was early in my career and I was scheduled to speak for a group of wealthy businessmen and their wives. I had, in my mind, overprepared because I wanted the speech to go well, and I hoped the chapter of this organization would then recommend me to their brother chapters across the nation.

I stepped onstage and used my usual opening, the one that always got a laugh and a huge round of applause. This time, there was no laugh. There was no applause. They just sat there, staring at me. Thrown by their cold reception, I nervously jumped to a hilarious piece that I normally reserve for the middle of my speech. This chunk had killed the week prior in Chicago. Rather than getting the expected belly laughs, I got a few soft chuckles and maybe a smile of pity from one of the wives.

A painful silence filled the room because now my speech was out of order and I was lost. I could actually hear my heart beating—thump, thump, thump. Then I felt a blast of cold air, and couldn't tell if it was the air-conditioning or the audience freezing me with a chilly vibe. Sweat poured down my face, over my eyes, loosening one of my false eyelashes. The single lash hitched a ride on the sweat river that was now my entire head and floated over my cheek toward my upper lip. I pulled it off my mouth and tried to make a self-deprecating joke about it. The audience stared at me with the exact same horrified expression I had when watching the movie *Snakes on a Plane*. I had no idea how I would endure the next hour and frankly, I don't even remember the rest of that speech. Somehow, I had lost them at hello and I had no clue why.

When I got back to Los Angeles, I asked a friend of mine, a former West Virginian, to watch the video of my fiasco and tell me why I bombed. I braced for the footage with a sip of my cocktail (all right, all right, a slug of my cocktail), and squinted against the horror of re-living the nightmare. We pressed play and sixty seconds in, my friend turned off the video and said, "I don't need to hear anymore; I know exactly what happened."

What?" I screamed. "You only saw sixty seconds!"

"That's all I need to see." My friend leaned back on my sofa and prepared to school me. "You talk too fast. As soon as they heard your voice they pegged you as one of those fast-talking, snotty Yankee Northern lawyer types."

I was shocked. "You mean it was the *speed* of my delivery and not what I said that turned them off?" Suddenly, it all came back to me. He was right. I came on with high energy and it repelled them instead of attracting them. Then, the quieter they got, the more insecure I felt and the faster and louder I talked. By the time I reached the end of my speech, I sounded like a New York auctioneer on crack cocaine.

My friend continued. "The nail in the coffin was following up that opening with a West Virginia joke. These folks are proud of where they live. The rhythm of life is slower there and they don't consider that a bad thing." He topped off my drink, knowing I would need another swig. "The first words out of your mouth made it clear that you were different from them. You lost them at 'Hello.'"

Fortunately, there are easy ways to avoid an awkward opening or a mad dash to the nearest local Kenyan airport. After twenty-plus years of touring and speaking, I've figured out the secret to a great opener. Remember that rule I mentioned in the previous chapter, It's All About Them? It's time to put that rule into action and I assure you, if you do, within one minute you can get applause, connect to your audience, establish your expertise, empathize with your audience's problems, tease a solution, and even get a few laughs.

Sounds impossible to do in one minute? It's not. You just need to prepare and use these three simple techniques:

1. Control your image

2. Force a reaction

3. Announce an abbreviated version of your Core Promise

CONTROL YOUR IMAGE

Picture this situation: You've spent hours and hours prepping your speech and researching your topic and now, the big day has arrived and it's your moment to step onstage. The emcee/host takes the mike and says, "Ladies and Gentlemen, have you watched *The Tonight Show* or

The Daily Show? Well, this next speaker . . . watches them, too!" Then they project a picture of you they downloaded off the Internet, forgetting to crop out your ex-boyfriend, the Hell's Angel gang member. All that work you've done is suddenly null and void. You're going to have to spend the next ten minutes trying to win over an audience that now thinks you're a nobody. In other words, you can't leave the intro to the imagination of that emcee. They usually don't have one. It's up to you to control your image, and that starts one month before you even get to the gig.

This is why, before I walk onstage, I track down my emcee, politely introduce myself, and hand him or her the following text, typed out in a LARGE & BOLD font. Sometimes, the emcees have "forgotten" to wear their glasses. Make it impossible for them to screw this up and make it clear to your emcee that you want your intro read exactly as it is written. If the VP of accounting says, "Don't worry, I'll just improvise," just say politely, "No, thank you." Then hand them your copy.

EXERCISE: MASTER YOUR EMCEE

A good introduction goes a long way toward establishing your credibility, establishing you as an expert, and getting the audience excited to meet you. Besides, it's much more effective to have someone else brag about you than to do it all yourself. Use this outline to write your own introduction and keep it to one minute or under. Anything longer than that starts to feel like a speech—and hey, *you're* the one giving the speech!

1. Make sure your introduction has a humorous line and includes your name.
Having a little joke in the intro tests the temperature of the audience. If they laugh during the intro, you'll know it's a hot audience. If they don't, this audience is going to need a warm-up. I have in my intro, "Judy Carter is the Goddess of Comedy, but she says you can just call her 'Goddess.'" Humor is also an attention getter that will push focus to the stage.

2. Let the emcee brag about you.

This is no time for modesty. Put your impressive credits right up front—books you've written, programs you've founded, awards you've received, impressive jobs you've held. Look back at your list of successes from the exercises on pages 67–68. Let your audience know, before you even step onstage, that you're a Pro.

3. Mention a down moment in your life.

Reveal your journey by letting the audience know about your "down" time. From the exercise you did in chapter two, *briefly* mention a challenge that you had to overcome. This will actually make your success so much more impressive. It's one thing to have spoken at Fortune 500 companies, but it's even more impressive if an audience knows that you had to overcome a speech impediment to achieve it.

ADD A MULTIMEDIA INTRODUCTION

"I like an intro that is very brief and excites the audience about what is to come. One of the best intros I saw was where the speaker, who was a reporter, had a brief introduction and then a video showing her in action, establishing her expertise and laying the foundation for her speech.

—Bonnie Wallsh, meeting planner, MA, CMP, CMM

"But Judy, won't that undermine my credibility? Shouldn't an intro impress an audience?"

Yes, your introduction needs to highlight you as an expert and mentioning your challenges will make you look even more impressive as it reveals that you had to work hard to achieve your successes. It's one thing to be a world-class speaker who has shared the platform with presidents, but it makes it even more impressive if, as a child, you had a speaking impediment. (That's my story. Don't use it.) Be authentic on this as it's your downs that make you more likeable and interesting.

Remember: this is just a *quick* mention of the low place that started your journey and not the full story in all of its glory.

(For examples of speaker's video introductions, go to MarketYour-Speech.com/videos.)

4. Sneak in a subtle sales pitch.

If you have product to sell, like those books the emcee just mentioned, then make sure your audience knows that they will be available after your speech. You can do this by having the emcee announce that you will be autographing copies of your book, DVD, CD, or wind-up dolls at the back of the room. If you're just starting out and don't have any products, announce that you will be available at the back of the room to answer any questions.

5. State your speech title.

The audience wants to know exactly what to expect from you. They want to hear that the speech is going to be relevant to their lives. If the announcement of your speech title elicits a groan, it's time to rethink your speech!

6. Wrap it up with another mention of your name.

If your name is anything other than Jane Doe, then spell it out phonetically. It's horrible coming onstage to the wrong name. Review this example introduction from speaker Mimi Donaldson:

> Mimi Donaldson excites, educates, and entertains audiences all over the world. She frequently shares the stage with prominent keynote speakers such as Colin Powell, Katie Couric, and Maya Angelou. She has thrilled and inspired over half of the Fortune 100 companies as well as some less fortunate.
>
> Before starting her own consulting business in 1984, she spent ten years as a Human Resources Trainer at Northrop Aircraft, Rockwell International, and Walt Disney Productions.
>
> She has a B.A in Speech and Communications from the University of Iowa and a Masters Degree in Education from Columbia University. Mimi is co-

author of *Negotiating for Dummies,* selling over a million copies and translated into six languages.

Mimi's topic today is empowering yourself. She knows personally about this subject, having survived a life-threatening disease *and* something even worse—installing a Windows update.

After Mimi speaks today, you can buy her new book, *Necessary Roughness: New Rules for the Contact Sport of Life.* You can also buy *Bless Your Stress: It Means You're Still Alive!* Mimi would love to autograph her books for you.

Her new CD and DVD program is also available to us. It contains her most dynamic presentations to give you the competitive edge.

So today, talking about "Tactics to Triumph in Tough Times," welcome Mimi Donaldson.

Read the above intro out loud and notice how the six elements were included. Now, it's your turn to do the same. Take the next fifteen minutes and write your emcee introduction. Once you're done, have your Speaker Buddy read it out loud while you sit and listen, just like an audience member. Ask yourself the following questions:

- Did I hear everything clearly?

- Was anything confusing?

- What was most impressive?

- What needs explanation?

- Was it too long?

- How can it be improved?

Now that you have your emcee introduction, it's time to get onstage *fast* before the applause dies down. It's nice being applauded for just showing up, so get some of that love. Once you're onstage, you want to . . .

FORCE A REACTION

The very best thing you can do when you arrive onstage is take a deep breath in and out. It just takes a moment, but it has a calming effect that will center you for the rest of your speech. Once you've taken that breath, your main goal is to wrestle control of the audience's attention. You can accomplish this by asking the audience to do something.

Thank the emcee and encourage the audience to join you with their applause. You can also say something nice about him or her. You might even get a laugh. One time, my emcee had a deep voice. As I walked onstage, I looked right at him and said, "Thank you, Darren. That was a great intro. Let's give him a hand. (Applause.) You have a beautiful voice. I realize now it was you who played Darth Vader." (Laugh). So in less than twenty seconds, I accomplished the following:

- Everyone was looking at the stage.

- They had to put down their BlackBerries to applaud.

- I communicated appreciation, which gave me bonus points.

- I established I was in charge by getting the audience to applaud.

- I got my first laugh.

You can pretty much ask the audience to applaud anything and they will. You can usually get a laugh just by mentioning things that happened prior to you going on even if they're not that funny. "And let's also have some applause for the caterer who gave us for dessert both apple crisp *and* rhubarb crisp." People just like

GET A LAUGH—SAVE THE DAY

"When I hear a speaker get laughs in the first minute I can relax a bit, knowing that I booked the right speaker for the audience. Then I hope they don't screw up in the next hour."

—Cheryl Ducharme, senior trade show/event manager

to feel that they are "in" on the joke, so mentioning something obvious and inclusive will accomplish that goal. They want to feel that you're being spontaneous and if they see you, working, "in the moment," they will react!

So, how in the world do you appear spontaneous while sticking to your script? You have to set up a spontaneous "throw-away" moment.

Setting Up the "Throwaway"

Remember all that research you did when you became your own advance team? Here's where it pays off. You're going to reference a moment the audience just witnessed and combine it with your research to create a throwaway line that seems effortless. This gets the audience participating with applause and shows them:

- You are confident.

- You are spontaneous.

- You are in the moment.

- Your speech is not a "canned" speech.

WARNING:

Don't make cruel or sarcastic jokes:

"Let's hear it for the crepe paper lanterns! Guess you guys were on a budget this year, huh?"

Someone worked hard to hang those decorations so don't sweep into the room and dis' their efforts.

Keep your comments short, sweet, and positive.

You want to build a sense of commonality with your audience but you don't want to get a laugh at someone's expense.

Even if the speaker before you was a total bore, only acknowledge them in a positive way.

And remember, if you can't say something nice about somebody, then don't say anything at all.

For instance, right before I stepped onstage in Merced, California, they had a demonstration of tactics by the local SWAT team. When I was introduced I ran onstage, asked for appreciation for the emcee, then asked for applause for the handsome and talented SWAT team. During my advance research about the city I learned that the primary industry in Merced is agriculture. So my first moment onstage went like this:

"Let's hear it for Sandy. Thanks for the great intro." *(APPLAUSE.)* "And the handsome and talented SWAT team." *(APPLAUSE.)* "Though I'm not sure why Merced needs a SWAT team." I then acted like a cop aiming a gun at a criminal and shouted, "Drop the strawberries, now!" *(LAUGHTER.)*

You may not know what this throw-away line is going to be until you actually get to the gig. That might scare you, but here's the bonus of being spontaneous: you can get a good laugh without having to be über-funny. When the audience knows you just made it up, they give you a lot of leeway. In that one moment of spontaneity, you get instant respect as audiences are usually awed by people who are able to be spontaneous and improvise. Some ideas about who to target for your "spontaneous" moment:

- The guy who just fixed the air-conditioning, the bathrooms, the lights, the mike.

- The very generous bartender from the party last night.

- The volunteers or organizers of the event who have been up since 3 a.m.

- The waiters who served chocolate for dessert.

- The audience themselves for surviving three days of meetings.

Spontaneity is a skill of an experienced speaker. Your ability to risk being spontaneous in the first minute will grow with stage time. If you are a Novice, you will probably spend your first ten gigs just getting comfortable onstage before you dare to improvise in the moment. Give yourself time, but eventually you will need to take this courageous step and trust your instincts.

Okay, now you are ten to twenty seconds into your speech and you've gotten a few laughs, a round of applause . . . it's time to state clearly and succinctly the promise of your speech, the "why" they should listen, your Core Promise.

ANNOUNCE AN ABBREVIATED VERSION OF YOUR CORE PROMISE

Here is where you introduce your Elevator Pitch—the problem/solution version of your Core Promise. You don't want this transition to be jarring. You've just established yourself as spontaneous and comfortable and you don't want your Core Promise to sound memorized and stilted. An easy way to smoothly transition from unplanned to planned material is to bounce it off the introduction the emcee just read. For example, you could say something like:

> "As you heard our emcee say, I help people find their own style. Many of us buy our clothes to impress someone else. Today you're going to learn how to *stop* dressing to IMpress and *start* dressing to EXpress your own unique sense of style."

That was from speaker and stylist Mary Kincaid's speech, "How to Dress from the Inside Out and Do Business with Style."

WARNING

Don't allow this spontaneous moment to turn into endless chatter about your travel day.

You want to connect with your audience using a shared immediate experience—something that everyone in the room is currently experiencing together.

You included!

You don't need to tell them the "how" yet—you're just teasing them with the promise that they will be learning a new skill that will be valuable to them personally. You are going to motivate them, but you want to simply state what they are going to learn—in other words, announce the promise of your speech. Let's look at another example from speaker Mimi Donaldson:

> Many of us have trouble with eyeball-to-eyeball confrontations. Today, by using the lessons of America's most popular spectator sport, football, we will learn to use a bit of "Necessary Roughness." The results will be: we will talk straight, stand our ground, say no, and negotiate everything.

Mimi is a prolific speaker. She's spoken at over a thousand events in dozens of industries, in over 100 cities across North America and Europe. Mimi has spoken at company events for over half of the Fortune 500. She's been the subject of over 200 articles in newspapers and magazines, but despite her impressive credentials she makes sure that when she announces her Core Promise, she avoids saying, "*I'm* going to show you" or "*I'm* going to tell you."

Mimi explains, "Using the word 'I' turns people off. They hear 'I'm going to tell you something' and their mind automatically says 'No, you're not!' So I always use the word 'we' when I announce my Core Promise. It's more inclusive and less dictatorial."

DON'T WRITE YOUR SPEECH ALONE

Speech writing tools, videos, and tutors are available at KeynoteU. com.

EXERCISE: CORE PROMISE INTRODUCTION

Now, using the formula below, write your transition from cold opening to Core Promise. Keep it to five or six sentences, about forty seconds, and *never* make a joke out of your Core Promise. Your Core Promise is serious business. Joking about it would diminish its power.

Use this formula to introduce the abbreviated version of your Core Promise:

- Many of us are dealing with (INSERT A SUMMARY OF THE PROBLEM).

- Today we're going to learn that by (INSERT A BRIEF SUMMARY OF YOUR METHODOLOGY).

- We can (INSERT YOUR EXPECTED RESULTS).

Okay, you've got everything you need for a strong opening, so let's practice by getting you off the page and up on your feet.

EXERCISE: WARM UP YOUR OPENING

Call up your Buddy and make a date to meet in person. You're going to practice your cold opening until its red hot! Take turns practicing the following:

1. Have your buddy read your emcee introduction aloud.

2. Get onstage quickly and subtly take your deep breath.

3. Take command of the room by asking the audience to appreciate and applaud.

4. Improv a spontaneous throw-away about the shared audience experience.

5. Casually present an abbreviated version of your Core Promise.

 COMPLETED SPEECH TIME: One minute

CHAPTER TEN

STEP TWO: MAN, DO YOU HAVE PROBLEMS!

Remember the fundamental problem and solution you identified in Part One, chapter five? For the next section of your speech, you are going to use the research you did to convince the audience in detail that not only do they have problems, but it is just those problems that stand between them and prosperity, higher sales, well-adjusted teenagers, getting out of debt, happiness, buying their own home, or whatever it is that your Core Promise addresses.

SHOW ME THE SOLUTION!

"Speakers need to address problems. After all, the reason a business gathers its employees is to address company problems. So a speaker must contribute by inspiring the audience to think differently, to learn something new, or to fire up the staff."

—Cheryl Ducharme, senior trade show/event manager

This section of your speech must accomplish the following objectives:

- Show the audience that you understand them.

- Help them closely identify with your message.

- Create trust between you and your audience.

- Get some laughs (hard to believe, but true).
- Make them desperate to receive the solution.

Why is spending time examining the details of their problem so power-ful? Think about what makes you feel close to certain friends. Aren't they the friends who really listen to your problem rather than just giv-ing advice? When close friends ask us, "How are you?" we don't give them the impersonal, glib answer, "Fine." It's our close friends that we count on to help us unload our emotional baggage. It's our nearest and dearest who listen, ask questions, and make us feel heard, rather than someone who rattles off advice without first empathizing with our problems. When speaking, you want the audience to trust you as they would a dear friend. In order to do that, don't give them any hint of a solution until every person in your audience understands the extent of their problem and how it impacts their lives.

Speaker student Rene Pena is a military spouse who wanted to speak to other military spouses, giving them hope and solutions to relieve their stress. Here's how she starts her speech:

> How many of you military spouses have to deal with stress on a daily basis? You're separated for long periods of time. You feel like a single parent. You have to be completely independent when the reason you married was to have a partner and a teammate. There's the stress of hoping that time and distance doesn't change your relationship in negative ways. Many of you move every two years, uprooting your children from their friends and school. Uproot-ing yourself. Changing and adapting, always changing and adapting. And when your husband or wife is deployed to a war zone, or a dangerous area, it's hard trying not to dwell on the bad and worst case scenarios like, them losing a limb, losing their personality, their mind, their love for you.

Rene knows her audience because she *is* the audience! You better believe the military spouses in those seats trust that Rene understands them and they are more willing to listen to her solutions as a result.

THE PROBLEM HAS TO CLICK WITH THE AUDIENCE

This is a touchy moment in your speech. You don't want to come off as a judgmental know-it-all. You don't want to seem critical. But you do need to make the audience aware of the negative results of their having this unresolved, unaddressed issue. You must present the information in a way that keeps the audience on your side, but still causes them to take the problem seriously—so seriously, in fact, that they want and demand immediate help from you! But they have to keep listening if they want the secret of your Action Steps.

BOY, DO I KNOW HOW YOU FEEL!

"When you speak to a group, if you hit home with *the specifics of their problems with stories and examples*, you will have them in the palm of your hand. Then, when you finally get to your Action Steps, the audience will consider them truly viable options that they can apply to their own lives."

—Karyn Buxman, former nurse turned professional speaker

The way you accomplish this is by being super-specific and relating the audience's problems back to the big three: health, wealth, relationships.

For instance, asking an audience, "Is anyone stressed?" is too general and vague. If you want your audience to nod their heads in agreement or shout "Amen," you've got to show the future consequences of their behavior, show how it's hampering their pursuit of health, wealth, and relationships, and get them to commit to be engaged with you for the rest of your talk.

So, rather than the problem being a general statement of stress, you've got to get more specific such as:

- Taking stress home and ruining your love life. (Relationships)

- Finding yourself getting sick more often. (Health)

- Not getting a promotion because you are burnt out and it shows. (Wealth)

A student was writing a speech for Women in Business. She presented the problem as:

> "You know how you can feel overwhelmed from spinning 980 plates at once? Working to get ahead, balancing being married, having children, being in a relationship, and trying to have that elusive 'All'?"

That is an accurate description of the challenges facing Women in Business, but it doesn't present how the *consequences* of those challenges relate to the big three. Why are those things a threat to your health, wealth, and relationships? Does having it all lead to depression? Can the pursuit of having it all destroy a marriage? If you're constantly spinning plates, will you ever get ahead in your job?

A way to reframe it would be, *"[That] in trying to have it all—money, success, and a family—women are sacrificing their happiness and health, and end up not truly ever feeling successful."*

See the difference?

THE PROBLEM SETS UP THE MESSAGE OF YOU

The problems that you introduce in this section of your speech need to be the same problems you will later solve with Action Steps, as well as be similar to The Problem you address in your Heart Story. The audience can have many problems, but the *only* problems you need to include are the ones you are qualified to solve based on your professional and personal experiences.

For instance, one of my students was speaking on improving sales. He went into a long description of how salespeople go from winning streaks to sales slumps and they don't know why. That's a good choice of problem, but his speech didn't address it. Only bring up a problem if you have the solution.

As you continue writing your speech, you may want to circle back and tweak the specificity of these problems so they better complement your Heart Story or your Action Steps.

In other words, if your Heart Story becomes about your journey from low self-esteem to confidence, than the issue of low self-esteem *has* to be one of the problems you address at the beginning of your speech.

Mistake: You Present the Problem as Criticism

Be careful not to present the problems as criticisms or judgments. There is a thin line between bringing up problems and reprimanding people for having them. You can see from the example below how presenting the problem with a judgmental tone can turn an audience off:

> "You scientists have a hard time explaining complex environmental issues in a way that ordinary people can understand. You go into too much data and acronyms and no one can understand you."

A better way to present The Problem would be to relate it back to how it affects their daily lives:

> "Isn't it frustrating when you get really excited about a project and you go to share what you are doing with a nonscience friend and they just can't understand what you're talking about?"

You want to present the problem in a way that shows you *care* rather than *judge*.

WARNING

There's a thin line between exploring problems and criticizing. Make sure you're on the exploration side of that line!

Mistake: Your Problem Doesn't Ring True for the Audience

One of my students was putting together a speech on diversity. He started like this:

> "You know how your fellow coworkers, your boss, or even just people you meet in business settings have a problem dealing with diversity? They're not sure how to approach people of different races, or cultures, and when they do attempt to speak to someone outside their own ethnicity it's always with some joke they thought would break the ice but was really just stereotypical and inappropriate."

Chances are that no one in the audience would say, "Yes! That's so true! I do that all the time—make rude jokes about other races!" After he did more research on the topic, he came up with a better way to describe the problem that hit home:

> "Has anyone here ever walked into a meeting and immediately felt like the foreign diplomat for your gender, race, or religion? You know, like you're the only woman in the conference room and you realize you're basically starring in your own personal episode of the TV show *Mad Men*? Anyone feel that you have to constantly prove yourself? Because of a few outer differences many of us have cut ourselves off from making connections with people who could lead us to our next great idea, or bigger and better opportunities."

EXERCISE: PREP WORK FOR THE PROBLEM

Using the information you obtained from your research and interviews, you're going to now complete the next ten minutes of your speech.

Write out the problems you've identified.

Next, write out the details of each problem and how the consequences can damage the audience's health, wealth, and/or relationships. You'll have to provide proof of why the problem relates to the big three as just saying "Living in Chaos" costs you money, doesn't mean it's true.

Have your Speaker Buddy read over what you wrote and answer these questions:

1. Is what you are presenting truly a problem or is it a criticism?

2. Are you successfully convincing the audience that the consequences of the problem affect their wealth, health, and/or relationships?

3. Will the problem you are presenting truly resonate and cause the audience to nod in agreement?

4. Is the problem something that you are qualified to address with personal and professional stories, examples, and solutions?

GETTING LAUGHS AND APPLAUSE FROM PRESENTING THE PROBLEM

Here are five techniques you can use to write this passage so you can present the problem in an entertaining way. Do all of these exercises even if they seem redundant. Some of you will end up using one of the exercises for the content of your speech, and some of you will end up sampling from all of them.

1. Rhetorical Questions

2. Humorize & Futurize

3. Failed Solutions

4. Turn Staff Interviews Into Stories

5. Quotes & Stats

6. Go for Shock Value

Technique One: Rhetorical Questions

Speaking is a two-way conversation with the audience. You, the speaker, might ask a rhetorical question, and the audience will nod their heads and you nod back. They laugh, you then acknowledge their response.

They applaud, you smile. They are moved and you all take a breath together. They look at their watches and you quickly go to the end of your speech. The audience is constantly communicating with a speaker, and good speakers understand how to acknowledge an audience's response and use it to empower their arguments.

One way to engage an audience in this two-way conversation is by asking rhetorical questions. Like all the other techniques listed above, the goal of asking questions is to convince the audience they have a problem that is interfering with their happiness. If your questions are vague, general, or don't hit home, you will hear crickets chirping, but if your questions are relevant and thoughtful, you'll have the audience yelling their enthusiastic replies.

I was hired by a large telecommunications company to speak on stress reduction, and as part of my advance research I asked the CEO what issues were stressing out his employees. He responded, "Well, what's on everyone's mind is the worldwide shortage of copper. It's a huge problem as we are getting orders that we can't fill. Copper is what we use in our fiber optics."

I asked for the names of three people who worked in various departments and asked them how stressed they were about the copper shortage. They had no idea what I was talking about but they all mentioned a different problem. One was: "The parking lot doesn't have enough spaces. In the middle of the day, I have to go out and feed the meter! What a hassle. I've already got two tickets."

So, after I announced my Core Promise, that I was there to reduce stress, I asked the audience:

"How often do you wish you didn't have so many meetings?" Rumbles of recognition.

"How many of you feel that you can't get actual work done at work?" A few hands go up.

"Or, how many of you are already stressing out that my speech is going to be too long so you won't have time to feed the meter?" Huge laugh and applause.

COMEDY TIP

Be serious on the first two questions, but shoot for funny on the third. This comedy technique is called a "List of Three" and it guarantees a laugh.

To learn how to use the technique, chapter fifteen.

Notice how I started each question with "How often do you . . ." rather than "Do you ever . . ." I learned this from professional speaker Patricia Fripp, who says, "Asking 'How often?' actively engages your audience in thinking about a specific number. It gets them wondering about the size and scope of their problem."

EXERCISE: THE RHETORICAL THREE

Using the information you obtained from your research, interviews, and the previous exercise, create a list of the top ten problems your audience is facing. Let's use speaker Rene Pena's list as an example. Her list for The Problems facing military spouses included:

- Married but being separated for long periods of time, sometimes years.

- Having to be the mom and the dad and not doing so well with either.

- Being completely independent when you wanted a partner and a teammate.

- Hoping that time and distance won't change your love for each other.

- Moving every few years and uprooting your children from their friends and school.

- Uprooting your own life—your friendships, your career.

- Changing and adapting, always changing and adapting.

- When your spouse is deployed to a war zone, trying not to dwell on every worst-case scenario imaginable—staying in the present.

- Fear that your spouse will lose a limb, have a massive change in their personality, lose their mind, lose their love for you.

- Fear of becoming a widow.

Once you have that master list, identify three problems your speech will address. Again, using Rene's list as an example, she chose to focus on these three problems in her speech:

1. Having to be the mom and the dad and not doing so well with either.

2. Uprooting the family every few years.

3. Fear of becoming a widow.

Now that you've chosen your three problems, try writing them out as rhetorical questions using "How often do you . . . ?" or "How many of you . . . ?" Let's look again at Rene's rhetorical questions for guidance:

> *How often have you moved in the last two years?*

> *How often do you feel like both the mom and the dad?*

> *How many of you wake up in the middle of the night, terrified your spouse isn't okay?*

Now, rework your questions. Experiment with the order of the questions for maximum impact. Try to make that third question a laugh line but make sure that it still addresses a real problem facing your audience.

> *How many of you wake up, in the middle of the night, worried about your spouse?*

> *How many of you feel like you have to be the mom and the dad to your kids?*

*And how many of you have moved so many times that you
need GPS to guide you to your new bedroom?*

The reason Rene's rhetorical questions work is because they are related
to one of the big three issues: relationships. Your questions have to not
only address the specific issues facing your audience, but they must also
address the larger universal issues I mentioned before: health, wealth,
and relationships.

For instance, one of my students was speaking on the topic of organizing. She started off by asking the audience: "Have you ever found
yourself racing around the house looking for car keys that you know
you left on the table by the door? How many times have you backed out
of the driveway and realized you can't find the sunglasses you always
leave in the car?"

These are good questions, but they don't describe a problem. "Looking for car keys" is only a problem if you can relate it to the consequences
of losing your keys. Losing car keys every morning can make them
late for work, which threatens their job money security. Maybe losing
their keys makes things chaotic for the family, makes the kids late for
school, or angers their spouse. Maybe losing their keys starts each day
in a stressful way and is an indicator that their level of stress is un-
healthy leading to ulcers, depression, overeating. You've got to find a
way to relate to your three main problems to the larger issues that will
motivate them to actually listen and take action.

Once you're happy with your rhetorical questions, call up your
Buddy and run these past each other to see if they ring true.

Technique Two: Humorize and Futurize

This is a two-step process.

Step One: Turn Your Research into Lists
Using your research, write a list of the problems that your speech addresses. Make them as *specific* as possible. For instance, rather than
saying "Your company is facing stiff competition," it would be better to

point out, "Home Depot just opened a megastore fifteen blocks away and they've stolen your customers." Getting specific will let your audience know you are taking their problems very seriously. Shoot for five to ten problems.

Step Two: Futurize the List

Using The Problem list you created, you then imagine the future consequences of those problems if they are allowed to run rampant and unchecked.

Here's an example of how to use this technique. We'll start by using a common list of problems that cause stress in the workplace:

- Staff feels they spend too much of their work day in meetings and can't get work done.

- Censorship of Internet makes it hard to research information for upcoming projects.

- Downsizing means that hours are too long. Parents can't get home to their families.

- The cafeteria is out of spoons. Every single day.

- Too much candy on desks around the office. People are gaining weight.

COMEDY TIP

Act-Outs are comedy gold and they can be sprinkled throughout your speech. They are particularly effective when you're presenting The Problem to the audience.

To learn more about using the Act-Out technique, turn to chapter fifteen.

Then we futurize those problems.

Censorship of Internet makes it hard to research information for upcoming projects. *Next thing you know . . .* I have to be home to get anything done. My boss asked me, (Act-Out) "Bob, did you finish your report?" "No, I haven't had a chance to go home."

Downsizing means that hours are too long. Parents can't get home to their families. *Next thing you know . . .* if you come home before midnight, the dog thinks you're a burglar. Your kids say to you, (Act-Out) "Hmmm . . . you look familiar, have we met?"

The cafeteria is out of spoons. Every single day. *Next thing you know . . .* you're at the doctor's office with burns from stirring your coffee with your tongue.

Too much candy on desks around the office. People are gaining weight. *Next thing you know . . .* you can't fit into any of your work clothes unless they have elastic waistbands. You ask your husband, (Act-Out) "Do these pants make me look fat?" He doesn't lie. "The pants are fine. It's your butt that makes you look fat."

Now you try it:

EXERCISE: FUTURIZE TO DRAMATIZE

Watch out! To those of you who didn't feel the need to research the problems of your audience, you'll find yourself in trouble here. Completing this exercise is dependent on being able to not only identify your audience's current problems but to also imagine the long-term implications of that problem continuing into the future.

1. Write out ten problems you've gathered from your research.

2. Select three or four problems that when mentioned, the audience will nod their heads. "Yes! The speaker knows us!"

3. Futurize just how horrible their problems will become by adding this phrase to them: "Next thing you know . . ."

4. Call up your Buddy and see which of these futurizations gets a laugh or rings the most true for them. If none of them land, it's time to try again.

Technique Three: Failed Solutions

You've got them laughing, but their problems are serious business. In order for your audience to really feel the pain of their problems, you need to remind them that they have already tried to implement solutions but those solutions failed. Once you show them that their solutions were useless, they'll be hanging on your every word to help them out of their problem. Here are a few examples of ways to present a failed solution. Again, you want to use humor to help draw the audience in and to avoid a judgmental or critical tone.

> Staff feels they spend too much of their workday in meetings. And I know you've tried to decrease the number of meetings . . . by adding an additional meeting to discuss if you can decrease the number of meetings.

> I hear there's too much candy on desks around the office. People think if they do a lap from their desk to reception, they'll burn off that Hershey's Kiss. I had a friend like that. She was convinced she could eat anything she wanted as long as she fell asleep listening to subliminal weight-loss tapes. Fifty pounds later . . .

EXERCISE: FAILED SOLUTIONS

REMINDER

During this "problem" section of your speech, you must keep the stories you tell very, very short.

These stories are not your Heart Story.

This is not your big moment.

These are support stories.

They do not offer a solution.

> Yet . . .
> They are only used to illustrate the severity of the problem.

Write out two or three of the failed solutions that your prep work revealed that people in your audience have tried. Look back over your collection of stories and find the stories that relate to these failed solutions.

These stories should be very, very short. One minute max. Three or four sentences max. You don't want to get off topic. You don't want to venture too far from the topic of "them" into the land of "you."

Try out these failed solution mini-moments on your Buddy.

Technique Four: Turn Staff Interviews into Stories

Remember those staff interviews that you did? This is where they come in handy. Use the information you gained to open with a short story about them. It can be a story you collected when you asked a committee member what defined a bad day at the office. It could be something that just happened at the conference that caused a new problem or that relates to a problem they also have at work. An example of this would be if you're talking about customer service, it could be helpful to point out the awkward check-in at the hotel where everyone is staying and how now they're on the receiving end of bad customer service.

No matter which approach you use, in your story the main character has to want something and can't get it because of an obstacle/problem. If you choose to talk about one of the people you interviewed, you don't have to mention them by name unless you've already gotten their permission to do so.

Sometimes, I come to a gig with my "problem story" set, but while I'm observing people at the event, I get an even better story. The closer your story is in time to your speech the more dynamic it is. Ever notice that successful stand-up comics say, "I *just* broke up with someone . . ." They just say that to make the setup more dynamic. I know comics that have "just broken up with someone" for the last fifteen years. The reason they phrase it this way is that it gives their story immediacy and appears to the audience that they are the first to hear this story. It makes the audience feel special, especially if their story includes a member of the audience.

Here is an example of a successful story I lucked into when speaking about "stress" for Boeing.

> "When I pulled into the parking lot a few hours ago, I saw a man walking aimlessly. I asked him, 'Are you all right?' He said, 'I'm lost. I'm trying to find my way to a Boeing meeting and I keep going in the wrong door.' I said, 'Oh, you're in luck, I'm speaking at the Boeing meeting and I know where it is. Why don't you just follow me? By the way, what is it that you do?' He said, 'I'm a Boeing navigational engineer.'" *(Laughter and applause.)*
>
> "Yes, you people might want to hear what I have to say about stress." *(More laughs.)*

Of course I asked the navigational engineer permission to include this little story in my speech. Obviously, the universe doesn't always line up to give me a great opening story such as that one, but after speaking for so many years, I have tons of stories and I will pull one out if I am speaking at a similar group. Matter of fact, a year later when speaking for another aerospace company, Northrop, I used the same story, but set it up by fudging the time. "I know working in the aerospace field is very stressful—matter of fact, last week I was speaking at another company, and walking around the parking lot was . . ." It still got a huge laugh and once again, set up their stress problem.

The more you speak, the more you will gather your own collection of stories that will be dead-on for presenting the problem.

EXERCISE: THE PROBLEM INTERVIEW

Look back at the interviews you did and the stories you've collected to see if there are any that match up. If not, feel free to flip back to chapter five and re-brainstorm stories that are based on the problems identified by your client.

For example, I was hired by a company whose employees all complained about their boss. In my speech, I told a story about how working in an office I found that I was heckled at work by my boss even more than I was heckled onstage by drunks at a comedy club on Long Island. The employees knew exactly what I meant even if the boss didn't.

Technique Five: Quotes and Stats

A quote or statistic from a reputable source gives your speech further credibility and drives home the point that The Problem you're addressing is relevant to a larger audience. If you are speaking on childhood obesity, it is one thing for you to remind the audience of the issue but when you start pulling quotes and stats from *The New York Times,* scientists and researchers, doctors and the president of the United States, you've got an army of proof onstage with you.

Lisa Ford speaks on customer service and illustrates The Problem that if companies don't hear customers complain, they assume everything is fine. "Not true," Lisa tells her audiences. "Most customers avoid the hassle of complaining and that's why you have to beg for complaints." Lisa then uses statistics that backs up her theory, so the audience has proof that her techniques will truly affect their bottom line. For example, research shows that if you have one hundred unhappy customers four will tell you and ninety-six won't.

But just reciting statistics can be boring, so Lisa makes them entertaining, by telling a personal story about having rotten service at her dry cleaners that backs up her point. As she says, "I was a typical customer, as I did not bother to complain. It is not worth the hassle." Then Lisa drops in the statistic about how only four out of ninety-six will complain. She then drives home her point with a call to action. "And that's why you have to beg for complaints. You cannot let yourself risk 96 percent of your customers not telling you and letting problems go unresolved. You've got to beg for complaints."

COMEDY TIP

You can add humor to a quote or statistic by pausing then making an "aside" remark about that information. Andy Core is a professional speaker who speaks on health and exercise. He uses quotes, statistics, and humor to open his talk.

"In 1982, 15 percent of the people living in Arkansas and Mississippi were obese. [pause] The other 85 percent were sucking in their gut."

And check out Ellen DeGeneres on her show or watch her standup clips on YouTube. She's a master of this comedy technique.

Sandra Sellani is a marketing and brand consultant and speaker. She scares the audience into action by using this quote when speaking to business owners about providing relevant services to an aging American population: "On January 1, 2011, the first of seventy-seven million baby boomers turned sixty-five, and a member of the baby boomer generation will continue to turn sixty-five every eight seconds—for the next eighteen years. Companies that do not understand this important demographic can miss significant business opportunities."

As Sandra says, "A good statistic can hit your audience between the eyes and give them a reason to believe your message."

EXERCISE: YOU CAN QUOTE ME ON THAT!

Who are the people who've inspired you? What wisdom did they pass down to you? Are there writers, philosophers, politicians, scientists, or athletes who have spoken or written about a problem similar to your audience's? Without plagiarizing, let's find a way to weave their wisdom into the fabric of your problem story.

1. Get online and find ten quotes from ten different experts that relate to your problem.

2. Once you have the quotes, keep searching and find five to ten statistical announcements that also back up the validity and seriousness of the problem. These should be "bad news" statistics

that further prove to the audience that they desperately need solutions. Your solutions!

3. Add humor to the quote or the statistic by commenting or disagreeing with it. Later on in chapter fifteen I'll show you how to make this work for laughs.

4. From the lists you made above, try out all of your material on your Buddy and see which ones get a laugh. Those are the ones that are keepers.

WARNING

Plagiarizing any part of your speech is bad form.

The speaking community is small and word gets around quick. Even if you don't get sued from profiting from someone else's material, Karma will catch up with you and torpedo your speaking career. You can't build a career on stolen material because once your reputation is damaged, you won't be able to repair it.

Make sure your material is original and if you do quote someone, give them credit.

Technique Six: Go for Shock Value

Imagine this. I had a gig for a Fortune 500 company where they wanted me to speak about the lighter side of change. Prior to the gig, when speaking to management, they told me, "We have some changes going on and we want our people to know that change, although scary, is inherent in life and we all need to accept it." Later, when interviewing staff members, I found out the change they were talking about was an announcement that everyone was losing their bonuses this year. This is where management makes a mess, people are extremely disgruntled, and they think the solution is to bring in motivational speakers to clean things up. It rarely works and usually it's the speaker who ends up going to the slaughter.

At 8 a.m. sharp, I watched as the first speaker's Core Promise that "change was good" was met with rolling eyes and even heckles. Practically everyone in the audience was on their BlackBerries or napping. There were a few people looking at the podium, but with their middle fingers extended. I decided that this called for drastic measures. In order to get their attention and respect, I would have to derail their apathy and hostility and the only way to do that was to open with something shocking. I got an idea.

Here is exactly what I said:

> "I've been asked to talk about how to use humor to handle change and I want you to know that I'm perfectly qualified to talk about this because I used to be a man." Huge laugh. And you better believe they put down their BlackBerries to stare at me. (BTW, for the reader, I'm 5'3" with cleavage that is visible from outer space.)
>
> I went on: "No, I'm kidding, I didn't used to be a man . . . I still am . . . technically." Another huge laugh.
>
> "No, I'm kidding . . . that was a joke to get your attention and show you that when we joke about something it makes you take a second look at it. Some of you are still looking. No, these are real and I'm about the only woman in L.A. who can say that." Huge laugh.
>
> "So, now that I've got your attention, I'm going to convince you to take a second look at some of these very uncomfortable changes going on, and at the least, we can have some laughs."

I had them in the palm of my hand and that attention and respect continued for my entire speech. Now, this was one of my rare bouts of inspiration and it doesn't happen all the time, but the more you speak, the more you will gather these gems that you keep in the database of your mind and roll them out in case the audience needs some shock therapy. However, it's not shock for the sake of shock. It still has to set up *their* problem. One of my students, Jessica Halem, speaks on diversity issues. She opens with:

> "I'm a radical-feminist-Jewish-lesbian. Hey, it's a niche! Today, you're going to learn how use your sense of humor in constructive ways—to joke about yourself rather than put down others."

Just hearing the word "lesbian" in a corporate setting is a wake-up call for an audience, but you can't say that if you have a husband at home. A shock statement has to be authentic.

EXERCISE: SHOCK THE SH*T OUT OF 'EM

This technique can be a little tricky, as you don't want to shock the audience into retreating from you. But, sometimes a speaker needs to present the problem in a way that is a wake-up call. Look through all the exercises you did in this chapter and see if any aspect of the problem reminds you of a personal story, an incident, or a comment that packs a wake-them-up punch. Try out your material on your Buddy. If their mouth drops open and their eyes bug out, you've got a winner.

EXERCISE: PICK A TECHNIQUE

Look over all the writing you did for this chapter and pick your two strongest pieces. Get together with your Buddy and present two versions of this section of your speech to each other. Ask your Buddy the following questions:

1. After hearing that section, were you convinced that you actually had a problem?

2. What was The Problem?

3. Was The Problem presented as a judgment or as a concern?

4. Were you convinced that The Problem was severe and needed a solution? If not, why not?

5. Is The Problem something that your credentials qualify you to talk about?

6. Which approach worked best and why?

I hope I didn't overwhelm you with so many techniques to present the problem that now you have a big problem—which one to use. Here's the thing: there is no one right way to write this part of your speech. Some of you might do an exercise and bingo, it works. Some of you might need to try out all the techniques mentioned in this chapter in order to find the right one. Some of you may even find that you'll choose a technique once you step onstage based on how the audience "feels" to you. It's all about which one best fits your style and your needs.

COMPLETED SPEECH TIME: Ten minutes (for half an hour), twenty minutes (for one hour)

CHAPTER ELEVEN

STEP THREE: WHIP OUT YOUR CREDENTIALS

Have you ever been in trouble and needed help? A few years ago, I realized my poor investing skills had left me with a negative return on my retirement fund. If I wanted to be able to eat more than Top Ramen Noodles when I was eighty years old, I needed to find the right person to help me sort out my future. I wanted someone able to relate to my life and my work. Someone who had other clients in showbiz. Someone I could trust. I got referrals for investment advisers, checked out their credentials, as well as their education and past jobs and I picked someone. As it turned out, the market crashed and I would have done better if I had left my money under my mattress, but that is not my point. When people need help, they need to be able to trust someone—they seek out the right person with the right credentials.

If you've done your job well in the first two sections, your audience may like you and agree with your assertion that they have problems. You've established the Core Promise of your speech, hinting that you have a way to help them out of their misery and you've gone into some detail about their problems using stories and/or statistics with just a dash of humor. Now it's time to convince your audience that you are the person who can rescue them. After talking extensively about *them,* now it's time to mix in a story about how you successfully helped someone or an organization find solutions to their problems. This should be a story where you demonstrate how your methodology helped someone else become happier, richer, healthier, better. In this section, you'll learn how to qualify as an expert by including in that short story not only how you know what you know, but also one or more of these items:

1. Name-dropping

2. Referring to your published works

3. Reminding the audience of your business experience or training

This story is not your Heart Story. It's one of your Support Stories. It should illuminate why you qualify to speak on your Core Promise but it should not, as of yet, reveal any solutions. You're just setting up why the audience should pay attention to you. Very often speakers start this section out by saying, "I know how you feel, because . . ." So keep that phrase in mind as you work on this chapter. Think of this as the "I feel your pain" moment and "I've got the credentials to help."

The structure you'll use to tell this story is: Point—Story—Question / Call-to-Action

Meaning, you announce the point of why you're telling the next story.

You tell the story.

You reframe the point of the story as a question to the audience asking them to take action. The question is also called a Call-to-Action.

This is a structure you will use over and over again throughout your speech. Here's an example of how I use it in my speech called "Laughing Your Way Out of Stress." I start by giving the point of the story first:

"It's not what happens to us that causes stress. It's how we react to it and I've learned how to combat stress by making a humor choice."

Giving the point sets up the story and lets the audience know why they should listen to this story and what they will get out of it.

I then tell the story of teaching stand-up comedy and how the process of turning my students' problems into punch lines actually transforms them from Drama Queens to Comedy Queens. As I tell the story, I mention the names of several famous former students who got their start in my workshop, such as funny person and movie star Seth Rogen. I then tell the story of one specific student who was struggling to find the funny in her life. Her breakthrough moment came when she got honest about a rather difficult divorce and said, "We had one thing in common—we were *both* madly in love with *him*!"

I describe in detail her Eureka Moment and how feeling the power of laughter helped to heal her pain. I also share that her breakthrough inspired me to write my book, *The Comedy Bible*. ". . . And when I went on the Oprah Winfrey show I was able to show housewives how they could turn their problems into punch lines and not only feel better about themselves, but make a living as a stand-up comic."

QUESTION / CALL-TO-ACTION

So, after telling my story, I then directly confront the audience and ask them:

"So when bad stuff happens, how do you react? Do you get angry? Or are you able to see the humor? You have a choice. You can get mad, or you can get funny. I say, don't get mad . . . get funny."

Pick a Point

As you've just come out of talking extensively about the problem, this is when you want to tell the audience a general point about the solution. This is not where you go into detail about your specific Action Steps. This is where you give the audience a rephrasing of your Core Promise. This is where you introduce your methodology that introduces a short story of either, how you found your method, or how you've helped others solve the problem using your technique.

Pick a Story

Your story will most likely start with "I understand how you feel . . ." This is not going to be your big Heart Story. This story should illustrate you helping someone solve the problem. The main character in this story should not be you, but rather be someone you helped. Start the story describing the problem this person (or company) had. You intervened. End with the positive results that you assisted them to achieve.

Question / Call-to-Action

Coming out of your story, ask the audience a rhetorical question along the lines of, "If that was you, what would you do?" Then give a Call-to-Action, telling the audience something that they could do. This is not where you go into detail about it, as that's coming up next. This is where you are introducing the idea of the solution.

MAKING YOUR CREDENTIALS POP

Okay, now that you understand the basic structure of Point—Story—Question, let's move on to rewriting this section of your speech. Just remember that as you're telling this story, you want to drop in your credentials casually. You'll notice in my story, I managed to mention I'd taught workshops that launched the careers of famous people, and that I was featured on the Oprah Winfrey show. I did all that without seeming like a jerk because I made the story relevant to the issue at hand—stress reduction and I spoke about the person I helped rather than bragging about myself. It's a lot to accomplish in such a short time, but I assure you, it's possible. Here's how:

Technique One: Name-Drop

This technique is exactly what it sounds like—you casually drop the names of important people you've worked with or associated with in order to enhance your own credibility. It's best if these people are somehow related to or well-respected within the same industry or company for which you're speaking. For example:

"When I was consulting at Facebook, we were facing the same challenges you're facing now. Could we bring in enough capital to make payroll?"

Even better, if you can name-drop a major celebrity or a famous face, you're sure to keep their attention. Such as:

"When I shared the speaking platform with Katie Couric, backstage we talked about these same methods."

EXERCISE: BRAINSTORMING NAMES

Take a moment now to make a comprehensive list of any important, famous, well-known, or well-respected people with whom you've rubbed elbows, or impressive companies you've spoken at, or worked for. If you can't remember off the top of your head, look back over the list you created in chapter four for memory prompts.

- In the story, the hero—which can be you or your famous name— is dealing with the problem that is the topic of your speech.

- The obstacles of solving the problem mount and if your famous name gets involved here, mention it.

- At the end of the story, the hero finds a way of dealing with the problem and is perhaps recognized by the famous name as a result.

Technique Two: Your Published Works

You should refer to any books or articles you've published, or any media appearances/accolades that would indicate that the media perceives you as an expert. Especially if your book was a best-seller, you want to find a way to sneak that information into your speech. Make sure you do this in a casual way bringing up the "before" aspect of your success. For example:

"Before my book, *Seven Ways to be Successful,* hit the *New York Times* best-seller list, I was broke with no job and I didn't know what to do with my life."

"Before I started my blog, I was rolling quarters to pay for my daughter's diapers. Now, companies send me Gucci bags to profile on my Web site."

Technique Three: Reminding the Audience of Your Business Experience or Training

If you're speaking about how to succeed in a job interview, and you've worked for twenty years in Human Resources interviewing job applicants, your experience makes you an expert. Or, if you're conducting a sales training and the participants increased their sales by 20 percent, that's a great story to tell here. Ask yourself these questions:

- How do elements of your job relate to the subject of your speech?

- How has your training taught you how to deal with this problem?

- What kind of effect has your message had on an individual or an organization? Tell that story here.

Your main qualifications might be your personal background. If you are speaking about credit repair, having been bankrupt and later raising your credit scores to above 800 would convince most people that you know something about the topic. Speaker student Naomi Lopez's expertise was being the mother of a child with behavior issues. Her journey of finding a way to deal with her child made her a sought-after speaker for parent groups. She speaks about the journey from feeling her child was a burden to understanding her challenges were a blessing in disguise. At this point in her speech, Naomi doesn't do her Heart Story, but rather a story about a mother who heard her speech and went from despair to hope.

EXERCISE: QUALIFY & TESTIFY!

Remember in chapter three, I had you write about your journey from failure to success? This is a great place to mention that journey in relationship to how your experiences helped someone else with the same problem. Go back and choose one of the stories you wrote that relates to the topic of your speech. Ask yourself these questions about that story:

- Have you made a difference in someone's life by helping them deal with the specific problem that you just detailed?

- Who were they? What did they want in their life and what obstacles got in their way? How did you help them overcome their problem?

- Has a company or organization used your techniques? What were the obstacles? What were the results?

- Did your speech, book, blog, radio show help someone to be healthier, wealthier, or happier?

Answering yes to any of those questions means the story will stand as proof of your expertise. Once you have that story, find a way to pepper the story with the information you created above: drop those names, mention those books, brag about your jobs.

Next, set up the story by picking a point. Read over the Core Promise you wrote and find a way to generalize the methodology you will be teaching the audience by telling this story. Make your point no longer than a few sentences.

Finally, after you tell the story ask a rhetorical question and give a Call-to-Action. "So . . . what would you have done? Would you be willing to live a healthier life style by doing thirty minutes of exercise a day?"

Call up your Buddy and read this section out loud to each other, then switch and read each other's aloud. Make revisions based upon what you hear.

 **COMPLETED SPEECH TIME: Fifteen minutes (for half an hour), thirty minutes (for one hour)**

CHAPTER TWELVE

STEP FOUR: AND . . . ACTION!

By now you have captured your audience's full attention, stated your Core Promise, convinced your audience that they have a major problem, and established yourself as an expert in just that issue. At this halfway point, everyone should be salivating for a solution. It's time to let your listeners off the hook and provide them with definitive, concrete steps they can take to solve their problems and enrich their lives. These are your Action Steps—solutions you know work because you've used them yourself. Remember those life lessons you explored in Part One? It's time to pull them out and boil them down to three very practical steps your audience can use to become richer, healthier, happier, more organized—insert your issue here.

Let's face it, most people want the answers to life's big problems to be super-simple and not require much effort. Whether it's out of laziness or fear, people love when solutions are broken down into doable, easy to follow, and easy to remember steps. They don't want to hear that they need twelve years of expensive psychotherapy or that they have to confront their long-lost father face-to-face. Remember, this is a speech you're giving, not a book you're writing. The audience can't go back, study and reread your steps. They're not taking notes so you have to give them the sound-byte version of your solutions.

Generally speaking, three Action Steps are the magic number, but in my speech on using humor to reduce stress, I only offer *one* Action Step and it is so simple people remember it and practice it for years. I tell them when things get stressful, they should yell "Whoo-Hoo!" to remind them to lighten up and face challenges with a positive attitude. Reducing my message to one word ensures that my audience remembers the Action Step and remembers me.

With that said, you still want your Action Steps to resonate and be truly helpful. I had a client who came to me with three Action Steps she wanted to use to help women overcome adversity to become role models. Her Action Steps were:

1. *Have a Good Attitude*

2. *Don't Get Upset*

3. *Smile*

As my client presented her case, I flashed back to an extremely depressing time of my life. In one year I lost my mother, my grandmother, and my relationship. As I was walking my dog, I must have had a glum expression on my face because as I crossed the street someone in a car shouted, "Smile!" He had the unfortunate timing of being stuck at a stoplight where he was met with the full force of my sorrow and rage. I used words that would ban this book from public libraries. "Smile" is not an effective, well-thought-out Action Step.

BE THE BEST OF BOTH TO GET BUSINESS

"Event planners are always torn between two worlds—what their audiences want, and what management and bean counters want. Audiences do want to learn, but more than that, they want to have fun and be moved. The speakers who can fit in both worlds will win."

—Brian Lord, speaker agent, VP, Premiere Speakers Bureau

Just imagine how glib those three above Action Steps would feel to someone in the audience who was dealing with a life-threatening disease. "Just do it" might work for a fifteen-second Nike ad but to resonate with an audience, your Action Steps need to be based on your real life experiences rather than shallow slogans. Action Steps are *your* original methodology. These are the steps that can become your trademark process, your brand, and your calling card.

Step into the self-help aisle at any bookstore and you'll see what I mean about the creation of methodology. Every author is promising their reader a fast solution to their problem and they are using catchy titles, alliteration, numbering, and acronyms to convey their message quickly— *The 17 Day Diet, The 7 Habits of Highly Effective People, The Secret, The Power of Now, The 4-Hour Body, The 4-Hour Workweek.* Get the point?

At first glance, creating Action Steps seems simple, yet identifying your methodology is anything but. Believe me, I speak from personal experience. (See how I worked that in there?) A few years ago, if you'd asked me if I knew of a system that would ensure a powerful speech as its end result, I would have told you I didn't have a clue. I thought I just floundered around in a hit-and-miss fashion until I found components that worked and since, like most people, I was constantly focused on upcoming challenges, I never really evaluated my process. It was only when I started coaching other speakers that I stopped to examine the actual steps it took to put a speech together. That's when I realized that there was a method to my creative process; I just wasn't sure what that method was. I'd been working instinctively for so long, it all seemed "second nature" to me. I needed to CSI my process.

PEEK IN AT JUDY'S WORLD

You can actually watch my day-to-day process in putting a new speech together on my online workshop at KeynoteU.com

---

When a client booked me to write a brand-new speech, I decided to pay attention to my process and observe myself. Although there was a lot of wasted time devoted to the steps of being crazy, worried, insecure, scared, and tipsy, there were also some chunks that really worked. Initially, I had a lot more than seven steps and they were in a different order. Coaching other speakers became a research project to see if the same steps that brought me success worked for others. They did. I further finessed the steps and the results were the "Seven Steps of Writing a Speech," of which you are now on step four.

Finding your Action Steps requires a left-brained search of your success. It's not easy, as many experts just can't explain to people how they became successful. Most people just think in terms of doing it and not *how* they do it. In other words, finding your Action Steps requires a thorough investigation of how you, your company, or others overcame The Problem. Unless you give great thought and attention to your Action Steps, the solution part of your speech will be met with a frozen stare, or worse, hostility from the audience.

So . . . how will you create your Action Steps?

Technique One: Consciously Watch Your Subconscious

Subconsciously, you already know your Action Steps. You're using them currently or you've used them in the past to overcome your problems. In fact, you're writing this speech because you are an expert, and you got to be that expert by using your natural zigzagging instincts between "Wow, this worked," and "I don't ever want to make that mistake again."

Look back and ask yourself, "Exactly what did I do to get out of debt, survive that life threatening disease, or attract the perfect mate?" If you can't remember the details of your journey, look back over your diaries or journals or sit a friend down and ask them to tell you the story of your success. Sometimes, our friends can see our triumphs and our tragedies with a more objective eye. Break out the old photo albums and see if those images jump-start any memories. Meditate and visualize that time in your life. Try to conjure the old emotions and if all else fails, put a blank notebook by your bed. Just before you drift off to sleep, announce to yourself aloud, "Tonight, I will remember the steps I took to conquer (insert your problem here)." Then let your subconscious do the work for you. Upon waking, immediately jot down the ideas that occur to you.

Technique Two: Practice Investigating Your Success

You can practice unearthing Action Steps by investigating a process that has nothing to do with your current speech. Pick something at which you've been successful, like learning to play the guitar, becoming an expert Scrabble player, becoming fluent in French, etc. Look back at that accomplishment and parse out three steps you used to succeed.

An example of this: when I turned forty, I decided to learn to snowboard. I'm not an athletic sort and growing up in my family, I was discouraged from even playing with a Slip and Slide, as I might slip and slide. Physical risk taking was so frowned upon that my grandmother even railed against the dangers of hopscotch. "Hopping on one foot on cement—oy!" So snowboarding down a mountain with no way to "steer" or stop absolutely filled me with terror, especially after having dislocated my shoulder and broken two ribs just getting off a ski lift during my first lesson. But I didn't let those broken ribs stop me. I got back on the board and became a black diamond snowboarder at forty years old.

Using this success story to practice finding Action Steps, I identified the five most important steps I took to become a snowboarder that I could pass on to someone else:

1. Commit to three days of trying. You are going to fall. That's a given. So don't give up on day one.

2. Take lessons with someone who has been teaching more than one week.

3. Give yourself small challenges and stay on the bunny slopes until you feel confident and then go find easy intermediate runs so you don't scare yourself.

4. Whistle when you get scared, which will be all the time.

5. Know that the pain of learning will be worth the bliss of snowboarding.

6. Have your medical insurance paid up.

Technique Three: Coach Others to Find Your Methodology

Like a fine wine, your methodology will deepen and evolve as you give your speech. In the development stage, it is essential to get feedback on your ideas. The ways that you can refine your steps are by offering to give free coaching on your topic to anyone who would be willing. By having others test drive your Action Steps, you'll not only get a clear idea how they work for others but by coaching others you'll find stories to add to your speech as well as testimonials to add to your marketing materials.

Now you try it.

EXERCISE: CREATE YOUR ACTION STEPS

In some speeches the Action Steps are the longest section, while in other speeches the steps are extremely short. In Aron Ralston's speech, his story about being stuck under the rock is the bulk of his speech. He offers only one step: The time to love your family is now, because you never know what is going to happen. With that said, let's discover your Action Steps:

MAKE A POINT, TELL A STORY

"Stories are happening all around us every day—you just have to keep looking for them. And then use them!

"During your speech, after you make a point, tell a story. Not only will it keep your audience interested in your topic, it will also help them remember your message because they will remember your stories."

—Ken Blanchard, speaker and best-selling coauthor of *The One-Minute Manager* and fifty other books

1. Write a top ten list of Action Steps that can solve the audience's problem.

2. Arrange the steps in the order you think is most productive.

3. Give the steps short clever names that will make them easy to remember.

4. Test them out with your Buddy to see if they relate and understand them.

5. From your test run, pick the top three steps.

Now, use this formula to create the Action Step portion of your talk:

- Give the overview point of the step

- Tell a short story about the step that can include:

    ⊚ How the step works.

    ⊚ How it's useful.

    ⊚ How you discovered the step.

    ⊚ Or, how you or people you know successfully used the step.

- Question (Call-to-Action): Ask the audience if they are willing to immediately implement the first step. Then give them a Call-to-Action on something they can do to implement it.

THREE IS THE MAGIC NUMBER

Comedian and author Dan Rosenberg wrote *The Book on Hosting: How Not To Suck as an Emcee,* so I asked him to speak to my stand-up class.

In the first class, he gave fifteen tips and nobody bought his book.

For the second class, I told him to say, "I only have time to tonight to give you three tips but if you want all twenty-three tips, I'm offering my book at the end of class."

Everyone bought the book.

Then repeat Point—Story—Question with all three Action Steps. Here are some additional tips in presenting your Action Steps:

Consider Customizing Your Action Steps

Many speakers tweak their Action Steps depending on their audience. Award-winning professional speaker and author Glenna Salsbury has a way of presenting her Action Steps, which she calls P-S-A.

Point—Story—Application.

This is very similar to what I refer to as Point—Story—Question.

Glenna frames each story starting with a point, tells a story, and ends with what she calls the application (Question/Call-to-Action) where she asks listeners, "What's in this for you?"

One of Glenna's Action Steps (point) is, "We can make a difference in someone's life by acknowledging them, calling them by name, and providing genuine, authentic recognition."

She then tells a story that illustrates how she found this Action Step.

"When I was twelve years old, there was a girl in our grade school who was basically an outcast. Her parents were garbage collectors and the family lived near the dump, wore clothes from the dump, and smelled like the dump. No one wanted to sit next to this young girl. One day Mae came walking toward me in the hall at school. Her hair was matted, her dress was filthy, and she was shuffling along the wall with her head down like people with low self-esteem often do. For whatever reason, that day I looked into Mae's eyes and said, 'Good morning, Mae. How are you?' I saw the most amazing thing happen. Mae looked at me with this incredible sense of wonder and she stuttered out her response, 'I . . . I . . . I'm fine, Glenna. How . . . how are you?' Now I'm not sure, as a twelve-year-old, that I knew in my mind what had happened, but I knew in my viscera that a life can be changed by looking into the eyes of another and calling him or her by name."

Glenna then gives her "Application," or what I refer to as a Question / Call-to-Action by asking the audience a question: "How many of you are looking for every opportunity to touch lives in a transformational way by simply calling people by name and honoring them with the recognition of their presence?"

Glenna then customizes her Call-to-Action, for each audience. If she is speaking at a hotel, she says, "Maybe as you leave this conference tonight you might want to thank the valet who parked your car, look him or her in the eyes, call them by name."

When she is speaking at a school, she says, "Kids, did you know that your teacher would love to hear that you like her? So today, how many of you will tell your teacher what she means to you?"

By customizing the Action Step directly for your audience, you have a better chance that the audience will actually implement your steps.

Consider Using Your Action Step as the Title of Your Speech

Mike Rayburn's keynote is entitled "What if . . . ?" which is also his first Action Step. In his presentation he uses music and comedy to teach what he calls "Three simple, powerful tools you can use immediately and forever to be able to leap beyond your perceived limitations."

Mike frames his steps by telling the story of how he got from playing cover songs for drunks in a bar to playing at Carnegie Hall.

As Mike says, "I found the tools I give to the audience by examining my own life success. But I wanted to make sure that my technique of success not only worked for me, but was for people who could apply it to anything including, business, teaching, financial management, and leadership. After all, we all have a Carnegie Hall type of success that we would like to achieve."

Mike Rayburn's Action Steps:

1. Ask yourself this question, "What if . . . ?"

2. Set your dream goals.

3. Become a virtuoso and resolve to be the best.

Mike gives his steps to the audience with a heavy dose of humor, stories, as well as songs. And the results? Mike Rayburn has been inducted into the National Speakers' Association Hall of Fame as well being booked at high fees, keynoting for hundreds of companies and organizations.

Use Audience Participation . . . Smartly

Very often speakers will design a simple exercise that the audience can do for one, or all three of their Action Steps. I personally don't like it when a speaker tells me to raise my hands, or hug the person next to me. As Jon Stewart would say, "Awkward!"

Nobody likes to be forced to do things against their will, so I suggest that if you are going to have audience participation, use it very carefully, and be respectful. Not everyone likes to participate. According to meeting planners, one of the biggest complaints from an audience is a speaker who "forces" audience members to do thing that they don't feel comfortable doing.

Tips on involving the audience:

1. Keep your exercises simple and fun.

2. Never put anyone on the spot, or make them look foolish.

3. Don't force someone to stand up in front of the group.

4. Create exercises where they can turn to the person seated next to them to practice your particular exercise.

Keep Your Action Steps Simple

Make the first step easily to implement. You don't want to start out with "First you have to decode the human genome." Very often, step one is small and the action for the audience is to "Question" "Realize," "Imagine," or "Understand." Creating a step one that requires a mind shift is far less demanding than, "Write," "Find," or "Make a list."

Arrange Your Action Steps in a Progressive Order

In order to do step two, they have to complete step one.

Create an Acronym or Use Alliteration

In Connie Podesta's popular talk, "Stand Out from the Crowd: How to Out-Think and Out-Perform the Competition," she gives her action steps a rhythm by repeated use of the prefix "re."

Step One: "RE*COMMIT TO CHANGE."

Step Two: "RE*THINK YOUR CHOICES."

Step Three: "RE*ASSESS YOUR EXPECTATIONS."

Keep It Fun!

Keep these steps entertaining rather than presenting your steps as homework.

COMPLETED SPEECH TIME: Twenty-four minutes (for half hour), forty minutes (for one hour)

CHAPTER THIRTEEN

STEP FIVE: OPEN YOUR HEART AND GET YOUR STANDING O

Caroline Casey may not be a name you recognize but she is one power-house of a woman. She is known internationally for changing attitudes and perceptions of disability within the business and media markets. In 2004 she founded Kanchi, an organization established to influence this change. She named the organization after the elephant she rode across Southern India during a 1,000 km personal journey. Through Kanchi, she launched the Ability Awards to recognize progressive and sensitive companies and build awareness for disability issues in the business world. The awards are now being rolled out internationally across five countries.

Oh, did I mention that Caroline is legally blind?

Caroline Casey is invited around the world to speak on her leader-ship work at eminent events including the Global Competitiveness Forum, the Clinton Global Initiative, and TED. At the end of any talk Caroline gives, the audience applauds her with a standing ovation and there is never a dry eye in the place. Caroline has an amazing story to tell about overcoming the limitations of her blindness to take on the world.

Caroline wasn't born blind. Her blindness came on slowly, stealing from her day by day. As her vision worsened, Caroline became more and more secretive. She was terrified she would lose her job. She was terrified to face reality. Then, one day, she realized she couldn't fake it any longer. She had to tell her boss she was blind. She had to face her

CELEBRITIES DON'T GET ALL THE GIGS

"Here is why honing your craft as a speaker is so important. Most people don't realize that event planners—those making decisions about who will speak at events—are rarely looking for Olympians, *New York Times* best-selling authors, or Fortune 500 CEOs. They're looking for speakers who have an incredible story to tell."

—Brian Lord, speaker agent, VP of Premiere Speakers Bureau

fear and when she did, she realized that by hiding her disability she had bought into the mentality that she was no longer competent. That she was limited. And that just wasn't true. If she wanted people to believe in her abilities, she had to first believe in them herself! Using that Eureka Moment as a force of inspiration, Caroline asks her audience to do something as daring as she did: to take a chance, to try something new that will make their lives and career more successful. Casey teaches her listeners how to look past their self imposed limits to achieve greatness in life and to reframe the word "disability" into "ability." Caroline is on a mission to convey her message and actually has changed the global social landscape for people with disabilities.

Just think about that.

A Heart Story with a Eureka Moment can transform others and the world.

Stories are powerful tools for a speaker. We use them to drive home a message, make our points memorable, and emotionally grab an audience. Some speeches have one long story and others have many different stories drizzled throughout their speech. But all speakers have a Heart Story that beautifully and poignantly communicates the message of their speech and illustrates how their Action Steps work in real-life situations. Heart Stories get under people's skin and take them on an emotional journey that can truly inspire change and transformation. No speaker gets a standing ovation because their Action Steps were so informative. Audiences will give you a standing ovation because you've touched them emotionally. You've captured their hearts. And the way to do that is with an authentic Heart Story. It's time now to write yours.

"But Judy, I'm not blind, I don't have a rags-to-riches story, and I've never had to cut off an arm! How the hell am I going to get a Heart Story?"

I can relate to those of you who are not Survivors.

As a former stand up comic, I was unaccustomed to having poignant moments in my speech. Coming from an occupation that required me to tell jokes to drunken hecklers didn't exactly lead me to being vulnerable. I had one job and one job only—making people laugh. I was used to the club owner standing at the back of the room listening to make sure his paying customers were happy. That is not to say that my stand-up wasn't personal or revealing, but all intimate details of my life had to be couched in fifteen-second jokes.

Revealing my own past didn't exactly come easily. During my first speech, which was essentially my stand-up act with a brief message to "Lighten Up," I dreaded the upcoming Heart Story. Although it was a story with tons of laughs in it, it also included a hospital scene of my mother's death, where the laughs stopped dead cold. No pun intended.

As a comic, a quiet room always meant I was bombing but this was different. Usually when a comic bombs, audience members will look away from the stage because they feel awkward and embarrassed. This time, even though the room was silent I could feel the entire audience staring at me, not with embarrassment but with intense interest and some with tears in their eyes.

Telling my first Heart Story was a memorable moment. It was so different from being a comic where I was busy trying to win the audience over, get their approval, slay them, and control them. This was a simple moment of solidarity where I wasn't trying to win them over. I wasn't trying to get their approval. I was just telling them my story as if I were speaking with a dear friend.

After the speech, something different happened. I got a standing ovation. As a comic, I had always done well, and had occasionally gotten a standing ovation; the kind where a few people in the front stand and then the people behind them do the I'm-standing-because-I'm-guilty sort of ovation. But I had never had this kind of ovation, where the entire audience stood up as a group.

Coming off stage, the differences continued. After a good stand-up set, I would often get audience members saying to me, "Hey, you're really funny!" But after giving a speech with a Heart Story, people lined up to see me. Some wanted to hug me, some still had tears in their eyes, and some just wanted to share with me how much my story affected them. And the best news, in all my years of performing I had never had so many people line up to buy my books and other products.

You may argue . . .

"Judy, I don't need a Heart Story. I'm just presenting new software to my company and people just need to know the logistics of how to use the equipment. There's no need to get all mushy about it. I don't feel it's appropriate to spill my guts to an audience of accountants."

I beg to differ.

A Heart Story is by no means just an act of spilling your guts onstage to manipulate or gain sympathy. Your Heart Story must also provide information about your subject matter. It just happens to be a story that has an emotional component to it. It still has to address the problem and the Action Steps you used to solve that problem.

And trust me, everyone loves a good story. People will pay to read them in books and watch them in theaters and every audience being asked to tackle a new challenge—even if it's "just" new software—wants to be assured that they can do it, that they will succeed, and that change is a good thing. It doesn't mean you have to reveal the story of your abusive childhood to convince people to learn Excel, but maybe you can share a story about learning how to golf or snowboard and how you tackled the challenge of a new sport. Maybe your story will inspire your colleagues to actually listen instead of checking their email.

There is no subject matter that can't be enhanced by telling a Heart Story. As a matter of fact, the more technical, statistical, or dry your speech, the thirstier your audience will be for a Heart Story. Besides which, your Heart Story doesn't necessarily have to be about you. It can be a story about a client, an acquaintance, or even a story you heard about someone else that moved you. Even accountants love a good story. Especially one where the hero is someone like them. After all, when was the last time you went to the movies and the hero was a bean counter? Uh . . . nearly never. You can start a trend.

Plus, your story doesn't have to be a dramatic life-or-death tale. Beginning speakers most often pick obvious life-changing moments for their Heart Story, such as a parent's death or a car wreck, just like I did when I was first starting out. It took me many years to figure out it's not necessarily the epic scope of the event but the little details that can transform even a small life moment into a great Heart Story. Matter of fact, at the core of every Heart Story is one Eureka Moment where everything changes.

In my "Laughing Your Way Out of Stress" speech, my Heart Story is very simple: I'm stuck at the airport, trying to get to a gig, and my plane's been cancelled. As I stand in line with a lot of angry people trying to reschedule, I decide not to be another angry person. It is in that Eureka Moment that I decide to make a "humor choice" and rather than yell at the gate agent, I choose to make him laugh. Cut to me, sitting on the next plane out, in a first-class seat while all the other bitter people in line were shipped to a nearby Motel 6.

Simple story, huh? Not very funny, right? Matter of fact, if it happened to you, you might not even feel it's worthy to tell at a dinner party. Yet, this ten-minute story has twenty-five laugh breaks and ends with thunderous applause from the audience. It's all about the delivery and really milking your Heart Story, sharing your Eureka Moment and the Life Lessons you learned, explaining how that moment and those lessons led to your Action Steps and how your life has changed as a result.

WHAT'S YOUR EUREKA MOMENT?

Your Heart Story is not a monologue. It is not the chronological narrative of your life. If you want to detail every year of your life, you should rent a theater and do a one-person show. Speaking has to be about the Message of You, and this speech has to address your Core Promise, not just function as a collection of remembered moments. In fact, all you need to really communicate your Message of You is to identify the *one* moment, your Eureka Moment, when life bonked you over the head so hard that you went "A-ha!" This is the moment where you overcame the same problem that you started your speech with.

If we're lucky and we're paying attention, we'll realize that our lives are full of these moments. We call them "hitting bottom" or "having an epiphany" or "the straw that broke the camel's back" or "a lightbulb went off" or "something just clicked." No matter the terminology, these are the moments you want to share in your Heart Story—just not all of them at once! The only Eureka Moment you need to focus on is the one that is relevant to your audience and their problems.

My client Emiko Hori came to me with considerable experience speaking at her local Toastmasters branch, but she wanted to take her speech to the next level. Emiko was the only female manager at a software firm where she supervised a staff comprised entirely of men. This may not seem remarkable in and of itself but when placed in the context of her childhood, it was extraordinary journey.

Emiko told me the story of growing up in a very restrictive household in Japan where she was taught to be submissive, not to talk, and wasn't even allowed to look her parents in the eyes. Her family immigrated to California when she was ten years old and, unable to speak English, Emiko felt incredibly isolated from the world. She spent all her free time playing piano, saying in music what she couldn't say in words. She became a concert pianist and at a concert, she met her husband. She transitioned from music to technology and rose through the ranks of the industry to become one of only a handful of female managers working in that capacity. Emiko had spent her childhood in submission and near silence and now she was a woman in charge. It was a huge journey and as a result, her speech was a patchwork of many different themes and topics. It was confusing for an audience to understand how exactly Emiko's stories were relevant to them.

One month into our coaching work, Emiko found her Eureka Moment. She remembered an English tutor she'd had when she was twelve years old. The woman taught her not only to speak English, but to speak up and be heard. She realized this teacher had been her Annie Sullivan, the character from her favorite movie at the time, the Helen

Keller story *The Miracle Worker.* She also realized that she had identified with Helen Keller, feeling cut off from the world, unable to communicate, to look anyone in the eye, to participate in life. It was this English tutor that gave Emiko her voice. It was through their lessons together that Emiko got over her fear and found the courage to speak aloud in her classroom. Once Emiko identified her Eureka Moment, not only did her Heart Story come together, but her whole speech. She now speaks to women on the "Power of Speaking Up."

As you can see from Emiko's journey, your Heart Story is not the chronological time line of your life, but rather an isolated moment in that life that illustrates one of the major life lessons you learned. A Heart Story takes the audience on a journey from powerlessness to powerful, from chaos to organized, from resentment to appreciation.

How do you identify which story should be your Heart Story? Well, first, you have to understand the difference between telling a story and telling a Heart Story. The chart below is a helpful guide to help you determine whether your material qualifies as a Heart Story.

STORY VS. HEART STORY

Story	Heart Story
The storyteller tells a story usually leaving it up to the listener to determine the message.	The speaker tells the audience the message of their Heart Story upfront. (Point)
The audience is passive. They are required only to listen.	The audience is active. They are required to act on the information they are hearing.
The story remains the same no matter the audience.	The Heart Story is adapted to relate to the needs of the audience.
The emphasis of the story is on the main character and how he/she either overcame or succumbed to obstacles.	The emphasis of the Heart Story is on the obstacles of the audience, and the Heart Story is used to inspire them to follow the speaker's solution.
The character in a story learns something new from what happened and changes.	The audience learns something new from the Heart Story and understands how they can use the Action Steps to change their own lives.
The ending can be happy or sad.	The ending must inspire.

With all that said, you don't need to worry about finding the perfect, super-original, nobody's-ever-heard-this-before Heart Story. It's rarely about *what* happens in a story that inspires an audience, but rather *how* you tell the story. As a matter of fact, two people can have a story with an identical plot and yet, in one speaker's hands, the story is a dramatic tragedy and in another speaker's hands, it's a comedy. And both speakers can communicate two different Core Promises using the same exact Heart Story.

I was having lunch with Ed Tate, who was the recipient of Toastmasters World Champion of Speaking Award in 2000, and asked him about his Heart Story. As he spoke, my mouth dropped open. We had the exact same Heart Story!

In Tate's story he is at the airport (just like me) when he intervenes as an angry traveler is verbally abusive to a gate attendant (just like me). At the end of Tate's story, the airline shows him appreciation for sticking up for an airline employee and they upgrade him to first class (just like me!). But at the end, Tate's story in his speech "One of Those Days" culminates with a Core Promise of courage, as he asks the audience a question and a Call-to-Action:

> "How do you react when others are in trouble? Every now and then we must step outside of our comfort zone. We must answer that voice in our head and heart. The voice inside all of us. It is the voice of our conscience. The voice that questions, 'What is the right thing to do?' The voice that cries out, 'If not you, then who?' It was like I said all along, I knew it was going to be [audience completes the sentence] one of those days!"

My ending was very, very different and focused on my Core Promise of using humor as a life tool:

> "Who are you? Are you one of those angry people in line? It's not what happens to you that makes you angry, it's how you choose to react. So, make a humor choice—don't get mad, get funny."

You've already heard the explanation of why my Message of You centers around humor so you know why I approached that Heart Story the way I did. To understand Ed's Core Promise, you need to know that it was heavily determined by his childhood, when his father left his mother stranded, broke, and struggling. Ed grew up feeling powerless to make things less difficult for his mother. When he finally met his father and discovered that the man was wealthy and had been living a life of ease while his own family struggled in poverty, Ed was enraged. He channeled that anger into living a life of courage and doing the right thing. It's almost as if Ed's father is in each audience as he implores his audiences to do the right thing. His speeches teach others how to have the courage to intervene when they see an injustice. This is the broader Message of You that Ed weaves through all of his speeches, materials, and books. So when Ed saw a gate attendant being verbally attacked by a hostile customer, he acted in a way his father never could. Ed saved the day. You might want to think, who needs to hear your message?

That's why similar Heart Stories can have multiple meanings. That's why several people can experience the same event and yet, come away from that Eureka Moment with completely different life lessons. A Heart Story is more about the speaker than the plot, which is good news for you. It means there is no *elusive* perfect Heart Story that you have to magically find among the pages of your writing. It means instead that any Eureka Moment you choose to launch your Heart Story can be constructed to get laughs, tears, and to reflect the Core Promise of your speech.

So, as a magician will say, pick a Eureka Moment, any Eureka Moment and stick with it through these exercises. Perhaps your moment has a message that someone in your life needs to hear as well.

CASE STUDY
TRACY SUTTLES, "PERSONALIZE YOUR SALES APPROACH THROUGH THE ART OF CONVERSATION"

Tracy Suttles helps sales people improve sales. Her Eureka Moment happened at age fourteen when she was caught ditching school by the school nurse. She thought the usual would happen—detention, a call to her mother, and punishment. But the nurse didn't turn her in. Instead, she listened past Tracy's lies and excuses to hear what was really going on in her life at home.

For the first time Tracy was truly heard and told the nurse about the verbal and emotional abuse she was suffering at home. The nurse took action and Tracy was removed from her home and began her process of healing.

It's a powerful Heart Story after which Tracy gives her Call-to-Action to the sales people: "Are you just following a script, or are you truly *listening* to your customers? Right now, turn to the person next to you and ask them, 'How are you feeling right now?' Then listen. Truly listen and say, 'I hear you.' Those are words that can not only change your sales, but turn you into a hero."

EXERCISE: PICKING A EUREKA MOMENT

At the pinnacle of any story is a moment where you either:

1. Overcame an obstacle.

2. Solved a mystery.

3. Resolved a problem.

4. Brought order to chaos.

5. Went from innocence to experience.

6. Experienced personal growth by realizing something.

Find that Eureka Moment and you will find your Heart Story.

I was consulting with Robert "Chuck" Rose, who owns many restaurants and speaks on customer service. He wanted to speak to his audience about finding a healthy life/work balance. He told me his story in broad strokes: "I was a complete workaholic—growing my business and nothing else mattered. The consequences were that I lost everything."

Broad strokes. This is how many people tell a story—summing up months or years of their life rather than pinpointing the exact moment when life changed. When I asked Chuck what he meant by "complete workaholic," he then pinpointed one particular Thanksgiving. He was working late and kept calling home to tell his family that he would be there, but to go ahead and cut the turkey rather than wait.

"I promised them that I'd be there for Christmas dinner, but the marriage did not make it that far. By Christmas, my wife had filed for a divorce."

Chuck's Eureka Moment was waking up on Christmas morning alone in a friend's windowless basement. He'd lost his family. He'd lost his business. That's the moment when he understood the life lesson that if you don't take care of what's important, you will lose everything. By identifying, and reliving that Eureka Moment, the audience understood the Core Promise of Chuck's speech.

He then drives his point home by asking the audience this question: "Are you waiting until you reach some milestone before you can be happy? Take care of what's important or you might lose everything."

Now, let's find your Eureka Moment. Go through the story notebook I asked you to create earlier in chapter three and see if any of those stories contain moments that best illustrate how you overcame a similar problem that your speech addresses. In other words, if the problem you announced in the beginning of your speech was "bullying" you must share a moment in your life when you triumphed over a bully or realized you were the bully or stood up for someone being bullied. You get the idea. You want to illustrate in a personal way how you have lived your message. Don't worry if the story isn't funny, as later we will do a "Comedy Pass" that could turn a painful trip to the dentist into a laughfest minus the gas.

CASE STUDY

MARY KINCAID, "CLOSET ZEN: HOW TO DRESS FROM THE INSIDE OUT AND DO BUSINESS WITH STYLE"

Speaking student Mary Kincaid is a fashion stylist and founder of the popular blog Zuburbia. Her speech is full of useful tips on how to find your own style rather than dressing to impress others.

Her Eureka Moment came when she was in her closet, packing her clothes after her divorce became final. She brought in a huge stack of packing boxes, but as she held up each dress she realized that each bit of clothing was something she bought to impress someone else—her ex-husband, her former corporate job, or her friends. She left the house with only a few outfits and began her journey to find her own style, her own life.

EXERCISE: FINDING YOUR EUREKA MOMENT

1. Read back on The Problems that you discuss at the beginning of your speech.

2. Pick a moment in your life when you had an Eureka Moment about a similar problem.

3. Picture that moment—where are you, who is with you, what are you wearing?

4. Spend no more than fifteen minutes writing out the story that contains that moment. Write your story out in present tense as if you are "in" the story as you tell it. Telling a story in present tense makes your story more immediate and dramatic. So, rather than writing, "There I was . . ." write, "There I am . . ." Rather than writing, "And he said . . ." write, "And he's saying . . ." Write quickly without stopping to spell check. The important thing is to get a draft of your story on paper. Don't worry if it's the right story. We will turn whatever story you pick into the right story.

Now that you have a rough draft of your Heart Story, let's put it through a serious rewrite process. This is what separates the Novices from the Professionals—reworking and rewriting until a lump of coal becomes a gleaming diamond. Oh, how I wish everything I wrote came out perfectly like a newborn colt that gets up and walks. No such luck. Those of you who will be successful are the ones who have the stamina to examine and rewrite your Heart Story over and over again, discovering each and every nuance.

The following exercises will assist you in rewriting your Heart Story to make it an unforgettable experience for the audience.

THE HEART STORY WORKSHOP

Step One: Clarify Your Objective

Every story has a main character, the hero of the story, the protagonist, who is in pursuit of a worthwhile objective. Most likely the hero of your story is you, the speaker. Tell the story just right and the audience will be rooting for you to get your goal. So, then the audience needs to know right away what you want. Usually, a character is driven by two desires.

1. Conscious Objective. This is the obvious objective that a character wants to achieve. In my story, at the airport, my desire was simple—I had to get that plane to go to Denver for an audition that would get me on a TV show. In setting up my story, I explained how important this was by having my new agent say to me, "Don't let me down, Judy. This is your big opportunity and they don't come around twice." That simple moment set up how important it was for me to get to Denver. The audience needs to have an understanding of the importance or urgency of your objective as well as the worthiness of the objective. If you tell a story of a character whose main desire is to drown kittens, chances are there won't be any sympathetic listeners.

Using Tracy Suttles's story of being caught by the school nurse for ditching class as an example, her conscious objective was to skip school. Her obstacle was the school nurse and to overcome that obstacle, she had to lie to pursue her new objective—to not get in trouble, to avoid getting detention, and to be left alone to do as she pleased. She wanted that nurse off her back.

2. Unconscious Objective. There is always a back story that explains why the hero of our story wants what he or she wants. In my case, I had spent one year writing a book that fifty-six agents rejected. As a result, at thirty-two years old, an audition meant everything to me. Also pressuring me was my emotional baggage. I grew up with an older sister who was severely disabled. Being an "able-bodied" child, the hopes and dreams of my mother were yoked tightly around my shoulders. It was my responsibility to become someone famous or rich so that my mother's life would not have been in vain. My unconscious desire was not to fail and to make my mother proud. When telling a story, the unconscious desire is unapparent to the hero, but usually comes out during the telling of the story.

Using Tracy's story again as an example: From the outside, she looked like a kid who wanted to be left alone and to fly under the radar, but really, Tracy desperately wanted to be heard and helped by an adult. By skipping school, she was unconsciously asking someone to pay attention to her and to ask her what was wrong. Fortunately, the school nurse was listening with her heart as well as her ears.

The stronger your desire, the more drama and comedy will be available to you when telling your Heart Story.

I was coaching a student, Sheri Strong, whose speech was about the life lessons she learned while healing from a massive car accident. She was severely injured, broke every bone in her body, had to be fed through a tube, and lost her ability to speak. When working with her on her Heart Story, she was convinced that her primary desire was to regain her health, so she started her Heart Story with the car accident.

But something didn't feel right for me. The conclusion of the story was a no-brainer. Clearly, she had recovered or else she wouldn't be standing in front of an audience speaking. We had to find her deeper objective. Going on instinct, I asked her to do a scene for me when she was eight years old. The scene went like this:

She said, "I'm singing a song I wrote. I want to be a singer. I want to write music."

"Now what is going on?" I asked.

"I'm showing my mother what I wrote."

I asked her to Act-Out her mother (a process I will describe in greater detail in the final chapter of Part Two) and then watched her transform into a *Mommie Dearest* type, angrily ripping up her daughter's song saying, "This is crap. Stop messing around and do your chores."

I asked her, "Did you ever perform as a singer?"

"No," she said sadly. "I got married, had three kids, and my husband was so controlling. He would have never let me have a singing career. We divorced. Then I married another man who turned out to be an alcoholic. I was supporting him as well as my three children. And that's when the accident happened. We divorced during my therapy. I then spent all my time getting myself well. Part of my therapy was singing."

It might appear that the car accident derailed her life, but it actually put her back on track to living her passion. She'd been shut down by her mom and the car accident forced her to sing again. It was singing that brought back her voice, literally. It gave her the will to recover. After forty-five years of silence, she even started writing music. Now, how powerful do you think it is for an audience, after hearing that Heart Story, to witness her sing? There isn't a dry eye in the house! And it makes her message of Do It Now! even more personal and effective.

If you followed the exercise above, you will have a solid story. Don't worry about if it's funny as later in the Comedy Pass chapter, we will go over it and work in humor.

EXERCISE: DESIRE ON FIRE

Read over your story and spend only ten minutes answering these questions:

1. What is the main character's conscious desire and how does it relate to the message of your speech?

2. What is the main character's unconscious desire, based on their history?

3. When did this character first realize what they wanted?

Step Two: Set Up the Obstacles . . . Lots of Them

As your character pursues his or her objective, there will be obstacles. If you don't have obstacles, you don't have a story. In *The Wizard of Oz,* if Dorothy didn't have to deal with flying monkeys, poisonous poppy fields, haunted forests, violent apples trees, and the Wicked Witch of the West, getting back home would be a boring, uneventful trip to Kansas—a place not known for excitement.

So, in your story, your character is running into obstacles trying to get to their objective. When obstacles prevent your hero from getting their objective, he or she makes an adjustment, perhaps a new attitude, a new point of view—and zigzags their way to the end of the story where they either get or don't get their objective.

Depending on the nature of these obstacles, the character readjusts how they go about getting to their goal. Obstacles can be other people, circumstances, forces of nature, or inner obstacles.

The obstacles in my story were other people—the long line of travelers standing in front of me and the gate attendant who held our futures in his hand. There were forces of nature—bad weather in the East that had cancelled a number of flights, and then there were my circumstances: I was a rejected writer, getting older, who had to be in Denver by a certain time or else I would miss my only and maybe last chance at success.

At first glance, that seemed like a good enough Heart Story, but I kept digging. There were other obstacles I forgot to mention and comedy is in the details. Smaller obstacles included the body odor of the man in front of me in line, the muffled, incomprehensible airline announcements over the PA system, the overpriced bottles of water, the embarrassing hole in my sock that everyone saw when I had to take off my shoes at security, and especially the "No Joking" warning signs by the airport security entrance. (Complete torture for a comic.)

Added on top of the external obstacles were my internal obstacles—trying to get through an airport with my literal baggage and my emotional baggage: low self-esteem; needing to be liked by the people around me; anger of feeling out of control in the larger universe; fear of missing my last shot at stardom. There were a million emotions coursing through my veins. I was tempted to include them all in my Heart Story, but I knew I had to pick and choose those that best dramatized my struggle.

Let me help you do the same.

EXERCISE: OH, THOSE OBSTACLES!

Let's really dig into your Heart Story and milk it for all its worth!

1. Make a list of all the obvious obstacles that prevented your character from getting what she or he wanted.

2. Go through your story again with a microscope and find the smaller obstacles that you might have missed originally. Go into the details of what people said and how they looked that made your journey difficult. When writing the story again, write it thinking of all five senses. Was there a horrible smell? Flickering lights? An irritating song playing? How did the character of your story react to the obstacles? Did the obstacle make them change their course of action?

3. Rewrite your original story and add at least five new physical, external obstacles that could have been overlooked. How does that change your main character's behavior?

4. Now, add three more internal obstacles to your Heart Story. How does that change the meaning of your main character's actions?

Step Three: Finale

Your story ends in one of two ways:

1. Your character obtains their objective.

2. Your character does not obtain their objective, but all is well because they learned a lesson they needed to learn.

At the end of my Heart Story, I don't get to the gig in time for the audition, but in first class I meet a book agent who ends up representing my book and *Standup Comedy: The Book,* goes on the Oprah Winfrey show, becomes a best-seller, and launches my unexpected career as an author and a speaker.

Missing my plane becomes a life lesson for me and for my audience. We learn that it's not worth stressing out over the small bumps of life because sometimes the universe gives us something even better than what we were chasing. Having a sense of humor can even help get us what we want.

EXERCISE: WRITE YOUR OWN ENDING

Take ten minutes and write the ending to your Heart Story. Does your character get everything their heart desires and then answer the question: How did obtaining their heart's desire teach them something valuable?

Now, do the exact opposite. Take ten minutes and write the alternative ending to your Heart Story. What happens if your main character does not obtain their objective? What lesson is learned from that result?

Call up your Speaker Buddy and tell them both endings. Discuss each ending and determine which best serves the needs of your speech.

GETTING YOUR STORY PERFECT

Beth Lapides created the Un-Cabaret, a live show that became an important venue for the Los Angeles alternative comedy movement. Here's Beth's advice on questions you can ask yourself to get your story ready for an audience:

1. Have I cut enough? Just because something happened doesn't mean it is part of the story. Can you start farther into the story? Do we need the back story? Is there a chunk of dialogue when you only need one line?

2. Is there anything I can milk? Is there part of the story you are rushing over that is juicy and deserves more attention? In terms of pacing it shouldn't feel like a metronome is running.

3. Do I need to tell this story so linearly? Linear time is an illusion. You are allowed to loop back for back story as it is needed. Or tell the end first. Think about *Lost* or *Memento,* liberate yourself from linear time.

4. Why am I telling this story now? That might shift over time and subtly affect the focus of the story. Stories get stale, but can be refreshed. New dimensions and levels emerge over time. Also the context in which you are telling a story can subtly affect how you are telling it. Every now and then it is too soon to tell a story. Either the ending is too unclear, or you are uncomfortable with it. If you are uncomfortable with it, the audience will worry about you. You can tell an audience anything, no matter how humiliating, as long as *you* are comfortable.

5. What's funny about this story? Even if you are not a comedian, there is something funny about your story. Usually it's the most painful part.

EXERCISE: FRAME IT!

Once you have your objectives, your obstacles, and your ending determined, place your Heart Story within a frame using the same structure we used to illustrate the problem portion of your speech: Point—Story—Question.

You announce the point that will be illustrated by the Heart Story. You tell the Heart Story.

You remind the audience why you just told the Heart Story and ask them if they are willing to apply the lesson to their life.

And then . . .

You repeat how your Action Steps helped your main character achieve their success.

You've already written your Heart Story above, so just tackle the intro and the exit to frame it. When you write the introduction to the story, keep it short—no more than one or two sentences. Remember, you've just provided the audience with your Action Steps so you want to have a natural lead. "I know these steps work. I learned how to (insert your message here) the hard way. Back in 1982, I wanted to . . ."

When writing the exit out of your Heart Story, remind the audience of your Core Promise by asking these questions: How would you react in that situation? How do you handle people? What would you have done?

Then give people a Call-to-Action: "I learned the power of (insert your message here) and I know that you can (insert Action Step)."

EXERCISE: TAKE IT FOR A TEST DRIVE

Get together with your Speech Buddy and really listen to each other's stories. When listening to someone else's story, note:

- Is the character's objective authentic, believable, and a worthy pursuit?

- Do you understand why the character wants what she or he wants?

- Are the obstacles all believable?

- Are you telling the story in the present tense?

- Is the life lesson clear from the story?

- Does the story illustrate the Core Promise of the speech?

- Does the story address The Problem you brought up at the beginning?

- Is there any place where the story drags or is boring?

COMPLETED SPEECH TIME: Twenty-seven minutes (for half an hour), fifty-five minutes (for one hour)

CHAPTER FOURTEEN

STEP SIX: NOW . . . DO SOMETHING!

Eileen McDargh is an award-winning speaker who speaks on resiliency as a business and life tool. Eileen defines resiliency as "growing through challenge or opportunity to end up better." Her Action Steps present four categories of resiliency: adaptability, agility, laugh-ability, and alignment. When she comes to the last category, alignment, she talks about being lined up with that which is your highest core value. As she says, "When that is in place, and you're clear on that, it's what Austrian neurologist and psychiatrist Viktor Frankl noted, 'Any man or woman can survive any "what" if they have a "why."' My mother taught me how to have a 'why.'"

Eileen then tells her Heart Story about her mother, who was a Women's Air Force Service Pilot in World War II.

As Eileen says, "Although they did all the military domestic flying and 1,074 women earned Air Force wings, they were not considered official military. They flew sixty million air miles of official military duty and thirty-eight of them died in the course of duty. But because they were not considered official military, there were no benefits, and in at least one case they had to pass the hat to send the body of someone in their unit home to her parents. And when they were disbanded, women were not allowed back in the cockpits of military planes again for thirty years. Their grand experiment seemed like a failure. It wasn't until seventy years later, March 2010, when they were awarded the Congressional Gold Medal."

At the end of Eileen's story, she pinpoints the major life lesson of her story. "They didn't do it for the gold medal. They would have kept doing it because of their core values of service and love of country."

She then comes to the Call-to-Action of her final story and asks the audience this question:

"How many of you have days where you feel that what you do doesn't matter? I'm here to tell you that what you do does matter."

Eileen then gives her final Call-to-Action:

"Know what is most meaningful to you and keep that center. When you can stay connected to what is most meaningful to you, then that's the ultimate resiliency skill. And regardless of whether anyone acknowledges you or not, that's what keeps you focused. Keep your center and I guarantee you will be able to stay right-side up in a world that is upside down."

If we're going to change the world, we've got to get people out of their seats and motivate them to actually do the Action Steps you presented as the solution to their problems. And don't forget that the people signing your checks want your speech to do more than entertain. They want results. To wrap up your speech, you need to remind the audience of their problem, your solutions, your Core Promise, and the Action Steps. You also need to remind them that you know they can do it, because *you* already have!

This is the Call-to-Action I've mentioned doing after each Action Step. Now, at the end of your speech you want to summarize your Action Steps and give the audience one concrete, specific, and rousing assignment to do *immediately*. This is your one important final Call-to-Action. This won't work if you just list a bunch of things they have to accomplish. Nobody does something just because

I AM KEYNOTER—HEAR ME CLOSE!

"A speaker's positioning on a program depends on the power of their Call-to-Action. To be the closing keynoter, a speaker needs to leave the audience with a Call-to-Action that inspires and motivates them to take on their challenges."

—Mike Frick, President of Speakers.com speakers bureau

a stranger in a suit on a stage tells them to do it. You have to present this final call to action in such a way that they will *want* to do it. It's your ultimate motivational moment right after your Heart Story.

EXERCISE: THE CALL TO ACTION

First, you need to remind the audience about their problem and how bad it feels to have no solution to that problem. This is a great place to use rhetorical questions. The way I do this in my speech is:

> Who are you in life? Are you one of those angry people at the airport? (This is a reference from my Heart Story about being angry at the airport.) How is that working out for you? Is getting angry getting in the way of what you want to have in your life? Are you losing friends, family members because you are not so much fun to be around?

Keep the summary of The Problem short and sweet and then ask the audience if they want to try something different. This is where you bring it home.

Boil down your Action Steps so they are easy to remember and easy to do. Don't end with "So tomorrow, how many of you are going to redo your will, set up a living trust, and restructure your retirement?" Give people something very simple that they can do, such as "Sign up." "Vote." "Believe." "Start [insert action]." "Stop [insert action]." "Visit this Web site." "Donate."

Your Call-to-Action can become your tagline, posted on your T-shirts, mugs, and other merchandise. Billionaire owner of the Tampa Bay Lightning hockey team turned speaker, Art Williams's Call-to-Action is "Do It Big!" He wears it on a T-shirt during his speech.

Since my Action Step is extremely simple, "Make a humor choice by saying, 'Whoo-Hoo!' when things get stressful, I ask the audience in my Call-to-Action:

> "When your mom asks you if you've gained weight, what will you say?"
> "Whoo-Hoo!"

"When they announce that your plane is cancelled, what are you going to say?"
"Whoo-Hoo!"

When writing your call to action, think about including the results that are possible if audience members will take that Action Step. It's one thing to say, "I want you to make five additional sales calls a day." It's another thing to say, "Anyone want to increase their income by 20 percent? How many of you are willing to give up an additional fifteen minutes of your workday in exchange for a week on the Italian Rivera? Well, we can do that by making only five additional calls a day."

See how I avoided saying, "I want you to do . . ." No one wants to be given a chore. Remember your mom telling you she wants you to take out the trash? How'd that work for her?

And please, for the love of God, know when to end your speech. Don't use the phrase "In conclusion" and then go on forever. Zzzzzzzzzz. And don't finish with a long-winded sales pitch of your merchandise. This is the number one complaint meeting planners get from conference attendees. This is not a good place for a commercial. Once your Heart Story is finished, burst out of there on a high note and don't blow it.

When done properly you will feel the rhythm of going from the emotional moment at the end of your Heart Story to your Call-to-Action. This means that you start slow and build in speed, intensity and volume, (although you should never, ever shout at an audience.)

Say "Thank you," and take a bow.

 COMPLETED SPEECH TIME: Thirty minutes or one hour

CHAPTER FIFTEEN

STEP SEVEN: THE FUNNY IS MONEY COMEDY PASS

Making speakers funny is my specialty and here's the good news about adding comedy to your speech: You don't need to be a trained comic to get a laugh. I have found surefire, specific techniques that will take your speech from a polite chuckler to a gut-buster.

You can do this.

You really can. Being funny as a speaker is a lot easier than being a stand-up comic. Speakers aren't expected to get huge laughs every ten seconds so when you deliver them, it's a happy surprise. Which means you'll work more often!

Plus, *you need to do this.*

WHAT DO MEETING PLANNERS *REALLY* WANT?

MEET FUNNY PEOPLE WITH A MESSAGE

The Association for Applied and Therapeutic Humor (AATH.org) is a nonprofit, member-driven, international community of humor and laughter professionals and enthusiasts. AATH provides its members the education, cutting-edge resources, and supportive community they need to excel in the practice and promotion of healthy humor.

Members include scholars, psychologists, counselors, allied health-care practitioners, nurses, social workers, physicians, funeral directors, business executives, human resource managers, educators, clergy, hospital clowns, speakers, trainers, and many others who incorporate humor in their life and work.

No matter how serious your topic, everyone who steps onstage needs to add humor to their presentation. Actually, the more serious your topic, the more you need some yuks. Let me use an example of something very unfunny to prove my point: the genocide in Darfur.

Recently, a speaker came to me needing a punch-up for his speech to encourage volunteerism in Darfur. Needless to say, his speech was serious business. I had no idea how we could find the funny in such depressing subject matter. It was like writing *Auschwitz: The Musical*—without the help of Mel Brooks.

What could I do? My only option was to dig deep for the details because that's where humor hides, in the specifics, in the obstacles rather than in overall topic. Turns out he had a few problems that needed solutions. He was in fierce competition with other nonprofits for a limited number of dollars, which sounded like . . . a contestant on a game show. "You must choose between these two suitcases! Suitcase One is 'Dollars for Darfur' and Suitcase Two is 'Twitter for Troubled Tots!'" His second big issue was credibility. Donors are never sure whether they can trust a charity, which sounds like . . . dating. "I mean, they invited me to the gala dinner, but then they never returned my calls. I think they're wooing that woman with the bigger, ahem, checkbook."

Relating something very niche/dark/specific that is unfunny to something very mainstream/light but still specific will help to guide you toward funny. Don't cheat yourself out of the discovery process.

Explore the depths of the darkness. Explore the problems. Have the guts to delve into the details. Where you find laughs might surprise you.

We comics make lists of possible funny stuff all the time. Most "civilians" will stop when they can't make something funny after three tries. Working comics will try twenty more times. It's a numbers game, just like sales. The more you try the better chance you have of hitting on something funny.

So, try out the different exercises in this chapter. If you find you are trying too hard or feeling frustrated, move on to another exercise. Some will work for you and some won't.

Remember, comedy is supposed to be fun and doing the comedy pass on your speech should be a hoot. There is nothing so dreary as someone sooooooooo serious about comedy. Lighten up and enjoy yourself.

The best place to start? Look right in the mirror.

HOW TO GET LAUGHS IN YOUR OPENING

YOU ARE ENOUGH JUST AS YOU ARE

Speakers think they have to change their personalities in order to seem funny. They try to "loosen up," be more physical onstage or even get a little nasty.

No! No! No! Funny comes from truth. Sometimes the painful truth.

Don't change who you are—*acknowledge* the truth of who you are. Make fun of the obvious.

See yourself the way an audience sees you.

Let's face it, when a speaker steps onstage, they are facing an inherent hostility toward "know-it-alls." The best way to curb that judgment and defuse hostility is to do some lighthearted self-mocking. Having the guts to get a laugh at your own expense can appease even the harshest critic. Poking fun at yourself not only creates laughter, it creates likability. We all love people who don't take themselves so seriously and besides, the first part of your speech is about problems, so why not start with your own? That's right. That's not an expanding waistline—that's a punch line.

When I boasted that my book, *The Comedy Bible*, could make anyone funny, National Public Radio put me to the test—to do a comedy makeover on the most unfunny, humor-impaired person they could find. I agreed and Captain John Heinzel was picked. He is a navy officer at Port Hueneme, California, who lectures on "The History of Civil Engineering." The captain had a special talent of making a boring topic even more boring. He was supposed to educate the cadets, but the problem was—he was putting them to sleep. His wife also complained about his ability to clear a room when he told a story. He spoke in a deep robotic monotone that made Mr. Spock sound exciting. Captain John Heinzel was a buzz kill and he knew it.

"Judy, I know I'm so serious. Can you help me be funnier? How do I get more confident? More animated? More relaxed when I speak in front of others?" John was approaching being funny and entertaining the way most people do—they assume that they have to change, be something other than their drab selves. That's far from the truth. Actually when speakers try to be funny is when they become inauthentic and off-putting.

The captain was shocked to find out that his comedy makeover didn't include changing his personality—it included making fun of it.

I told John, "I don't want to you change. I don't want you to talk faster or use more modulation when you speak, or smile more, or wear party hats. That's not who you are. Trying to be funny makes you unfunny."

"Well, then, how can I be funny?"

"What do people joke about behind your back?" I asked.

The captain had a list of the things that people joked about him: his seriousness, his monotone, his emotionless tone.

The next time the captain did his presentation in front of his cadets, he said, "I know you think I'm uptight, well, I just want you to know that last night I got wild . . . I drank milk one day past the expiration date!" The place fell apart.

If you want to get a laugh when you first come onstage, the best way is to joke about something obvious about you that the audience sees.

MAKE COMEDY FIT

When making fun of yourself, it has to relate to your Message. You can't just have a joke for the sake of having a joke and then back to your speech. The joke has to illustrate a point. One of the best ways to use this is during the problem. So, you might be talking about how difficult their lives are and then say, "I know how you feel. Look at me!" Then go into one of these formulas.

EXERCISE: MAKE FUN OF YOURSELF

1. Make a list of what people see when you walk onstage—your weight, hairline, age, gender, clothes, and attitude. Anything that makes you different can be comedy gold.

CASE STUDY
I KNOW WHAT YOU'RE THINKING

Speaker and stand-up comic, Diane Kawasaki is a Little Person. She creates quite a buzz as she comes onstage as she is all of 3' 4" tall. She is also of Asian heritage. After the audience gets a good look at her, she takes a pause and then says with attitude, "I know what you're thinking so let's clear this up right away. The politically correct term is . . . Asian American!"

People laugh so hard, they literally fall off their chairs.

---

2. Make a list of any qualities you think the audience might notice, such as whiny voice, seriousness, awkwardness, aggressiveness, high energy, low energy. Note that none of these things should be funny, but they should all be *real*. Keep your list focused on the things the audience can actually see or notice. "I'm short" is better than, "I'm lactose intolerant."

3. Using the lists you've created, play with these formulas:

"I KNOW WHAT YOU'RE THINKING" FORMULA

"I know what you're thinking?"

Act-out of what the audience is thinking, i.e., *"Boy, does she know that her hair is the color of Cheetos?"*

Then, give a retort. *"Yes, I do know and, actually, part time I donate my head to guide planes into the gates at the airport."*

STUPID QUESTION WITH FUNNY RETORT FORMULA

People say stupid things about you when you're (insert quality).

I say, (insert funny retort).

Have you ever had someone say something stupid and then a week later you thought, "Oh, I know what I should have said in response!" Using this formula, you can recreate the stupid thing that someone said about you and what you should have said when it happened.

Make a list of stupid things people say to you and see if you can find a funny retort.

Award-winning humorist Jeanne Robertson gets reams of laughter by joking about the odd things people say to her regarding her 6' 2" height.

"People are always asking me silly questions: How is the weather up there? How tall are you? I was on a plane and a woman commented, 'Wow, you're tall.' I looked down at myself and said, 'Oh, my gosh, I wasn't when I got on the plane! It must be the peanuts!'"

The audience roars.

As Jeanne says, "My message is to show people how to laugh at the things that we can't change."

USING FUNNY RETORTS WHEN
QUOTING STATISTICS

In chapter ten, I suggest using statistics or quotes to give credence to The Problem. You can bounce off these statistics or quotes to get a laugh. The formula is to give the quote or statistic and then insert your funny comment or disagreement.

I presented summarizer, author, and comedic speaker Dale Irvin with a few quotes and statistics. Here is what he came up with:

Statistic: "One-third of Americans feel they are living with extreme stress," says *USA Today*.

Dale's Retort: And the other two-thirds are giving it to them.

Quote: Charles Darwin said, "A man who dares to waste one hour of time has not discovered the value of life."

Dale's Retort: But a man who has discovered the value of Xbox will waste the rest of his life.

Now you try it. Make a list of stupid things people say to you or what people in the audience might be thinking about you and see if you and your Buddy can find a funny retort. Some of you might not have an obvious characteristic that you can joke about. No worries, just move on to the next comedy formula. Don't bother making up something people might say. If they're not saying stupid things, congrats—you've got smart friends.

COMEDY FORMULA:
SELF-MOCKING—RELUCTANT ADMISSION

ANYWAY!

The beauty of the reluctant admission is that there is no limit on how many times you can use it. Use it during any story, or whenever you over-exaggerate a statistic or a result.

There is something very funny about someone admitting that they lied or exaggerated something. And even more funny *and* endearing when the honesty comes from a respected professional.

In this exercise, you make a big, bold statement of "truth" and then reluctantly admit that you were caught telling a lie. Here's the formula:

- Lie

- Admission One (quiet)

- Admission Two (quieter)

- "A-n-y-w-a-y . . ." (loud)

- Continue with speech

RELUCTANT ADMISSION

"You need to find a coach that inspires, motivates, and will push you to your physical limits! My swim coach has me swimming
five hundred meters each and every day! Actually . . . it's more like a hundred meters daily . . . Well, okay, six laps around the
hot tub. Anyways!"

—Eliot Hoppe, professional speaker, "Body Language: The Truth Lies Here!"

Here's how to put it into action:

Lie (bragging): "I lost 120 pounds!" Admission One (quiet): "Well . . . I didn't exactly lose all of it at once." Admission Two (quieter): "Well, actually—I just lost and gained the same ten pounds twelve times. A-n-y-w-a-y (loud) . . . Continue with message: "But today, I'm going to show you how you can make a difference in your health and maybe not lose 120 pounds, but five."

I was so excited to find this formula. But here's the secret: it only works if you say, "A-n-y-w-a-y!" really loudly and then quickly move on. Getting laughs can be finicky. Sometimes, changing one word can make the difference between a laugh and no laugh.

So using the list of "defects" you made above, give this one a try by turning a defect into an initial brag and then have to admit that you're lying. Use the formula above. This formula always works! Well . . . maybe not always in every situation. OK, it only works between the hours of 8 a.m. and 10 a.m. A-n-y-w-a-y . . . Get it?

COMEDY FORMULA: SELF MOCKING—THE MASH-UP

WARNING

Don't lie about your mash-up.

Only joke about your religious, cultural, or ethnic stereotype if you actually are that religion, culture, or ethnicity.

Corporations are particularly sensitive to politically incorrect jokes, but if you're joking about yourself, Human Resources can't take issue with it!

It's hard to listen to speakers who qualify as experts by droning on and on with lists of information that don't include a laugh: "I'm from blah blah, I went to school in blah, blah, and I got a degree in blah, blah."

Boring! This is a lost opportunity for a laugh! Here is a way to introduce your credentials that I call The Mash-Up. Let's say, for instance, you want to tell the audience that you're a nurse and a stand-up comic. All you have to do is to add the words, "So that means I . . ." and then add the mash-up of the stereotype.

For example, speaker and comic, Judy Oliverio says, "I'm a nurse and a stand-up comic, *so that means* that I never get a break from asses."

Here's how to use The Mash-Up formula:

WHERE TO USE THE MASH-UP

Consider using The Mash-Up during the step two: the credentials portion of your speech.

It's a great way to get a laugh while also bragging without bragging. Make people laugh and they'll actually remember your credentials instead of being turned off by your bravado.

EXERCISE: MASH IT UP

You may need some help to use this comedy formula so let's do some brainstorming.

- Make a list of your ethnicity, parents' nationalities, your hobbies, and your current and past professions.

- Pick two of the items you wrote above and put them in the formula below:

You may not know this, but I'm half _____ and half (or you can say, "part this or part that," or "I'm an engineer during the day and an actor at night") _____ so that means, I _____

Okay, now that you've got them laughing through your first minutes onstage, let's bump up the laughs on the problem section of your speech.

HOW TO GET LAUGHS AS YOU INTRODUCE THE PROBLEM

Those of you who have read *The Comedy Bible* know it's not the subject matter that's funny—it's what you do with it that makes people laugh. The problem section of your speech is a natural for mining laughs. Getting laughs when detailing the audience's problems serves two purposes:

1. Laughter makes the audience happy and entertains them.

2. Turning their problems into punch lines is transformational.

The first point is obvious, and anyone who books speakers knows that speakers who entertain as well as educate get more bookings and higher frees. But the second point is less obvious: when someone can laugh at a problem, it tends to make The Problem seem smaller in size and more manageable. Once someone can laugh at a problem, they feel they have more power over it, and it doesn't dominate their lives. In truth, getting the audience to laugh at their problems can be even more powerful than your upcoming Action Steps. But it has to be done in the right way. It can't appear that you're mocking the audience or not taking their problems seriously. You can't "poke fun," as your mom used to say. You have to walk a fine line between getting the laugh and still being respectful and treating The Problem seriously.

Sometimes just revealing you know about The Problem is enough to get a laugh. From my research interview with a pet food company, I learned that a big employee complaint was that they were only allowed one picture on their desk. I simply acted out that problem. "It's hard just having one picture on your desk because you have to decide who that's going to be. You're going, 'Cat or husband? Cat or husband? Cat!'"

Huge laugh and applause.

WHAT'S UP WITH COKE?

"I'm very careful who I poke fun at. I don't even poke fun at my client's competition. If I'm working for Pepsi, I don't poke fun at Coke because I might be working there next week."

—Connie Podesta, speaker and author

There are two big rules about joking about your client's problems. The first is:

ALWAYS REMEMBER, YOU'RE THE OUTSIDER

I was playing a small town that was not exactly a tourist destination. In fact, when I looked at the newspaper to see what was going on in town, I saw a picture of myself. That gave me an idea. Since I had time the day before, I walked around town with my camera taking pictures of possible tourist attractions. I took a picture of a bait shop, calling it "the freshest sushi in the world." I took a picture of their tattoo parlor and called it an art museum. The slide show got big laughs and I thought it was very successful. Then, I checked my e-mail.

"Thanks for flying in from L.A. to make fun of our home. It's a better place now that you're not here."

Ouch! Now, there will always be a few people in the audience who just don't have a sense of humor. But my job is not to turn people off. Reevaluating, the next time I did this I set it up a bit differently by telling them that I was looking for funny things, but I ended up finding some of the most wonderful people in the world and you can't find that where I live. No hate mail that time. A learning experience.

So, when you are an outsider, you want to make sure that you are respectful of where your clients live, how they talk, and your differences. You need to be the butt of your jokes and not them. So now when an audience laughs I say, "Thanks for laughing. Nobody laughs in Los Angeles, they can't. Too much Botox." Huge laugh, and now I'm one of them.

The second rule is:

NEVER DIS' THE PERSON SIGNING YOUR CHECK

That one needs no explanation.

Okay, now with those two rules are out of the way, let's talk about things you *can* do to be funny in the problem section of your speech. There are different techniques you can use to present the audience's problem. You can use some of them, all of them, or just one of them. That's up to you. They all work.

COMEDY FORMULA: LIST OF THREE

Just like three is the magic number for Action Steps in a speaker's speech, three is a magic number in comedy. Three has a comedy rhythm that just works. Using the "List of Three" formula, a comic sets up a pattern on the first two serious ideas and then "turns" on the third. Comics use this formula constantly and you should feel free to incorporate it into many sections of your speech. For example:

"I like Florida; everything is in the eighties: the temperature, the ages, and the IQs."—George Carlin

The first two set up a pattern of expectancy and the third one is the surprise.

Speakers can use this formula to get a laugh by putting the problem as the third one so it comes as a surprise to the audience.

When I was hired to speak to a cosmetics company, I was told management would be announcing that there would be no bonuses that year. Management actually asked me to do "something funny with that." Boy, that was a tough assignment. But using this formula helped me to come up with a laugh. I also knew, prior to my keynote, the audience would be doing a workshop on conceptual selling. So my "List of Three" was:

I understand that you learned today about conceptual selling. That means:

1. You aren't selling lipstick but rather the *concept* of beauty.
2. It's not about the mascara but the *concept* of glamour.
3. And I guess it's not about the money but the *concept* of a bonus.

People literally fell off their chairs. Now, that's a good joke.

The "List of Three" is a powerful comedy formula that depends on an authentic setup: leading the audience down a path, and then surprising the audience on the third one or what we comics call the turn. Those of you Techies who use PowerPoint can benefit from this by having a surprise when you do bullet points. That third bullet point should be a doozy. Remember: keeping the audience laughing will keep you employed.

EXAMPLE: LIST OF THREE

"It's tough being a teacher these days. You're expected to do a lot more than just teach:

You have to navigate school politics. You've got to keep the parents happy. You've got to squeeze into that bulletproof vest."

—Herky Cutler, professional speaker and teacher

EXERCISE: YOUR LIST OF THREE

Get a feel of this formula by practicing creating lists of three by filling in the turns of these unfinished lists.

"There are three subtle clues you're not getting your annual raise . . ." (subtle, subtle, and *obvious*)

1. Sales are down

2. They cut back on office supplies and

3. Insert your turn: (i.e., ". . . And the CEO has a second job as a pole dancer.")

"There are three subtle clues that your relationship might be on the rocks . . ."

1. You've stopped communicating

2. You don't hug at night

3. Insert some clue that's huge and obvious: (i.e., ". . . She's issued a restraining order.")

Go through your list of problems that you created in chapter ten and see if you can create a "List of Three." Write out a setup that relates to the problem, such as, "There are three subtle clues that you are stressed, or not healthy, going to get fired . . ." Then make the first two subtle and the last one obvious and big.

Try it! You'll love it when you get laughs.

COMEDY FORMULA: FUNNY FRUSTRATIONS

This is a great way to poke fun of some of the industry terms that are a part of the vocabulary that the audience uses. The formula goes like this:

"You may not know this, but, _____ (industry term) is actually a _____ term (language derived from Latin, Navajo, etc.), meaning _____ (insert problem)."

For instance, if you are talking to entrepreneurs and one of their problems is not being able to set boundaries between their work and their personal life, you might want to use this formula to say, "You may not know this, but entrepreneur is actually a French term, meaning 'I work in my underwear.'"

CASE STUDY
DARREN LACROIX 2001 TOASTMASTERS WORLD CHAMPIONSHIP OF PUBLIC SPEAKING

When Darren arrives at a gig, he observes what he can plug into this Funny Frustration Formula. By picking something that everyone has experienced, he is guaranteed a laugh.

As he says, "I observed that there was an unusually long walk at the Vegas Rio Hotel to get to the meeting rooms. Then I overheard people complaining about how far meeting rooms were from hotel rooms.

"Early in my speech, I said: 'Welcome to The Rio Hotel. You might not know this, but Rio is a Native American term meaning long flipping hallway.'" Killer opening as they all could relate, and it showed that Darren's speech was not canned.

As Darren says, "If you are giving a speech on presentation skills, rather than simply saying that most PowerPoint uses are boring, use this formula to give the same information, and get a laugh as well: You may not know this, but PowerPoint is a Sanskrit term, meaning 'boring-ass presentation.'"

In order to do this exercise, pick one of the industry words that is a part of the problem of the audience. This could be the name of a problematic computer system, the "so-called" help desk, complicated computer procedures, ROI report . . .

WHEN TO USE THE FFF?

A great place to use the Funny Frustration Formula is when talking about the problem. It's a surefire way to illustrate the audience's frustration *and* get a laugh.

So, make a list of the industry terms familiar to your audience. Then make a list of the frustrations associated with the problems of the audience. The more negative the frustration, the funnier the joke will be. Now, connect the two. Try them out with your Speaking Buddy and see if you get a laugh.

COMEDY FORMULA: ACRONYMS

Take the acronyms your audience uses at work and rework them into different meanings. You can use their acronyms to illustrate their problem in a funny way. Comic Steve Bluestein was doing a speech for the Ford Motor Company, and joked about their competition.

"I know you at Ford are concerned about quality. You don't want to end up like FIAT, which I believe means 'Fix It Again Tony.'"

So, again we start the way most joke writers start—by making a list. In this case, make a list of short signature words that are associated with the group you are speaking to.

For instance, it could be the name of their payroll system, the name of their cafeteria, or one of their many acronyms. Then do a list of the frustrations associated with that item. Next, take one of their frustrations and see if you can express it by having it fit into an acronym of one of their terms.

If you were speaking to the FBI and they had a party the night before, you could say, "Looking at your eyes, I can see that FBI really stands for *Fairly Bleary Intoxication.*"

COMEDY FORMULA: TOP TEN LIST

If you find yourself with long lists that won't fit into a "List of Three" formula, why not pull a David Letterman and create your own top ten list of their problems.

The trick here is to create a list that sets up the Core Promise of your speech. I do a top ten list of "Ways You Know You Are Stressed."

It includes things like, Number Ten: When you come home from work before midnight, the dog thinks you're a burglar. Number Nine: When you talk without holding your iPhone, your thumbs still move.

So, create a setup based on your Core Promise, such as the top ten ways you know you need to make more money; your marriage is on the rocks; your company needs more customers, and so on.

Start with number ten and count backward. Try it—it's fun, and easier to jam or brainstorm with your Buddy.

COMEDY FORMULA:
PRESENT THE PROBLEM AS A SONG OR A RAP

If you have a talent for music, singing, or dancing, it's always entertaining to present the problem with music. I used to write a "rap" about the specific stresses facing the audience, such as:

> *Meeting to see why my meeting is late.*
> *Meeting to see why I can't hit my date.*
> *Want to know why I'm not completing?*
> *'Cause I'm at a stupid meeting!*

Even if you can't sing, just for the fun of it, write out a song about their problem. Use rhymezone.com to help. Put some of the words from your research about the problem into this site and play with them. Even if you've never done anything like this, you might be surprised—you can write a song!

You can also use a well-known melody to help you along. Make up words and sing them to the tune of a pop song or nursery rhyme.

COMEDY FORMULA: GREATEST HITS

If you can't sing, or if it's just not your style, Darren LaCroix has found that the "Greatest Hits" Formula is another way to turn an audience's problems into punch lines. Here's how Darren teaches this technique in his Comedy Boot Camp for Speakers. I'll let Darren explain how this formula works.

Step One: Identify Industry Terms

"I have my students identify heavily used industry terms. These are words or phrases that are used each and every day by the audience. An example might be 'DPI—dots per inch' or 'W'inkjet (short form of Windows Ink Jet)' or 'bi-monthly' or 'fiscal'—the lists go on and on."

Step Two: List Song Titles

"My students then make a list of popular song titles, keeping in mind the age group of their audience. Humor works best if the songs are easily recognized."

Step Three: Mash-Up

"I have my students mash up their list of industry terms with the list of their song titles and they end up with titles like 'I'm Too Sexy For My DPI' or 'Let's Get Fiscal' or 'Don't Worry. Bi-Monthly.'"

Step Four: Set up the Laugh

"Once my students have their list of fake songs, I have them frame the list with a setup, something like, 'Have you heard you can download the CEO's (or some recognizable person in the group) greatest hits album on iTunes? It's called . . .' It's followed by the catchy title of album and then they begin listing the songs."

EXERCISE: GREATEST HITS

Using Darren LaCroix's steps, make a list of the problem and song titles and see if you can add this exercise as a way of presenting the problem in a fun and creative way.

BAD FOR LIFE–GOOD FOR COMEDY

Use a song, The Top Ten List, the Acronym, or the Greatest Hits Formula throughout discussing the problem.

We have a saying in comedy, "Bad for life–good for comedy." It's the problems that we all have that make the best comedy material.

And if you can get an audience to laugh at what is upsetting them, you're transforming them in that moment.

THE HOLY GRAIL OF COMEDY: THE ACT-OUT

Whether you're presenting a story about The Problem or you've launching into your Action Steps or you're winning them over with your Heart Story, using the Act-Out technique is a must. It's a technique that should be used constantly throughout your entire speech so make mastering these next few exercises a priority.

The Basic Act-Out

Most dull speakers narrate their speech, meaning that they narrate the ideas, stories, and advice by talking directly to the audience. A more dynamic way to get your point across and tell stories is by doing what I refer to as the Basic Act-Out.

When a speaker is doing an Act-Out he or she is no longer speaking to the audience, but rather is in a scene and speaking to another character in that scene. An Act-Out is where a comic or a speaker performs the people in a scene and scores the big laughs. Instead of *talking about* someone or something, you *perform* it. For instance, here is the same idea presented as narration and as an Act-Out:

Wrong Way

Narration: "It's hard getting work done when you have to go out and feed the parking meter right in the middle of a meeting."

Right Way

Act-Out: "It's hard getting work done when right in the middle of a meeting, some guy jumps up and yells, *'Oh, my God, I've got to feed the meter. I'll be right back.'* And that's the CEO."

As you can tell from the italicized sentence, the Act-Out comes when you become a character to say, "Oh, my God, I've got to feed the meter."

The Act-Out, even if it doesn't get a laugh, makes a speech come alive with immediacy. The more a speaker embraces the full emotion and tones of the character, the better the laughs—especially if you can convey the real frustrations of the problem.

ACTING IT OUT!

The Act-Out is used throughout your speech, especially when telling stories. Rather than telling an audience what someone is saying, become them and act them out taking on their mannerisms and vocal quality. Whomever you mention in your speech, act them out.

"But Judy, I'm not very good with doing voices or characters."

That's okay, neither am I. Act-Outs don't have to be Oscar-winning performances, and don't worry about accuracy if you are pretending to channel your mother or father. The comedy patrol isn't going to yank you offstage and say, "His mother sounds nothing like that!" You don't even have to be able to do different voices. There is nothing more offensive than a male speaker raising his voice to a squeaky high voice when doing an Act-Out of his wife. Rather, be in your body, feel it, be it, and then say it. You don't need to drop to the ground, pretending to be a dog barking. No need to be that dramatic. With that said, I believe that whomever you mention in a speech should be acted out. I don't mean breaking into a long scene, but I do think that whatever character you mention in your story deserves a short appearance.

As you can imagine, some Techies and Novices have a hard time with the Act-Out. I get it. It's completely outside your comfort zone. But, guess what? *Comedy* is uncomfortable. It's taking a risk. Just because something doesn't feel comfortable doesn't mean you shouldn't try it.

WARNING

Never use a joke you found on the Internet or you heard a comic perform during their set.
    That's called stealing. And it's not funny.

EXERCISE: THE BASIC ACT-OUT

Every person you mention in your speech should be acted out.

Go through your speech and underline every person you mention, and make sure that you are acting them out.

If you are uptight about acting someone out, then focus on their physical being rather than their voice. If you are telling a story about your mother, then see how she stands, leans over, walks, picks up something, answers the phone. Stand like her. Does she hunch when she walks? Does she always have a finger out reprimanding, shaking it? Does she chew gum? Bite her pencil? Pull at her hair? Stand stiffly? Take her stance. Become her. Feel her. The voice will take care of itself when you take on another person's physical attributes.

COMEDY FORMULA:
ACT OUT INANIMATE OBJECTS AND ANIMALS

The characters in Act-Outs don't have to be people. As a matter of fact, it's pretty much a guaranteed laugh if you act out animals or inanimate objects. Robin Williams gives voice to a chair: *"I wonder what chairs think about all day: "Oops," here comes another asshole.'"*

Richard Pryor's heart talked to him in this joke: *"Your heart gets mad, 'Think about dying now, ain't you? You didn't think about it when you was eating that pork.'"*

One tip for doing these Act-Outs is to do it as a character. There is nothing funnier than a cat with a New York accent: "Ya want me to cuddle wi'chu? Fuhgaddaboudit! Get a life!"

Go through all your stories and see if you can add an Act-Out of anything that isn't human—a tree, your keys, your car, your refrigerator. *"Oh, hello, again Fatty. Weren't you just here five minutes ago?"*

Adding humor takes guts. Many of my students are very nervous to try the techniques in this chapter, but there is always a big smile on their faces when they get the laugh. Boy, does that

"I'm not that funny. What I am is brave."
–Lucille Ball

feel good. Try adding one humor piece each time you speak. You might find that after a year, you are hilarious!

Being funny is not all in the writing, it's mostly in the performance. Let me help you with that in the next chapter.

PART THREE

TAKING YOUR MESSAGE TO THE WORLD

CHAPTER SIXTEEN

PERFORMING THE MESSAGE OF YOU—
FROM THE PAGE TO THE PLATFORM

Now this part of the book is where I'm supposed to lecture you about the do's and don'ts of performing a speech—how to gesture, how to use body language, voice volume, tone, tempo and pitch, and so on. Here's the problem—I don't believe there is one "right" way to perform. If there was one right way to present a speech, then all speakers would look and sound the same, like politicians who've been groomed for the national press. You're not running for office. You're not trying to win an election. You're onstage to relay The Message of You.

Your speech is the unique expression of your Message of You, and if you truly believe in your message then it doesn't matter if you stutter, mispronounce words, stand perfectly still, or gesticulate like an air traffic controller. If you're speaking from your heart, then you're presenting your speech the right way—even if you use language that is grammatically incorrect.

Speeches are not written to be great literary prose. They are written to be spoken aloud and in the authentic style of the speaker. Professional speaker Jeanne Robertson is from South Carolina, and her speech is full of "y'alls," and "'Melpya?" (May I help you?) Her colloquialisms authentically reflect her personality and make her speech appealing.

NOBODY LIKES A PHONY

In 2004 Dr. Howard Dean was running for the Democratic nomination for president of the United States. At the beginning of the primary, he had headed to the top of the Democratic ticket with his message of "Taking Back the White House." But his stab at being the Democratic candidate was doomed by one speech, and it wasn't anything thing he said, but rather how he said it.

After losing the Iowa primary, he came out to speak to his following. He started getting worked up and ended up ranting, shouting, and presenting what would later become his infamous "Scream Speech." The next day the press labeled him "angry" and "out of control." The label stuck and his campaign fell apart.

Watching his speech years later, I realized that it wasn't really that he was angry; it was that he was inauthentic. Perhaps he hadn't gotten enough sleep, or was so disappointed with his election results, that he thought it was necessary to pile on the enthusiasm to an extreme degree. But rather than being authentic to the moment, he perhaps overcompensated and pushed a performance that sunk his bid for the presidency.

Audiences will forgive everything but phoniness. Sounding literary or using big thesaurus words you would never use when talking to friends—these things just won't fly with an audience. Imagine if a high school English teacher got hold of Martin Luther King Jr.'s "I Have a Dream" speech. That teacher might have marked his page in red and exclaimed, "Redundant!" Speeches are meant to be experienced. When a speaker fills each moment with passion, connects with his or her message, that creates a rhythm, a tone, and a movement that powerfully engages an audience. Moving from paper to performance requires passion.

When I say passion, I don't mean louder and bigger. So many people feel they have to be full of energy, dramatic, or fast talking. I used to think that for people to enjoy my presentations I had to move around the stage a lot. Watching my early work is painful beyond belief. I bounce around the stage like I'm running an aerobic class. I must have given whiplash to people just trying to watch me.

All inauthentic movement, voice modulations, fakeness, and histrionics come from the disassociation of being in the moment with the truth of who you are and The Message of You. If you express your passion by whispering, shouting, moving, or being still, it doesn't matter. Your belief in what you say will determine your own unique style of performing. You can't even look to other speakers to find your performance style because that would be mimicry, but you can check YouTube for speaking videos to see the vast range of delivery techniques. The late Apple CEO Steve Jobs slowly wandered around the stage when he gave his famous speeches announcing a new Apple product. Storyteller and comic Bill Cosby performs sitting in a chair. Physicist and cosmologist Stephen Hawking is captivating, even though he can't use his voice or move a muscle.

It is only fear and self-doubt that will tell you that you need to be something different than you are. So, the first step to creating a dynamic performance is simply to own your message and accept who you are.

OWN YOUR MESSAGE

When I began my comedy career I got a call from a booker who told me he hated my act. "Judy, I don't think you're funny. Actually, your manager said if I ever wanted to work with his other clients, I had to book you."

Ouch!

The gig was that night. How was I to step onstage when my confidence had been so shaken? I was freaking out. I decided to take my act out for a walk. I broke up my act into small portions and recited each portion as I walked asking myself, "Do I like that material? If I heard someone else say that material, would I find it relatable?"

I had walked about two miles by the time I was finished going through my twenty-minute act. There were a few pieces that felt awkward to me, so I cut them. But the rest I kept because no matter what another person said, *I liked my material.*

That night, I hit a home run. Backstage, the guy who hated my act pulled me aside to apologize. Then he told me the truth. His wife had just filed for a divorce and I looked like her. Go figure.

What gave me the courage to stick with my material was my passion for what I had to say. The passion you have for The Message of You connects you to your audience. It is that passion that moves an audience. It is passion that drives your speech and gives you the confidence to perform and gives you your tone, your physicality, and your style.

Here's the thing—if you took the time to research your audience and followed directions, you have a pretty good chance of creating a speech that will inspire. But no matter how hard you work, not everyone will like your speech. In the end, there is only one person that has to love your speech—that's you.

Trust your instincts.

EXERCISE—TAKE YOUR SPEECH FOR SIX REWRITE WALKS

You need to go for six walks. Take each section of your speech out for a walk: the opening, the problem section, the Heart Story, etc. Speak each portion of your speech out loud imagining your audience as you walk. I like to walk with a Bluetooth headset in my ear so I won't look like a madwoman ranting and raving to herself.

Ask yourself about each section:

NOBODY DIES LISTENING TO A SPEECH

"The beautiful part of writing is that you don't have to get it right the first time, unlike, say, a brain surgeon. You can always do it better."

—Robert Cormier, author, columnist, reporter, and speaker

- Does your material feel comfortable to you?

- Have you picked the right stories? Do your stories serve your message?

- Is any material awkward? If you find there is a piece of your speech that you just can't wrap your lips around, cut it. That's right, get rid of it. There's a reason you can't memorize or say it—you probably don't want to say it. Very often material that is forced, weird, or uncomfortable might seem like a good idea when you wrote it, but getting your speech up on its feet will reveal the parts of the speech that don't belong. Can't remember it? Then cut it!

- Are your stories authentic? Do they still contain meaning for you? Do you still feel emotion as you speak the words?

- Are you expressing your thoughts in a clear, simple way?

Make the changes in your speech you need to make. If you need to break some rules then break them. In the end, you're not writing a Judy Carter–approved speech—you're writing your Message of You and you are the expert about you!

Don't overrehearse. There comes a time when you know your act, but keep rehearsing it out of fear of forgetting material. Know your intent, but not necessarily the words. It's okay not to know it perfectly. No one is going to say, "Well you were really insightful, but you left out a line." Memorize it well enough, but also know how to go off script so you can swing with the moments.

So, now that you've reworked and rewritten your speech, cutting anything that feels forced, inauthentic or just plain weird, the next step is to focus on memorizing and rehearsing.

Memorizing your speech without sounding like you've memorized your speech.

Speaking is *not* about memorizing your speech *exactly* and having every gesture and movement rehearsed. With that said, if you bring your notes onstage and read from them, that's not called speaking, that's called reading. If you want to be a highly paid professional speaker, you can't hide behind a podium, reading your speech. We connect to audiences with our words, expressions, emotions, and body language. If your body is hidden behind a podium, you are a talking head. There should be nothing between you and the audience. No podium, no papers, no Post-its, no empty dance floor, no display table. Especially if you want to get laughs. We comics call the empty dance floor the valley of dead laughs. Just like a dog sleeping between you and your spouse will prevent intimacy, that empty dance floor will isolate you from your audience. Don't allow it to happen, even if it feels "safer" to stand at that distance.

I was booked for a conference where the author of an uber-famous self-help book was scheduled to speak earlier in the day. I was such a big fan of his book that I caught an earlier flight so I could hear him speak. I still arrived a bit late and had to rush to get to the event. I was so disappointed to see hordes of people streaming out as I ran toward the main ballroom. I asked a woman, "Did I miss the speaker?"

She responded, "No, he's still onstage. I wish I had missed him."

I entered the room and saw this famous author reading his speech at a podium. He never even glanced up to look at his audience. If he had, he would have seen that half the people had already left. The remaining audience members were checking their e-mail.

Part of putting on a great performance is maintaining eye contact with your audience. To do that, you have to rehearse and know your material.

Think about what you've written as your bouncing off point. As you get your speech up on its feet, words, stories, and ideas will occur to you. Later, with more experience under your belt or if you've been at this for several years, you may feel comfortable mixing it up in the moment. Ideas might pop in your head as you're working and I always suggest going with that moment . . . as long as your idea is G-rated. It's fine to launch into another direction, react to something someone says, but in order to get back on track, you must know your speech backward and forward. Knowing your speech actually leaves room for spontaneity. And spontaneity is key. Spontaneity reflects authenticity.

The biggest fear my students have when performing is that they will forget their spiel. This fear leads them to possibly overmemorize their speech, making them sound like Robo-Speaker. Performing a speech should be a fluid experience, leaving room for spontaneity. On the other hand, some students don't rehearse it at all, making them look disorganized and lost. No matter how rehearsed you are, your speech will never go the way you rehearsed it in the shower. There will be unexpected disturbances that will happen. You will have to react in the moment. Cell phones will ring, microphones will short out, and audience members will ask surprising questions. Rehearsing a speech is a balance between knowing it and yet, leaving room for inspiration. In performing a speech, we are not going for perfect. We are going for authentic.

There are so many times I have overmemorized my speech, delivered it absolutely perfectly, but those are lackluster performances met with polite applause. My best performances usually happen when things go wrong. During one particular woman's conference, there was a loud audio *pop* that scared me so badly I jumped. I couldn't ignore the distraction. I had to acknowledge it. I quipped, "That sound was my Spanx bursting. The front row better back up as there's a tsunami of flesh coming your way." The audience burst into laughter and applause. That moment was the best moment of my speech. It was real and the audience showed their appreciation.

Learning to live in the moment is essential. These "mistakes" and "detours" from your content usually become the best part of your speech, as it makes you alive in the moment. For me, it's a reflection of my Core Promise of turning problems into punch lines.

"But Judy, what do I do if I totally go blank?"

In spite of what you might think, losing your place or going blank for a moment or two will not trigger the end of the world.

If you truly go blank, this simple technique works all the time. Take a deep breath in and out with no words. I've seen this happen time and time again with my students. They lose their place and just stop talking.

FORGETTING YOUR SPEECH?

Chew gum

"According to research, the act of chewing gum right before your speech increases the flow of blood to your brain. Researchers have shown that people chewing gum are able to concentrate more intently and remember new information better. Chew the sugar-free type to avoid a blood sugar spike. Don't forget to spit it out prior to going onstage."

—John Tesh, speaker, composer, and host of *Intelligence for Your Life Radio Show*

The moment might seem endless to them, but the audience never seems to notice. They take a deep breath in and out and their act always comes back. Sometimes, they will admit that they lost their place, and that honesty guarantees them audience empathy.

If you're still not convinced that a deep breath will save you, try these three other tips:

Have a cheat sheet.

Comics and musicians all use a cheat sheet and so do speakers. Get yourself one sheet of paper and a Sharpie and give each segment of your speech a short name such as "problem—cafeteria—leadership story." Do *not* try to write out your entire speech in small print as one look at that, with your adrenaline pumping, and you'll be lost for your entire performance. A cheat sheet is a security blanket. You probably won't need to look at it, but many speakers find that it's comforting to know it's there.

Give yourself visual clues matching your content.

Some speakers use PowerPoint along with their speeches. Many speakers misuse PowerPoint by having their entire speech written up on boring slides. This is a huge mistake as forcing people to read your speech will disconnect them from you. Steve Jobs would project pictures to set a mood. For those speakers who are more visually than auditory oriented, a slide can provide an excellent clue as to what's next as long as you don't make them wordy.

Deliver different parts of your speech in different physical places.

Speaker Darren LaCroix used this technique to win the 2001 Toastmasters Championship. He had certain places on stage where he delivered different parts of his speech. So, different parts of the stage represented different parts of his speech. Walking to a part of the stage jolted his memory to that part of his speech.

Tightrope walkers understand that mistakes are more entertaining than perfection. Apparently, walking a tightrope is not so hard and the pros know that walking across a rope is only interesting if it looks as if they might lose their balance and fall. That's how they make an audience gasp by teetering on one foot, wobbling, and then triumphantly reaching the other side. Perfect is boring. Risk taking, having real moments of not knowing what's next and then finding it, will make you a captivating speaker to watch.

I was giving a new speech to a college on Buddhism and comedy. When I stepped onstage, I put my notes down and accidentally knocked over my coffee, spilling it all over my notes, making them unreadable. I had to acknowledge what I'd done so I quipped, "I had prepared a wonderful speech on Buddhism, which I wrote out beautifully. Every point was so well illustrated. (I held up my coffee-stained notes) They are now unreadable. As Buddhism teaches us that the human conditioning is suffering. I agree. And we must go within to find truth. (Throwing away my notes) I'm going to now go within and find my speech." Huge applause and laughs.

You might be wondering, "So do you then take that accident and make it happen each time?" No, I wouldn't suggest that. You can't try to recreate that magic moment—the new audience will smell the setup and have a harder time believing you are what you say you are. But you can use that mistake by turning it into an opening story for other speeches.

Just remember: when things go wrong, all you have to do is be true to the moment. Admit your flaws and move on. However, if your speech becomes a constant stream of getting lost, missed audio cues, your PowerPoint not working . . . then you're clearly not prepared.

EXERCISE–VISUALIZE TO MEMORIZE

Memorize your speech using the technique athletes use—visualization. Before competing in an event athletes visualize themselves winning. Watch Olympic snowboarders. Before they drop into a run, they close their eyes and imagine their body going through each and every turn. They twist and turn while standing on the ground. They let their body practice the motions.

SMELL THE SPEECH

"The best advice for memorizing anything is to study in a way that appeals to as many senses as you can. By seeing, hearing, feeling, and even smelling your material, you reinforce it in your brain."

—Grace Fleming, speaker on "Strategies for Success"

Speakers can use this technique. Close your eyes and imagine each step of your speech. Imagine yourself talking about the problem. Imagine yourself telling the story that qualifies you as an expert. Imagine yourself going through your Action Steps. And imagine telling your Heart Story and giving your Call-to-Action.

Practice this visualization once each day. A great time to do so is in the shower. The key is repetition. If you visualize once a day and take your speech out for six walks, you'll remember the order of your speech.

TO MEMORIZE OR NOT TO MEMORIZE YOUR SPEECH

John Kinde, professional speaker and humorist, suggests finding a balance between memorizing your speech and being impromptu:

"Certain parts of the speech should be more precisely memorized. You try to deliver the memorized parts exactly the same each time, but don't freeze if you deviate a bit. You don't want to be a prisoner of a script."

The areas that should be memorized are:

Your opening. It sets the stage and should be well "word-smithed" and rehearsed. One of the reasons there are many fans of memorization is that there is only one best way of saying something. And you need to spend time determining what that best phrasing is and memorize it as best you can.

Your humor, especially the punch line. The setup is very important; the punch line is critical. Mess up the words and you may kill the laughs.

Your transitions. This is an area where I spend most of my rehearsal time. Great transitions are critical to the flow and organization of your talk. They help provide the roadmap that will tie the entire talk together for your listeners.

Your idea outline. You should have your key-point outline memorized to the point where you can recite it, item for item, just as if you were reading it from a note card. This is the only thing I actually write on paper.

Your closing. Your Call-to-Action is probably the most important part of the talk. It should be precisely crafted for maximum impact.

MUST-MEMORIZE MOMENTS

With all that said, there are a few moments you absolutely must memorize:

- Memorize the first sentence of each chunk of your speech. This way, even if you draw a blank for a second, you know how to segue into the next section of your speech.

- Know your last line. You don't want to stumble over your ending.

- Memorize any comedy material, as changing a word sometimes is the difference between a laugh and a stare.

PERFORMING YOUR STORIES

As we discussed in the comedy chapter, you don't want to *retell* your stories, you want to *relive* them. You want to act them out as if you are actually back in that moment, feeling the emotions as your story unfolds. There is always magic in the first telling of a story, but often the magic vanishes in the second, third, and fourth telling. Why is that?

The first time you tell a story you are in the moment, picturing the people involved and as a result, you get laughs. Usually, the second time you tell a story you are probably doing what we call "heading to the laugh." This means you are no longer in the story, but you are hoping to get the same reaction you got the first time you told the story. This projects a phoniness that will distance an audience from you. Picture the story and perform it in present tense as if it's unfolding before your eyes.

Your Heart Story should not be memorized word for word. Memorizing your Heart Story in that way will stunt its growth. A Heart Story is a living organism. While you're onstage, new images will crop up, and you could find yourself spontaneously acting out something your uncle said that you'd forgotten. Trust the work you've done through this book and know that the arc of the story is in you. Just be sure to memorize the last line especially if it's a laugh line.

Two techniques that will help you really milk the performance of your Heart Story for all it's worth are the Squeezing Time Act-Out, and the Expanding Time Act-Out.

THE SQUEEZING TIME ACT-OUT

"Sometimes you need to give the backstory so that the audience understands the circumstance in which the story takes place," say Mark

Travis, who specializes in coaching one-person plays and is the author of *Directing Feature Films* and *The Film Director's Bag of Tricks*. Mark coaches actors how to condense time in a way to make it dramatic, by condensing time into short phrases and breaking up the rhythm with repetitive sentences.

SQUEEZING THE CLOCK

Squeezing the clock is a great way to quickly give the audience your whole history in a few minutes of their time. It lets your audience understand your motivations and desires, and you'll get some laughs just from the repetition of the words.

Mark coached comic Dana Gould on his one-person show, *Insomnia,* about how comedy saved his life and gave him an identity, and how it eventually led to him having a nervous breakdown while performing. It was important for the audience to understand his emotional state of mind and the technique he used sounded like this:

"Fly to NY, *tell a joke.* Fly home. Fly to Seattle. *Tell a joke.* Fly home. Why can't I get an agent? Meet Anne. Fly to Chicago. *Tell a joke.* Meet a waitress. Don't tell Ann. Fly home. Why can't I get on the *Tonight Show*?"

This technique can be used to condense time whether it is a ten-year stretch or just a morning. In my speaking workshop, nurse Judy Oliverio tells the story of her very overwhelming morning using this technique:

Join me for the day in the life of a nurse. Does this look familiar?
Call bell.
"Doctor, what can I do for you?"
"I need the CT Scan results."
"Oh yes. I will get you the CT Scan results, ASAP. I will be right back."
Call bell.
"Mrs. Smith, how can I help you this morning?"

"My mother wants vanilla pudding, not chocolate."

"OK, I will call the kitchen, be right back."

Call bell.

"Mr. Depressed, what can I do for you?"

"I need my antidepressants and my pain medications. I hurt so much."

"What is your pain level from zero to ten?"

"Twelve."

Mine, too.

And it's only 8:15 in the morning.

Ever felt like you just worked a twelve-hour shift in fifty-nine minutes?

REMEMBER

Never rehearse your act without emotion.

Always picture what you are saying, as it will make your material more dynamic and immediate.

Don't practice in front of a mirror. You won't be looking at yourself when you perform, so don't do it while you rehearse.

Practice this performance technique by first finding a phrase you can repeat that relates to your Core Promise. For instance, if you are speaking about a tough time in your sales career, the phrase might be, "Lost another sale." If you are speaking on relationships, "Got dumped again." If you are speaking on a time in your life when your finances weren't so good, the phrase could be, "Bill collector called."

The essence of this performance technique is to be in the moment and physically act out the sequence.

EXERCISE: SQUEEZE THE CLOCK

Try this technique in two ways:

1. CONDENSE A LONG PERIOD OF TIME

Pick a bad year that led up to an emotional event, such as a relationship breakup, finally finding love after a bad string of bad dates, watching yourself get poorer and poorer, or even a year of watching your company go down the tubes. Write out the year using short sentences with a repeating phrase.

2. CONDENSE A DAY

Now do the same exercise in condensing a bad day, making sure your repetitive phrase refers to your Core Promise. For example, if your speech is on emotional eating, a day could go like this:

> "Got up and ate a reasonable diet breakfast, saw I had two hundred e-mails. Ate a bagel. Got into my car and was in traffic. Ate jelly beans. My boss yelled at me. Ate Hershey Kisses. Called my mother and she yelled at me. Ate pasta. Watched the news and got depressed. Ate caramel corn."

THE EXPANDING TIME ACT-OUT

Have you ever had an experience in your life when time stood still? Many people who have been in an accident describe it as everything moving in slow motion while they seem to take in thousands of details in two seconds. Moviemakers have long used this technique of expanding time where they use one entire minute of movie time to show what happens in one second of real time. This is also a useful technique to use when you come to your Eureka Moment in your Heart Story.

Mark Travis says, "In telling your story, you can use this technique to dramatize a critical moment in your talk. Go into slow motion and slow everything down and let the audience see what happens and feel what happens. For the expansion to really work, you need a trigger to send you into the expansion, and then you can go as deep as you want."

For instance, WWE pro wrestler turned speaker John "Morrison" Hennigan talks about the time he was bullied in seventh grade:

> "This bully backs me into the corner and I'm thinking, *Oh my God, run!* But I can't run. No, oh, no! No place to go. Going to get beat up. Shaking. Sweating. Scared. So scared."

According to Travis, "There is always a trigger that brings the storyteller out of an expanded time moment. It's usually another character who says something that snaps the character out of his inner monologue."

"Then the bully says, 'Give me your lunch money now, or you're dead meat.'"

In Morrison's story, this also sets up a huge laugh for him when he reveals . . .

"It's Cindy, from tenth grade. Her lip ring is practically touching my face. I see it's infected. Do I hit her? Do I run? I can't run . . . I'm going to get beat up by a girl! And that's when I hear my friend Susan say, 'Leave him alone, Cindy. He's cool.'"

BE YOUR BEST NATURAL SELF, BUT . . .

Tom Drews, presentation expert and founder of What Works! Communications, warns, "When you speak you want to be your best natural self. But if you are doing something that is genuinely distracting, then people are going to focus on that and not on your message. Record yourself and cut out any 'You knows,' 'ahs,' and 'it's like,' as well as any weird gestures or movements. Don't let anything get in the way of your message."

EXERCISE: STRETCH THE CLOCK

- Use short staccato sentences when acting out the inner thoughts of a character.

- Always be in present tense.

- Use the expanding time technique on the peak, emotionally charged Eureka Moment of your story, and do a good acting job by conveying the emotion the character felt at the time. In other words, if the character is scared, be frightened when delivering the character's inner thoughts.

- Videotape yourself doing your speech. Watch it back identifying any artificial moments, distracting gestures, or idiosyncratic vocal qualities, and then knock it off!

TIMING YOUR SPEECH

It's very difficult to time a speech, as you never know how long the laughter will be and you don't want to cut that off just so you come in on time. Here are some tips so you don't have to worry about going over or going too short.

1. Know the last ten minutes or the end piece of your speech, perfectly.

2. Practice being able to transition to your end piece from any part of your speech.

3. Set your Smartphone to airplane mode so it doesn't ring, and set the timer to vibrate when you have ten minutes left.

4. Simply go to your end piece when it vibrates. It doesn't matter that the audience just got two Action Steps rather than three. Closing strong is more important.

CONNECTING TO THE AUDIENCE–
TALK *TO* THEM, NOT *AT* THEM

Although it looks as though speaking is a one-way conversation, it's not. When speaking, you need to leave room for the audience to react— whether it's laughing, applauding, or just nodding their heads. Don't be frightened of using pauses to let them react.

CONNECTING WITH A PUNCH LINE

One of the scariest times of performing is the moment after a speaker tells a joke. To avoid the potential embarrassment of laying an egg, many speakers will look down at the end of a joke. Big mistake, as looking down can disconnect you from the audience right when you need them to react.

When performing humor material, at the end of a joke:

- Keep your head up.

- Hold for a moment.

- Lean toward the audience.

- Hold both hands out and nod your head as if saying, "Don't you agree?"

Some of you might even want to go into the audience and talk to people. If that's your style, then do it. Just be careful that you don't use audience participation as padding. The audience is there to receive your message, not to supply the content themselves.

Here is a great technique to guarantee that you connect with your audience. Find a friendly face in the front row. Every now and then nod or smile at the person as if they are saying, "I love that story!" "I love that point!" It doesn't matter that they aren't saying anything. You just react to them as if you're saying "I'm glad you love me." They will usually smile or nod back. This connection to one person in the front row can translate to a connection to the entire room.

There have been a few times when I couldn't find a friendly face in the front row. When I was sharing the stage with President Clinton, I was speaking to an audience of 8,500 strangers and I couldn't even see the front row because of the stage lighting. If I could, it wouldn't have mattered because no one was looking at me anyway. Everyone was watching me in the huge TV monitors. In this case, I pictured someone who *loves* me sitting in the audience and I nodded and smiled to my imaginary friend. It worked. I looked confident and secure despite the overwhelming size of the venue and the butterflies in my stomach because, yes, I still get butterflies and so will you! Here's the good news about butterflies . . .

JUST BECAUSE YOU'RE SCARED
DOESN'T MEAN YOU'LL SUCK

I find no correlation between how scared I am before I perform and the quality of my performance. From watching thousands of speakers as well as comics, I can tell you that the arrogant ones who don't feel nervous are the ones who seem disconnected and are the ones that don't do as well. Fear makes you vulnerable and although that might not feel good, it is a likeable, human quality.

You need to reframe your fear and realize . . .

Fear is contained excitement.

I *always* feel nerves before I go on, but rather than calling it "fear" I call that uncomfortable feeling "contained excitement." Standing backstage waiting is like a runner on the starting line. You're in a coiled spring position ready to run. It's the same way you feel when you're in line for a scary roller coaster. Your mouth gets dry, your hands shake, and you want to leave but, once you're on the coaster—Wheeeeeeee!

IT'S NOT ABOUT *YOU*!

One of the great speech coaches, the late Dorothy Sarnoff, used to suggest repeating the following words to yourself before giving a speech:

"I'm glad I'm here. I'm glad you're here. I know what I know and I care about you.

"When you get in the habit of repeating this phrase, you can affect your own belief system. You actually become glad you are there and glad the audience is there. You stop worrying about whether you're good enough because you know what you know. And if you're convinced that you care about the people in front of you, you lose your fear of speaking to them and your confidence soars. I often repeat these words as I prepare to speak to a large group."—Ken Blanchard, speaker and best-selling coauthor of *The One-Minute Manager* and fifty other books

So, how do you get over the fear of performing?

The only advice friends will give you is to imagine the audience naked. To me, that seems like terrible advice. Anytime I'm in front of naked people, the last thing I want to do is to *talk* and my God, with obesity rates soaring do we really want to imagine any of these people naked? I don't!

Here's the thing about getting over fear. You can't. And the day that stepping in front of an audience doesn't make you quiver, that's the day you should quit. Some performers might make stepping onstage look like stepping into a living room full of friends, but that's an illusion. Ninety-nine percent of performers suffer from contained excitement. Their hands shake, they pant, they pace, they sweat. But in the end, it's thrilling and it means you're alive. So enjoy it.

What if you can't enjoy it? What if you really do get so tense that you can't speak?

I've got a solution for that as well. This actually happened to me once. In the middle of a speech, my throat just spasmed and I couldn't even squeak a sound. Actually, I got a huge laugh when I admitted it. I gave the microphone to someone in the audience and whispered to him to tell some jokes until I could take a sip of water and a deep breath to relax my throat and my voice came back. Here's the thing—the audience thought it was a part of the speech, and that gave me the time I needed to regain my voice.

To prevent this from ever happening again, I developed my backstage routine. Let me share it with you:

1. Stretch your body before you go on. I always duck into the hotel kitchen or hallway and touch my toes, rotate my hips, roll my shoulders, and stretch my mouth.

2. Center yourself. Some people think that they should be hyper before going in front of an audience; I think that is a mistake. Rather than having "energy" it's best to be centered. Before going on, take some deep breaths and get still enough to feel/hear your heart beat.

3. If you feel your throat closing up, stick two fingers on the back of your tongue. Your throat will immediately open up. Then, consciously relax your neck and shoulders while taking deep breaths. Once your throat is open, voice all the vowel sounds and make them blend into each other: A-E-I-O-U.

4. If your mouth is dry, pinch one cheek (yes, the one on your face) and it will immediately create saliva.

5. Lastly, before going on remind yourself of your Message of You. You can't control how people see you. You may remind people of their ex-wife who dumped them, their brother who owes them money, their sworn enemy. That's not something you can predict or change. So focus instead on what you can control—your message. There is someone in the audience who needs to hear your message. I have to remind myself of this every speech. I usually imagine my mother and I think how different her life could have been if she had heard my message from a speaker. I then say, "Get over yourself, Judy. It's not about you. It's about that person in the audience who I'm here to help."

I've got one more crazy thing to say before you're finished reading this chapter:

You need to forget everything I've taught you.

All right, now you *know* I'm totally nuts. Why did I bother writing this book if you're just supposed to forget it? Here's the thing—you need to know all the rules before you can break them. You have to do all the homework to discover The Message of You and you have to know the steps so well that you internalize the structure of your speech so it becomes a part of you. When you walk on stage, what the audience experiences can't be the formula or the structure or the brainstorming or the endless rewrites. In the end, what the audience will experience *is* you. Have confidence that everything in your life has brought you to this moment. All the life you have lived and all the knowledge you've obtained is contained within you. You have become the speech and you must trust in the fact that *you are the message.*

CHAPTER SIXTEEN CHECKLIST:

☐ Took my speech out for six rewrite walks.

☐ Memorized the critical moments.

☐ Visualized my entire speech.

☐ Reworked my stories using the Squeezing and Expanding Time Act-Outs.

☐ Timed my speech.

☐ Imagined connecting to the audience.

☐ Practiced the antifear exercises.

You are now ready to perform your speech! In order to make sure your first performance isn't a disaster, let's cover what can go wrong so it doesn't.

CHAPTER SEVENTEEN

DISASTER PREVENTION 101

You've written a great speech, you rehearsed it, and now you get to the gig and they say:

"Oh, you need a stage and a microphone? We thought you'd just wander around speaking."

Sound impossible? I promise you, it's not. Because this actually happened to me at a full-fee gig! Not even a freebie! They thought I could walk from table to table serving up inspiration and motivation like a waiter handing over an entree. When I told them that I couldn't do that, they explained to me that it worked for last year's entertainer.

"Really? And who was that?"

"A mariachi band."

One would assume that if a client is hiring a speaker to address their group that they would think ahead to have lighting, a sound system, and chairs, but I have found in the speaking business, to ASSume only makes an ass out of you. More things go wrong for speakers than entertainers because speakers are usually not performing in a venue created for an audience/performer relationship. Speakers end up trying to make do with an Embassy Suites multipurpose room or even speaking at a restaurant with Muzak blaring in the background while their audience sucks down Sierra Mist and picks fish bones out of their front teeth.

If you don't have specific working conditions in your contract or rider, they will not happen. As a matter of fact, each section of my rider (a supplement to the contract) has an origination story because I had mistakenly assumed that these issues were no-brainers. I was wrong and now, those that can be avoided with advance preparation are included in my rider. Those that can't be remedied by a rider can still be spotted and sidestepped. I'm going to share these disaster stories so you don't have to live through your own.

- I was expected to perform on a revolving stage where each minute I had a different audience in front of me. "Hi! How are you doing?" "Hi! How are *you* doing?"

- I had to compete with a bartender blending margaritas right beside the stage. When I got to my Heart Story, "And then my mother, with her last dying breath said—" *RHUMMMMMM!*

- There were no chairs. People were milling around and fidgeting. "Wait, don't wander away, this next point is really life changing!"

- I was totally in the dark. All the lights were focused on the audience rather than on me. I could see them. They couldn't see me. "Anyone got a flashlight?"

- I was positioned to stand on a platform behind the audience so the audience had their backs to me. "Ah . . . sorry to interrupt . . . hello? Can everyone turn around . . . please?"

- There were children playing hide-and-seek on the stage. "Put my water bottle back, that is *not* a toy."

- The CEO of the company got drunk and heckled me as if I were a comic at a Long Island comedy club. "So, the second point about increasing sales is—" "You suck!"

- I spent the first five minutes talking into a dead microphone. "Can you hear me now? What about now?"

- I was booked for a speech for the Junior Blind only to arrive and find out that they were the Junior Deaf. "Can you hear me now? What about now?"

Sound awful? You're right. The good news is there are ways to avoid disaster by preplanning.

MISTAKE #1: YOU FIGURE A FREE GIG MEANS YOU DON'T NEED A CONTRACT

Most disasters start with the words, "But I thought you said . . ." You must have everything in writing or you may find yourself stuck with a random $25 parking fee, fighting to get your video camera back after it was confiscated at the door, or being pushed back on stage after your finale because the client assumed you were speaking for an hour when you'd been told it was a half-hour meeting.

Solution: Get it in writing!

Freebie or not, you have to have a contract. Go to MarketYourSpeech .com/legal to download contract templates.

Here is a list of what's in my contract:

- Contact person
- Date and time of talk
- Sound-check time
- Venue details (address, phone)
- Emergency cell phone number of contact person
- Travel arrangements including exactly what they are paying for
- Title of talk
- Length of talk
- Prices (nondisclosed, including dates money is due. Half payment up front, etc.)
- Cancellation policy

  In addition to the contract, you also need a *rider*, which is a supplement to your contract that has the details of the audio/video requirements and others you need in order to speak.

Here are some of the conditions in various speakers' riders:

- Internet connection and projector needed for PowerPoint

- Type of microphone needed (handheld, lavalier, etc.)

- Microphone stand

- Stage diagram

- Table and volunteer at the back of the room for speaker product sales

- Water onstage

- No children in audience

- Audience seated close to stage

- Stage lighting

- Raised 4' × 8' foot platform or a raised stage

- Sound person

- Permission to videotape and a person to man the camera

- Personal assistant to pick out brown M&Ms (No joke! It's in Van Halen's contract.)

FUN FACT ABOUT VAN HALEN'S RIDER

Van Halen started performing in smaller cities—Macon, Georgia, for example—and after a few shows where their rider had not been read (safety hazards!) they added "No brown M&Ms" in the middle of all of technical requirements. So, instead of checking everything for every gig, they just checked the M&M bowl.

- No brown M&Ms—the contract had been read.
- Brown M&Ms—everything must be checked.
- No M&Ms—cancel the show.

MISTAKE #2: YOU DIDN'T ASK WHAT HAPPENS BEFORE YOU SPEAK

You prepared a motivational speech on surviving cancer, but when you arrive at your gig you find that you're booked to speak after a beer-pong party. Your audience is drunk and they have no desire to think about life or death issues. You're screwed.

As I have repeated throughout this book, you must research your audience and the conditions under which you will be speaking by simply calling your client and interviewing them in advance of your gig. No amount of money can soothe the wounds of a miserable speaking experience. You'll walk away from that stage and feel defeated, or worse you'll be so afraid to try again that you'll quit when all you really needed to do was pick up the phone and ask a simple question: "Tell me what happens to the audience before I go on. I mean, from the moment they wake up until the moment I walk on stage."

Find out if the gig is a no-win situation. If they want you to speak after a full day of meetings, it's a no-win. If they want you to speak after an open bar, it's a no-win. If they're serving dinner during your speech, forget it. If your audience has sat through an awards ceremony where they gave out forty plaques, give it up. You could be the Second Coming and you still won't get a reaction. Try instead to negotiate a different time slot and if you can't, seriously consider turning down the job.

Solution: Refer back to chapter eight for advance research.

Also, go to TheMessageOfYou.com to download an up-to-date PDF questionnaire on what to ask clients *before* you step on stage. If you don't ask, then don't tell.

MISTAKE #3: YOU HAVE 35 POWERPOINT SLIDES AND NONE OF THEM ARE FUNNY

I have mentioned using PowerPoint in this book only because I'm not a big believer in it. Organizations pay a premium to have a speaker appear in person and you lose value if your audience spends more time reading a screen than listening to you. Also, PowerPoint is a sure way to broadcast to an audience that your speech is not spontaneous, as it is entirely mapped out and you are not going to deviate from your plan.

POWER UP YOUR POWERPOINT

"A mistake speakers make is having too much information on each PowerPoint slide. If a slide takes longer than three seconds to read, it's going to distract from your speech.
    "Tips:

- Simplify your text. It's better to have just one sentence and a picture than an essay.

- Break your complex points across several slides.

- Use animation to have one bullet point at a time become visible so people don't read ahead.

"Add an interesting and engaging photo to help support your points. Go to istockphoto.com for finding photos for presentations."—Tom Drews, presentation coach and productivity expert

---

In some cases, there *is* definitely a need for slides to illustrate a point you can't easily convey verbally, such as graphs of financial data or pictures that make a point so perfectly it makes more sense to show rather than tell. Techies have more of an excuse to use PowerPoint than other speakers, but it doesn't mean they should use them excessively.

People get bored quickly if you force them to read when they planned on just listening. Nobody wants to have to read slide after slide of text in tiny print with complicated graphs and data. They'd much rather have you simplify it for them and tell them in a way that's interesting and entertaining. (That's why you're getting paid!) Also, depending on PowerPoint means there will be a lot of places you can't speak such as the smaller, after-dinner events that don't offer screens or projectors.

Solution: Go for the laugh!

If you must use slides, you must make them interesting, dynamic, and funny, and rely more on the visual elements than the text. Otherwise, you'll annoy the older folks in management who forgot to bring their reading glasses! Refer back to chapter fifteen on adding comedy. The quickest and fastest way to get a laugh here is to use the "List of Three" comedy formula—two serious slides and then follow it up with a funny third. Easy, and you've even got a visual reminder of your joke! At MessageOfYou.com/services there are lists of sites that will assist you in making your slides visually funny as well.

MISTAKE #4: "OH, I DON'T REALLY NEED A SOUND CHECK . . . HELLO, IS THIS ON?"

All it takes is one technical issue to torpedo an entire gig, which makes it of utmost importance to schedule a sound check and coordinate with the sound person before you even arrive. Make sure your client has a detailed list of all of your tech needs at least two weeks before the gig. And as soon as you arrive, check in to make sure you are good to go.

Solution: The sound person is now your best friend.

The sound man can make or break your gig. I learned early in my career that not being nice to a sound person can ruin a speech. One sound man thought it would be very funny to play audio rim-shots

"Don't take on a technical problem alone. If something goes wrong, and you think that you alone have to fix it, the seconds it takes to do so will seem like eons. And if you can't fix it, you're toast. Instead, bring the audience in on it. 'Are there any computer experts in the room?' That sort of question will get you at least three engineers dying to help. Then, it's everyone's problem, not just yours."

—Nick Morgan, speaker and author of *Give Your Speech, Change the World: How to Move Your Audience to Action*

"To err is human, but it takes a computer to really screw things up."

—Anonymous

after every one of my jokes. Note that sound techs are usually not drug tested and get bored easily. This person needs to be treated with utmost respect.

Here are some tips for working with the sound person:

- Always get the sound person's name (avoid attitude problems).

- Thank them profusely for caring enough to make sure your set is glitch free.

- Always talk into the microphone to get levels. Know that microphone levels will need to be adjusted when the room is full of warm bodies.

- Those of you who have a PowerPoint, do a run-though in advance so you don't spend your time repeating, "Can I have my next slide, please? Please? No, not that one . . ."

MISTAKE #5: YOU POKE FUN AT THE AUDIENCE

As I said in chapter eight, *never* make fun of the people sitting in front of you.

Solution: Make fun of yourself and not them

Even if the committee who hired you tells you it's a good idea to poke fun at their CEO's Elvis-like hair, avoid the temptation. Even if before you go on, the COO shows endless boring slides from his vacation at Dollyworld, don't reach for the low-hanging fruit. Never dis' the person signing your check as, if you do, you might not get one. Review chapter eight once again to learn how to make fun of you rather than them.

MISTAKE #6: YOU'RE INTRODUCED AS A BUSINESS EXPERT AND YOU ARE WEARING JEANS

When I first got into speaking, I wore business suits. I felt I needed to look like the people in my audience. But, here is the thing—you *are* an outsider and you need to dress according to your message. Larry Winget, who brands himself the Pit Bull of Personal Development, wears jeans and punk shirts no matter where he speaks. He dresses to his message. It creates a disconnect if what your audience sees doesn't match what they hear. If you're introduced as a specialist in dealing with Gen-Xers, and you're wearing a business suit, you're in trouble.

Solution: Be a functional fashionista.

Consider the time of day. If you've got the 8 a.m. morning keynote, dress casually. If you're the entertainment for an evening black tie dinner, then put on a jacket or a beaded something. And it doesn't matter if you're a guy or a girl, overt sexuality will only serve as a distraction. Keep your cleavage covered. Finding the right thing to wear is about being authentic to your message and allowing that to be reflected in your style. And hey, if you still can't figure out what to wear, hire a personal stylist for a one-time private session. Have them pick out three or four options for you.

ARE YOU SPEAKING IN *THAT*?

Kathy Reiffenstein, speech coach and founder and president of And . . . Now Presenting!, a D.C.-area communications training firm, has some great tips for the wardrobe impaired.

1. Your image will speak volumes about you before you even open your mouth. Make sure it's saying the right things. Does your conservative suit and muted tie support your creative, innovative image? Does your blouse with the low-cut neckline cry senior executive? Certainly different corporate cultures will embrace different styles. But the point is to be sure your clothing is indeed communicating the desired image.

2. Dress for the audience. Dress so they get a visually pleasing picture but not so they're distracted by your array of nonmatching patterns, bold designs, or heels so high you look like you're going to trip. Your audience shouldn't be more engaged by your clothing than they are by your message.

3. Be the best-dressed person in the room. Always dress a notch (but not two) above the standard attire as a compliment to your audience. It adds to your credibility.

4. If you have pockets in whatever you're wearing, empty them before the presentation. There are few things more annoying than watching a presenter playing with pocket contents. And if those contents create noise (like coins or keys), it's doubly annoying.

5. Shoes deserve a special mention. In many cases, your shoes are at the audience's eye level if you're on a stage. Shoes should be polished and heels should not be worn down. Shoes shouldn't squeak. And ladies, if the three-inch heels that look fabulous are so uncomfortable you can't get your mind off them, you certainly won't be at your best for your audience.

6. Choose jewelry carefully. Jewelry is a striking complement to most outfits, but if it's huge and jangly, it will be distracting. If a bracelet slides up and down your arm every time you gesture, if there's jingling every time you make hand movements, if your earrings are so huge that people can't take their eyes off them, your audience is going to be focused on these distractions.

MISTAKE #7: YOU TRY TO CONTROL YOUR PRE-SHOW NERVES WITH SUBSTANCES

Yes, you've got the flu and you've only had three hours of sleep. You still don't need excess coffee or stimulants to give you energy. Adrenaline will do the trick. I've heard speakers ruin their connection with an audience because they were so revved up before they went on that they acted unnaturally speedy, zooming through an hour keynote in thirty minutes. On the other hand, there are those who feel it's necessary to "calm down" with a shot of tequila before they speak. Not a good idea. You'll find that it will dull your reactions, ruin your timing, and slur your words.

Solution: Know that you are exactly the way you need to be.

One of my best engagements was performed with the flu. I learned from this gig that it's not about having a high energy level, but rather it's about being authentic to yourself *in the moment*. This doesn't mean sneezing and coughing on the audience. Being sick with a high fever meant that I didn't have any extra energy for my "Please like me" shenanigans. There was no nervous pacing, no artificial gratuity. It was me and my message and it was more than enough. I stood still and spoke from a deep place of utter authenticity. Then with the sound of applause in my ears, I came off stage and collapsed.

The best way to be on stage is the way you are.

MISTAKE #8: YOU ASSUME AIRPLANES RUN ON TIME

You don't get paid if you don't show up.

Solution: Book an earlier flight and stay overnight.

Save yourself the aggravation and get to your gig city the night before you speak. You'll arrive relaxed (or if things go horribly wrong, you'll have time to chill out) and get a full night's sleep before you go on. And bonus, you may even have an hour or two for a mini-vacation. When flying into another time zone, I always ask for two nights' accommodations at a hotel on the client's dime. At first they might protest, but when I explain to them the consequences of missing a connecting flight and being stuck in Dallas rather than at their event, they relent. You can also use the extra time to sit in on meetings prior to your speech and really get to know insider information on your audience.

MISTAKE #9: YOU DIDN'T BRING A COPY OF YOUR INTRODUCTION WITH YOU

Even though I always e-mail my introduction to the meeting planner at least one week prior to the gig, very often it never makes it into the hands of the emcee. Your introduction is the first thing the audience hears about you. It sets the tone and receptiveness of the audience. If the person introducing you says, "Don't worry, I have your bio and I'll just wing it," *don't let them.* Chances are the CFO or the admin who got roped into giving the introduction has never taken a Second City Improv class. You don't want to have to spend the first ten minutes of your speech trying to repair the damage brought about by misinformation. "Yes, I did share the stage with President Clinton, but I didn't sleep with him as the emcee has suggested!"

Solution: Pack an extra copy of your intro in your carry-on bag.

MISTAKE #10: YOU'VE GOT A "DIVA" ATTITUDE

If you want to be a diva, you'd better find yourself another profession. No matter how much money you make as a speaker, there will still be gigs where you yourself will be getting your hands dirty—moving the chairs so people can see you, or grabbing a broom to adjust the lighting to focus on the speaking platform rather than on the chocolate fondue fountain.

Solution: Humility is a virtue.

You have to be willing to roll up your sleeves and make a gig work. Throwing a hissy fit or giving the meeting planner a big dose of attitude will only hurt you in the long run. Meeting planners talk to each other. Word gets around that you're "high maintenance" and that's it, you're done.

DIVAS NEED NOT APPLY

"Don't give a meeting planner the don't-you-know-who-I-am? attitude. The goal is to make the event successful and speakers need to be a partner in that rather than to become a problem. The speaker is there to help inspire us solve our problems not to add to them."

—Sandy Biback, CMP, CMM, founder, Imagination⁺ Meeting Planners Inc.

CHAPTER SEVENTEEN CHECKLIST

☐ Issued a contract with a detailed rider.

☐ Researched my audience.

☐ Know my speech backward and forward.

☐ Made my PowerPoint presentations interesting.

☐ Scheduled a sound check.

CHAPTER EIGHTEEN

FROM FREE TO FEE: ABSOLUTELY
CRUCIAL MARKETING ESSENTIALS

How does a clerk at the Little Rock Housing Authority, with no college degree, become one of the world's most highly decorated professional speakers?

Jim Cathcart was twenty-six years old when he joined a local Little Rock chapter of the Jaycees, a community service organization that promotes leadership training and self-improvement for its young members. Jim got fanatically involved and since he was one of the only members who actually took the time to read the Jaycees' procedural manual, he was often asked to give reports, as well as speeches on chapter leadership, community involvement, and how to motivate volunteers. In two years, he spoke 400 times. His big break came when one of the members of the Jaycees asked, "Can you do that presentation at my insurance company in Tulsa, Oklahoma?" To Jim, Oklahoma was practically an international gig. He spoke to the insurance agents and it went so well that Massachusetts Mutual Life hired Jim to do their sales training for insurance agents in Tulsa and then around the country.

Thirty-five years later, Jim Cathcart is one of the highest grossing and most award-winning motivational speakers in the business. He has delivered more than 2,700 presentations on relationship selling to audiences in every state of the United States, most provinces of Canada, and countries from Scotland to Singapore. He has also has published sixteen books, as well as been inducted into the National Speakers' Association Hall of Fame.

All from volunteering to speak at a local service organization.

You might think Jim was lucky, but talk to any successful speaker and you will hear a similar story over and over again. Pro speakers often start their lucrative careers by speaking as part of their job or by volunteering to speak for free. Your speaking career is not going to be launched by an agent or a client, but rather by you. It is hard work, and yes it takes a bit of luck. Just remember, luck finds people who are already in motion.

BEING A GOOD SAMARITIAN PAYS OFF

"The turning point in my speaking career came when I agreed to do an unpaid job seekers seminar at my church for about a hundred people. When I did the seminar, there was a leader of a large organization in the audience. That led me to a paying job as well as other opportunities and invitations. Volunteering to speak is the way to move into paying gigs."

—Bob Yanega, speaker,
"Helping Others Lead Successful Lives."

No matter where you are in your speaking career, no matter how terrific your speech is, no matter how much money you made last year, marketing your Message of You needs to be attended to as a serious business venture. The good news is you won't need a lot of capital to start your business. What you will need is time. Novice speakers would love to have Jim Cathcart's career but very few are willing to do what is necessary to achieve that level of success. Jim is one of the hardest working people in the speaker industry. Now in his sixties, Jim gets up early to run mountain trails as well as his business. He attends speaker educational seminars, constantly studies and improves his speech, and will still do free gigs to improve his visibility and increase his client base.

CASE STUDY
FROM CAVE TO CEO

How did a guy who grew up dirt poor in a log cabin, without basic necessities like running water or a flushing toilet, become an in-demand speaker and CEO of a multimillion-dollar company?

By believing in his message.

After graduating college, Jonah White knew he wanted to pursue a career in marketing, but was unsure how his path would guide him there. So he did something different. He decided to go back to nature to find clarity and moved into a cave on the land where he had grown up.

He then met Richard Bailey, a dental student. Richard, for fun, had made a pair of fake "hillbilly teeth." Jonah instantly saw the potential, sold his gun for $400, and started Billy Bob Inc., working out of his parent's house. Two years later, he made his first million and after his rags-to-riches story was featured in *People, US Magazine, The Today Show,* CNN, and others, calls poured in from Fortune 500 companies to hear his message.

"I've always have been different and there's power in that. That's my message when I speak—the power of being different."

In chapter seven, I gave you instructions on how to book nonpaying speaking engagements. If you apply yourself, you can work every week. In this chapter, I will be focusing on what you need to do after your gig to turn free into fee. You can have a successful career as a speaker. You can make a living at this. But I will not kid you—it's a full-time job. Turning free gigs into paying gigs means you're going into the "speaker business." You will have challenges; you will have times when you wonder if and when it will pay off, but those who make a living at this all have one thing in common—they never gave up. Those who persist, succeed.

"But, Judy, I'm just an actor. I don't know anything about running a company."

If you're an actor, then consider this the role of a lifetime. You just got cast as the CEO as well as marketing director of a production called

The Message of You. Put your acting chops to work and fake it until you make it. Act as if you are your own CEO. Talk to any CEO and after a couple of drinks, they'll admit they go to bed each night with self-doubt about their own abilities. I never went to business school; I don't have a MBA; but what I have always had is a willingness to work hard, learn from my mistakes, and make my business work. When things get tough, I don't give up. I try different solutions. Being an entrepreneur takes the same set of creative skills that I use to write jokes: the ability to see the world with fresh eyes and to think out of the box.

TO FREEBIE OR NOT TO FREEBIE?
THAT IS THE QUESTION.

All speakers do freebies, even the ones earning over $10,000 a gig. You just need to choose your freebies wisely. Professional speaker Mimi Donaldson only agrees to free gigs if they meet her seven qualifications:

1. The topic is chosen by me and must be related to products I sell.

2. I must be able to sell my products at the event and distribute order forms before I speak to all attendees.

3. I require a six- to eight-foot table in a prominent place where participants will be, not off in another room somewhere.

4. I require at least forty minutes of speaking time. I tell them it's not a commercial; it's content.

5. Location corresponds to number of attendees. If the venue is within an hour's drive of my house, the audience must be at least twenty-five people. Over an hour's drive, at least fifty people.

6. I always require an attendee list with names and e-mails. You grow your database, and this speech becomes your first *touch* with each member of the audience. Sometimes, it takes more than one *touch* to sell a paid speech. You can e-mail them after the speech, and send your valuable newsletter or a report.

7. I *never* accept a freebie for a corporation with the hope or promise they will pay next time. They never will. Why should they? You gave it away the first time.

MARKETING ESSENTIAL #1:
MILK THAT FREE GIG FOR ALL IT'S WORTH

Some people might dismiss nonpaying gigs as beneath them, but if you're smart and you work these gigs right, they can give you a lot more than a fee. They can give you everything you need to launch your career. Free gigs can provide you with the marketing materials you'll need to book future paying gigs, such as:

- Video clips
- Testimonials
- Fans
- Stage time
- Referrals
- Product sales
- Paying clients

Think about it. How much money would it take to get PR, reviews, a grateful audience to listen to you, a professional video, and feedback? A lot. A free gig can provide you with thousands of dollars' worth of promotion so play these gigs for all they are worth. And consider their worth in sales. Many professional speakers opt not to charge a speaking fee and instead make a bundle in the back of room sales of their products and services. More on that later, for now I need you to . . .

GATHER YE TESTIMONIALS

Post-speech is no time to become shy. You've done so much work, stopping the momentum after a gig is like dropping the ball ten feet from a touchdown. After you do a free booking, call the event planner the *very next day* and ask them if they have a few minutes for feedback. Most people I call are flattered to be asked. Ask them what comments people had about your speech and write down every single thing they say, both good and bad. You can learn from the bad and you will get marketing materials from the good.

AFTER A GIG, HANG OUT

1. Stick around. The good questions come up during breaks and after your bow.

2. Be available. If you're rushing or packing up your equipment, anyone who wants to speak with you will feel disregarded. Listen to people. If you have to vacate the stage quickly to make room for the next speaker, tell fans you'll meet with them in hall or at the reception.

3. Place yourself by the exit doors at the end of your presentation so you can visit, smile, shake hands, and make eye contact.

4. Offer to send bonus information via mail or e-mail to audience members. Ask them to specify the requested information on the back of their business cards.

5. Follow through by promptly sending out requested material.

6. Request the mailing list or cards of attendees. Send them a reminder note within two weeks of your presentation.

7. Offer to sign them up for your e-newsletter or an e-mail follow up.

8. Write an article for the audience's newsletter.

—Karen Susman, professional speaker, "Be at Ease Communicating With Humans"

They might be saying, "People loved you!" "We really appreciated that you customized your speech for us." "People said you were one of the funniest speakers that we have had." "A few people complained about having too much audience participation." "Your content was very informative."

"But, Judy, what if I sucked at the booking? I don't want to embarrass myself by calling the client."

If your gig didn't go as well as you planned, then it is doubly important to summon up your courage and call the client. Rather than blaming yourself, there may have been extenuating circumstances. I had one gig that didn't go so well. I called up the client and he actually apologized to me for having me speak at the end of a long day to a tired and drunk audience. Boy, that made me feel so much better! The meeting planner and I both learned a lesson—never speak to a crowd whose day was full of speakers, followed by an open bar. If you ask the right questions prior to signing a contract, you can make suggestions to the client. After all, both of you want your speech to be a hit. I've actually turned down bookings when clients insist on putting me in a losing situation. You always have a choice. In any case, you must open up the conversation by asking your client for honest feedback. Don't argue or defend yourself. Just write down everything they say. Then get together with your Speaker Buddy and see if you want to implement any of their changes into your speech.

If the feedback was largely positive, ask your contact, "Would it be possible for me to get what you said on your stationery to include in my press kit? I don't want to be presumptuous and I know how busy you are, so I've written down everything you said and I would appreciate it if you could copy and paste it to your stationery, sign it or change it as you see fit, and either mail it to me or PDF to me." I've never had a client say no.

Within ten minutes after hanging up the phone, I send them my thank-you letter, minus any of the negative feedback. I have been in this business a long time and I still collect these testimonial letters—what I refer to as Happy Letters. Usually, their Happy Letter is returned right away. I scan it into a PDF and put it on my computer. I edit it for quotes, and then I categorize it according to industry such as health care, insurance, government, etc. Now, you have a letter and a name and you can turn this PDF into many bookings. By sending it to many people in the same industry, you can search for speaking opportunities at other companies.

GATHER YE REFERRALS

In that same phone call, ask your client if they can refer you to someone else in their industry. If you have spoken for a local chapter of an association or organization, ask if they know the person in charge of booking speakers for the statewide conference or for the national conference. Once you have the name of a new contact and the name of your referral plus your Happy Letter, you're in business! The way I frame this question is to ask, "Do you know of others who would benefit from hearing my message?"

REFERRALS WORK!

"There are solid reasons why referrals work. A referred client trusts the seller easily, because he trusts the referrer. Simply because the referred client's friend or relative has used the product and kind of vouchsafes its quality there is very little convincing required. It's only a matter of few additional questions and the sales person can close the deal."

—Doug Dvorak, CEO of The Sales Coaching Institute and author of *501 Sales Ideas to Win More Business*

Since you are putting them on the spot, give them some ideas to spur their memory. "Do you know any associations or other departments at your company who would benefit from hearing my message?" At first it was really hard for me to do these calls, but I found that 99 percent of the people were willing to talk to me. They gave me great feedback, wrote the Happy Letters, offered referrals and let me use their name as a recommendation.

MARKETING ESSENTIAL #2:
YOU GOTTA GIVE GOOD DEMO

Once you have your Happy Letters and Referrals, you can get on the phone and start calling for more nonpaying gigs. All you'll need is the EPK (electronic press kit) you created at the end of Part One and your demo video.

"Uh . . . wait, what? I have to have a video?"

If you want to work then yes, basically, you need to create a terrific, knockout demo video, but you don't need to spend a lot of money to do this. Most speakers who hire a production company to shoot their speech admit it was money flushed down the toilet. Hiring a crew puts unnecessary tension on you to film the "best" speech. Learn from my mistakes. Every time I spent a lot of money hiring a camera crew to shoot me, something went horribly wrong. The day you hire a camera crew, I guarantee that instead of a loose, spontaneous speech, they'll end up shooting you trying to be perfect. You'll inevitably end up mispronouncing words, rushing, and sounding strident. Then there's the audience. You just can't predict they will be a LOL-type crowd. Lighting might be a problem as well and the back drop has an 85 percent chance of looking cheesy. But that's nothing compared to the "hair" issue. I don't know what it is, but if you spend money to video your speech, you will have one single strand of hair that decides to stick straight up, making even footage of a great performance absolutely unusable. You don't want a potential client watching your video thinking, "What's up with that hair? She looks like she put Viagra in her hair."

In other words, your demo video cannot depend on shooting just one booking. You're going to need footage from lots of different gigs and there's no reason to pay professionals to do that job. You can get a great demo video in an extremely affordable way by investing in your own equipment and shoot every booking you do. Here's how you do it.

EQUIPMENT NECESSARY TO OWN

KEEP IT SIMPLE

Orvel Ray Wilson, senior partner of The Guerrilla Group, Inc., is a thirty-year veteran of the platform, and coauthor of five books in the legendary "Guerrilla Marketing" series. He believes that "Most speaker 'demos' are not really demos at all, but overdone puff pieces. These meeting planners are as smart as your mother, and you know you could never pull anything over on her. Send them something simple and genuine that they can trust."

1. You will need an HD camera that fits into your carry-on luggage. The quality on these cameras is amazing. Some of them are the size of a pack of playing cards, and the prices are low.

2. You will need a wireless lavalier omnidirectional microphone. You wear the microphone and attach the receiver to your camera. An omnidirectional microphone picks up both your voice and the audience laughs and applause. On a demo tape, meeting planners love hearing that your speech is going over well.

3. You will need a tripod. I use a sturdy video tripod that telescopes down to a small package so it fits into my carry-on luggage.

4. Get some headphones. Any type will do. You just have to make sure there is no buzz in the audio.

You can get this entire bundle for cheap. Go to MarketYourSpeech .com/video for a list of recommended equipment. Once you've got your equipment, you're ready to shoot, but keep these tips in mind so you don't give the speech of your life and then realize you forgot to press Record!

TIPS ON SHOOTING A GREAT VIDEO

1. Ask for a camera operator.

As part of your contract, especially if you are speaking for free, ask if your client can provide a volunteer to operate your camera. Sometimes they will set me up with a professional video guy whom I pay $50 to operate my camera. Fifty bucks is a small investment if your demo lands you a $10,000 booking. Plus, most clients are happy to do it and very often you get some skilled people. Sometimes they will already have a camera setup. In this case, ask if you can have a copy of the video and make sure to get the cameraman's card.

2. Make sure to frame your shot. You want a shot of yourself where the viewer can see your body as well as your facial expressions. I frame my shot at my knees and one inch above my head. This shot works well if you are standing still or moving around.

WHAT MAKES A GREAT DEMO?

The National Speakers' Association actually surveyed meeting planners on this very topic. What they said they wanted was:

NO fancy introduction with a bunch of special effects and a voice-over introduction.

NO highly produced videos shot in a studio. Anyone can look good in front of friends and family. Give us the "what I see is what I get" version. Production values are not as important as documenting a real event in front of a live audience. That being said, good production values do help your credibility. Good lighting and good sound are most important. Skip the fancy cuts, fades and effects.

Give us your BEST clip, 3–5 minutes, right up front, and then follow it with a complete performance, uncut. If we like the first bit, we'll watch the rest.

Cut in your PowerPoint slides (if you use them), so we can see what's on the screen. Audience testimonials are usually a waste of our time. You'll only include the glowing ones, anyway. Let us see your show with shots of the audience reacting and judge it for ourselves.

---

3. Deal with the lighting. Turn off any lighting that's behind you or cover any window so you don't look dark. Very often in hotel rooms, there aren't any lights on the platform. This is no time to be a diva. I ask for a ladder and a broom and swivel that lights around to focus on where I'm going to be speaking.

4. Shoot audience reaction shots. Meeting planners love seeing the faces of audience members enjoying your speech, laughing, applauding, and getting teary eyed. And if you get the opportunity to speak to a large audience, the shot of the packed audience is your money shot. Speakers who speak for large groups command higher prices. In order to get these shots, you can use a second camera, or even use your cell phone with a camera. Actually, once you have a lot of good video of your performance, use your free bookings to get audience shots. Or, here is another clever way to get audience shots without having to hire someone to do it: If there is a speaker on before you, stand up front and to the side and get video of the audience reacting to that speaker. You won't be using the audio from these clips, so it's easy to drop them into your demo video. This is exactly what reality TV shows do when they edit their shows together. However, it would be out of integrity if you shoot reaction shots of an audience that you were never in front of.

5. Shoot video testimonials. After your speech, shoot short videos of audience members speaking directly to the camera about how much they enjoyed your show. Meeting planners may not want to see this on your demo video, but you can use it on your Web page. Make sure that you get a variety of people (age, gender, ethnicity) to give testimonials.

EDITING YOUR VIDEO

1. Find a video editor. As the meeting planners said in the sidebar on page 298, you don't need anything fancy for your demo video. An

HOW TO GET A SPEAKER AGENT'S ATTENTION

"The days of sending [a bureau] expensive bulky VHS/DVD/press kits are over—thankfully! The best way submit to a speakers bureau is via e-mail. Send a brief introductory note, a link to your speaker's Web site, and a separate direct link to one or more video clips. It's important to put your best video clip link on top of the email since bureaus will watch your video first and if they like what they see, they will then review the rest of your information."

—Mike Frick, president, Speaking.com speakers bureau

endless parade of special effects will distract from your message. You can find a great editor on Craigslist or at your local college, or even high school. Better yet, your video editor might be you. Editing video has been simplified and is even available on an iPad.

2. Have a killer opening. Imagine a committee sitting down to pick the speaker and they have thirty video links to click. They will decide within the first thirty seconds if you're any good. So make sure those first thirty seconds rock. No pompous stuff. No voice-over. No special effects. They are looking for reality so just get right to it. Give them the best three to five minutes of your speech. If they want to see more, direct them to your Web site. I open my demo video with a shot of a huge audience. Then I have fifteen seconds of testimonials from famous people such as Oprah Winfrey, CNN, Diane Sawyer, and then *BAM*—I go right into a funny part of my speech. Don't fret if you don't have these sorts of testimonials right now. Just make sure the first clip they see of you is one where you look great, professional, funny, and it expresses the Message of You.

"Very often my client (the meeting planner) will watch a speaker's video while we are on the phone and that gets them hooked. Speakers have to have a video that wows a client within the first thirty seconds."

—Jonathan Wygant, CEO of BigSpeak Motivational Speakers Bureau

3. Constantly update your video. Another reason not to spend a gob of money on your demo video is you need to keep updating it with better clips. When you get to the gig, you want your client to recognize you and not ask if you are the speaker's mother! If you keep recording your gigs—every single one of them—slowly but surely you will find your demo video improving. So don't burn a thousand DVDs; in two months, you'll have better footage and you'll hate what you already shot. And honestly, it's been a long time since anyone has even asked for a DVD. Mostly, they want a link to your YouTube video or your Web site. So go to speakerdemo.com and upload your video, your Happy Letters, and create your own electronic press kit. By the way, it is *free*.

MARKETING ESSENTIAL #3: GET YOUR WWW ON

Once you have your video, it's time to create your most important marketing material—a professional Web site. Your Web site must contain these essentials:

- The Message of You on your front page, reduced to a very clear, short, and concise phrase that includes the results you give your audiences.
- Your video or short video clips.
- Your bio written to impress.
- A list of clients.
- Your keynote title(s) and short description(s). Starting off, it's perfectly fine to have just one keynote.
- Your contact information.
- A simple sign-up for your newsletter, or other free giveaway.

THE FOLLOWING ARE OPTIONAL:

- A form where a client can enter in what they are looking for, what their price range is, and what they want the speaker to accomplish.

- Your fee schedule.

CLICK YOUR SITE AND GET YOUR MESSAGE

"Don't try and be all things to all people. Be crystal clear on what you do and what a company will gain from hiring you. Describe what I call a 'positioning statement' that describes the concept and outcome of working with you. For example, my positioning statement is 'I work with speakers who want to book more business, make more money, and avoid costly mistakes.' That's the first thing people see when they hit my site."

—Lois Creamer, business consultant for speakers

Web site styles change all the time. Spend time researching how other speakers' sites look and feel and see what kind of style fits your Message of You. Keep it simple and don't do anything that is really campy, or all pink, or written in a cartoon font. This will distract from your professionalism, and people looking for speakers don't have a lot of time to navigate through multiple layers of Flash video. Also make sure that your Web site is cross-platform compatible as it needs to look great whether the client is on their laptop or their iPad. Finally, your Web site is there to catch the eye of a meeting planner who is surfing the Net and looking for a speaker such as yourself. SEO (search engine optimization) is extremely important when you are a speaker so that your site will come up when someone's look-

DON'T BE EVERYTHING TO EVERYBODY

"One of the keys to being active on social media without becoming overwhelmed is to create a long-term schedule of content that allows you to consistently post across the platforms. You want to be a magazine, not a newspaper. Pre-writing and planning your content will afford you the time to engage and converse with your audience."

—Lisa McTigue, marketing consultant

ing for an expert on your topic. Go to MarketYourSpeech.com/websites for tips on how to optimize your website.

MARKETING ESSENTIAL #4:
BECOME A SOCIAL BUTTERFLY

Social media is an essential way to spread The Message of You to a national—make that global—audience. We have come a long way from hiring kids to put stamps and labels on postcards and sending out huge mailings in order to publicize an event. Now we have Facebook, Twitter, LinkedIn, and more ways coming each day. Here are some tips to assist you in using social media to your advantage:

Rather than posting exclusively about yourself, remember the basic rule of speaking—it's about the audience. People care about themselves. They do not care about what or who you had for breakfast. Use your posts to create a dialogue asking others what they think as well as giving away useful information that brands you as an expert on your speaking topic.

BUILD YOUR FAN BASE VIA TWEETS

"Twitter gives everyone the ability to build loyal communities—while delivering content that is truly wanted by cocreating with your audience. That makes Twitter brilliant and highly valuable to the speaking industry."

—Michele Price @ProsperityGal, social communication speaker, Biz Radio host and founder, #Speakchat

Your Facebook friends can become your best PR agents, especially if they have jobs. I "friended" a childhood friend of mine. When his company was looking for speakers, he recommended me and I got the job.

Never post anything on Facebook you don't want a client to see. Be very aware of the privacy settings on your social media accounts. You don't want a potential corporate client to see the seminaked drunken pictures from your bachelorette party. I suggest having a private, nonpublic Facebook page for you, your family and close friends, and on that page you can have pictures of you winning the beer-bong contest or goofy pictures of your cat. But on your professional page, remember that everything you post on the Internet is your public face as a speaker. Don't do anything that will turn off a potential client. From the posts you do, to the pictures you share, the blogs you write, to the video—all have to be consistent with The Message of You.

DON'T FORGET THE "SOCIAL" IN SOCIAL MEDIA

"The secret to being effective in social media is to create and participate in communities. For example, join in on Tweetchat, or join speaking groups on LinkedIn. It's the fast track to getting well known."

—Lois Creamer, business consultant for speakers

With that said, it's not enough just to sit in front of a computer. You have to get out of the house and do the good old-fashioned meet and greets. In most cities there are business organizations, women's networking groups, entrepreneur groups, meetings of all sorts, classes, and workshops. Every time you step out of your house, you are meeting potential clients. If you are shy, get over it! You can't be a wallflower if you want to step on stage! Enter those networking meetings as if you are entering on stage with confidence! Always have business cards handy. Chambers of commerces are full of business folks who can get you work. Go to MessageOfYou.com/orgs for a listing of organizations and associations that book speakers.

MARKETING ESSENTIAL #5: WORK YOUR DATABASE

At eight years old, I learned the power of a database. My database at that time consisted of a wooden recipe box that ran my magic birthday party business. Every client had a separate card and a few months prior to their next birthday I did my marketing calls. "Mrs. Johnson, this year we have a new and improved birthday party. Now that your son is six years old we have added an accordion and the Hokey-Pokey!"

Although my database has gone from my recipe box to my computer, and now onto the Cloud, it is an essential marketing tool to keep track of my clients and fans. Every person who e-mails me, every business card I get, every person who takes my class, every audience member I speak in front of goes into my database and becomes a part of the audience for The Message of Me.

The strength of my database is what helps me sell my products, sell my speeches, and have an audience of fans that support me in my work. Go to TheMessageOfYou.com/databases to find templates for the latest databases that you can use to assist you in keeping track of your fans.

If you are truly motivating in your speeches, audience members will want more of you. Every time you speak, you want to increase your base by getting the names and e-mails of people in the audience. When you speak, every person in that audience can be a possible gig for you, especially if you are speaking to a diverse group of people from different businesses and organizations such as your city's chamber of commerce. You might have in front of you not only bankers and insurance people but also female entrepreneurs, scientists, engineers, and meeting planners.

So, how do you get everyone's business card? I like to have a drawing so everybody throws in their business card and then I give away one of my books. That way I am able to collect e-mails. Another way to get their e-mails is to have a bag on the table and everyone throws their business card in with a promise of receiving additional tips from you.

THERE'S AN APP FOR THAT!

Entering business cards doesn't have to be a hassle. Using a Smartphone there are apps that make entering data as easy as taking a picture. There are even apps that can turn your phone into a credit card machine. For a list of recommended apps for speakers, go to MarketYourSpeech.com/services.

Many speakers are now using interactive social media during their speeches to build their following. For instance, you can include an interactive Action Step during your speech, where you ask audience members to take out their Smartphones and Tweet comments or answers to a question. In a few seconds you've added a few hundred people to your social network and you didn't even have to enter in any e-mails. Can you say, convenient?

But having e-mail, Facebook, and Twitter followers doesn't mean anything unless you work your list by giving your fans value. Each week I send out a newsletter that contains my weekly blog giving free solid advice and helpful tips on my message that repeatedly establishes me as an expert in my field. Never send an e-mail without an unsubscribe link.

If you employ these steps, you will hear those magic words, "How much would you charge to come speak to my group?" If you have an agent, it will be their job to handle this question. If you're unrepped, you'll have to handle it on your own.

MARKETING ESSENTIAL #6:
GET INVOLVED—CAUSE-RELATED MARKETING

On the red carpet, the truly big stars are not just talking about what they are wearing, but rather, what cause they are serving. Paul McCartney is a fervent animal rights advocate. Lady Gaga sings and speaks out about gay rights. Justin Beiber lends his name to antibullying campaigns and you can't think of Angelina Jolie and Brad Pitt without also thinking about their massive charity causes. But you don't have to wait until you're a star to do cause-related marketing. Nor do you have to fly to Namibia to adopt an African baby.

What you can do is join a charity that is in sync with The Message of You. This means that by associating yourself with a cause that is larger than yourself, you will expand your contacts, mingle with people who are movers and shakers, get positive media exposure, increase speaking opportunities, and, but of course, do something good for others.

A win-win situation.

TO AGENT OR NOT TO AGENT

Here's how speaking agents work—they take 25 to 30 percent of your fee. For that service, they introduce you to their client, draw up your contract, and make sure you get paid. And of course, the best way to get a speaking agent is to already be working and making money as a speaker. In other words, if you don't need an agent, agents will want you. It's like getting married— once that ring is on your finger, suddenly all kinds of potential suitors come knocking. Go figure.

Basically, approaching a speaking agent is very similar to approaching your audience. It's all about them. If

SEE ME, HEAR ME, BOOK ME

"We only book speakers that have already been reviewed by our bureau staff. All our speakers have already matched our criteria: professionalism, presentation skills, testimonials, expertise in their topic area(s), and quality of their materials."

—Kelly MacDonald-Hill, senior VP, Speakers' Spotlight

MATCHING SPEAKERS TO CLIENTS 101

"How a speaker bureau matches a speaker to a client can be a complicated, long process depending on the client's needs. Factors include: themes the client needs addressed, the specific audience profile (everything from work and life experience, ages, professional development, gender, etc.), the overall event goals, program placement, past event speakers, and other speakers speaking at the event."

—Mike Frick, speaker agent, president of Speaking.com speakers bureau your speaking topic helps them make more money, then it's a no-brainer that they will book you. But make sure that you have your ducks in order *before* contacting them.

In order for a speaker bureau to be interested in you enough to submit you to one of their clients, you must have achieved at least one of the following:

- You're already making over $50,000 a year in the speaking business.

- You've got a hot book, movie, TV show, or a YouTube video that went viral.

- You're an expert on a topic that is popular and they don't have anyone on their roster to cover it.

- You're getting requested by an agent's client.

When you have achieved one or more of the above points, only then should you contact a bureau. Be very careful and research who they are, prior to contacting them. You'll only look foolish if you pitch yourself as a great health-care speaker and then find out they only handle sports figures. But if you qualify and can prove to them that you fill a gap in their current roster of clients, you can get them interested. Go to their Web site and do some research. If they don't have an expert in science, a female economist, a funny nurse, and you happen to be one of those things, then you might have a way to convince them that they need you.

Each speaker bureau has its own particular way of accepting new speakers, which is usually posted on their Web

HAVING YOUR DUCKS IN ORDER

"A speaker has to have a body of work prior to contacting a speakers bureau, including notoriety in the marketplace [already in high demand as a speaker], a particular expertise with proven credentials, and a unique positioning on their topic."

–Kelly MacDonald-Hill, Senior VP, Speakers' Spotlight

site. Again, do your research. Instructional videos on how to get a speaking agent are available at KeynoteU.com

If, however, you don't have an agent or you've opted out of handing over 25 percent of your money to a complete stranger, you're going to have to learn how to negotiate on your own behalf.

It's my favorite phone call—the one I get from my students screaming, "Someone wants to hire me! OMG! What do I do?" I love these happy, slightly hysterical calls. Call me needy, but I like affirmations that my advice worked and my students are getting paid.

NEGOTIATING YOUR FEE

Here are tips on how to negotiate your fees when someone asks, "I'd like you to speak at my organization. How much do you charge?"

1. Rather than answering their question, question them first. Even if you are a longtime speaker with a set price, rather than telling them your fee, you'll want to ask them, "What is your budget?" Right away this will tell you if this is the kind of booking that you will take. If you have told them you were a $10,000-a-booking speaker, when they said that they were looking to spend $2500, it would be hard to justify taking that gig. The best way is to avoid talking about money by replying, "Tell me first about your event."

2. Get the client talking about their event. Ask them specifically what results they are looking for from their speaker. *Always* take notes and really listen as this will give you a way to customize your sales pitch later on in the conversation. Knowing what they want a keynote to achieve will give you a better idea of how to convince them that you are a perfect fit for their audience.

3. Next, looking at your notes about the results the client wants from a keynote, reframe how your speech will give them the outcome that they are looking for.

4. Then, quote your price, and . . . shut up. There will be an uncomfortable silence, but don't be tempted to justify your price. Just be quiet. They will express concerns such as they have to go back to the committee, or your price is out of their budget. Or they'll ask you if you can do it for less. If they flat-out turn you down and firmly announce that your price is out of their budget, then find out how close you are. If you are a $10,000 speaker and their budget is $500, obviously that is too big of a gap to bridge. But if you are within 25 percent of your price you can say, "We are so close and I would like to help you make this happen."

Then use these negotiating strategies to assist the client in getting you your fee:

- Ask: "Do you have a company who can sponsor my appearance?" Very often associations have sponsors who will pay for a speaker in exchange for advertising in their program or other perks.

- Ask: "If I pay for my travel, will that help you pay my full fee?" You can always use frequent flyer miles to cover your travel expenses.

- Ask: "If I do a breakout session along with my keynote, will that help you meet my fee by reducing the need for another speaker?"

If they won't budge on their offer, then don't respond on the spot. Take a night to think it over. If you do accept a lower price, you need to have price integrity. This means that the client that paid you $10,000 doesn't want to hear that you did the same speech for $5,000. If you do end up accepting a lower fee, then have a clause in your contract that says, "This is a nondisclosed price." Meaning, if anyone asks the client how much they paid you, they are not allowed to say.

GETTING TO YES!

When negotiating your speaking fee, remember that the client may have more budget than they're sharing. Rebecca Morgan, CSP, CMC, has been a professional speaker and best-selling author for thirty-two years. Her advice is:

- If they want you to speak for free or a much-reduced fee because you'll get exposure, I always say, "I catch cold from exposure. My mortgage banker won't take exposure as payment. However, let's see what would work for both of us." Then explore options.

- Ask if they have a materials budget. If so, tell them you can charge a separate materials fee for your handouts and duplication rather than bundling it in your speaking fee.

- When you give a client your price, instead of asking, "Is that in your budget?" ask "Is that in the ballpark?"

- If they say they can't afford your full fee, ask, "What can you stretch to?"

- If they don't have your full fee, ask what else they could offer so you are fully compensated. A booth at their trade show, an ad in their program and/or on their Web site, and an extra night's lodging are options. Be creative! But don't just agree to a lower fee without getting something in return to make up the difference.

Here are some things to keep in mind in justifying a price reduction:

1. Is it a local gig? Many speakers have reduced rates if they don't have to get on a plane.

2. Can they professionally videotape you? If the event is on a big stage where you might get some great looking video clips, you might be willing to speak for a reduced fee if they will provide the camera operator, equipment, and arrange to shoot the speech.

3. Are they a local chapter of a larger organization? Ask the potential client if they have a national convention and if they could refer you to the planning committee for their larger event.

4. Will they provide e-mails of the attendees? This is a way to build your database of potential clients.

5. Will they publish one of your articles in their newsletter? Very often, companies have a newsletter where they can publish a short article of yours that will increase your visibility.

6. Do they have a materials budget to purchase copies of your book for everyone? Very often clients have an educational materials budget that allows them to buy your products in advance of the engagement.

7. Can you sell your product at the back of the room after your keynote? Many speakers make up the difference in their speaking fee in back of room (BOR) sales.

For sample contracts and more information about handling the negotiation process, visit MarketYourSpeech.com/legal.

YOU WANT FRIES WITH THAT?
CREATE MERCHANDISE FOR BOR SALES

To extend your reach, as well as to make extra income you need to turn The Message of You into a book, a DVD, a CD, an mp3 download, or even . . . a jar opener. That's exactly what Swedish speaker and comic Babben Larsson sells and here's why. While coaching Babben in my International workshop in Stockholm, I discovered the concept for the perfect product for her in her Heart Story, in which she explains why she couldn't leave her oppressive marriage:

> I didn't know how to change the tires on my car. I didn't know how to shovel snow. I couldn't even open jars. I'd give all the jars to my husband to open. Then, one day, I was in Helsinki and I saw these colorful items in a basket. I picked one up and it read, "Jar Opener: Put tool under top of jar, lift, and the vacuum will release." I just stared at that message.

It instantly struck me; this is the sign! With this in my hand I can open any jar myself! I bought the device, went home, and three days later, told my husband I wanted a divorce.

The jar opener became a symbol of Babben's message to the women in the audience—that we all have the power to lead happier lives. She contacted the factory in Denmark that made the jar openers and convinced them what good publicity it would be for them to be in her show. "They gave me a 60 percent discount on their retail price!" She then found a printing company to put her Core Promise, "I've got the power," on the openers. She bundles the jar openers with her book and CD and doubles the amount of money that she makes when speaking.

YOUR MESSAGE GOES HERE

Put The Message of You in everything you do—from your e-mail signature to your Facebook posts. By repeatedly broadcasting a relatable message, buyers will find you.

How do you create product? Your product needs to be a way for audience members to carry your message home with them. When people love your speech, they will want to buy something as a reminder of your message. Whatever you sell, whether it's a book or a T-shirt or even your services, it has to relate to The Message of You.

FIND YOUR NICHE

"Instead of doing one big generic book you try to sell to everybody, it's smarter to market to the pond than the ocean.

"Ironically, the tighter the niche, the larger the market. *Chicken Soup for the Pet Lover's Soul* sells more copies than a regular *Chicken Soup* book because it has a huge sell-through rate with that fan base.

"Plus, you can saturate a target market by promoting your book to related blogs and Web sites and preselling it as a premium to relevant retailers such as Petco, Hartz, Sergeant, and Iams.

"When you write a niche book, you are more likely to go to the head of the class in that industry and be paid to speak because you've established yourself as a topic expert. Don't worry about appealing to everybody. Focus on how you can be *the* go-to resource in a specific field. You will scale your writing, speaking, and media success as a result."—Sam Horn, speaker and author of *POP! Create the Perfect Pitch, Title and Tagline for Anything*

DO'S AND DON'TS OF SELLING PRODUCT

- DO include in your introduction that you will be selling your product afterward. That way, the person introducing you is selling your product, rather than you.

- DON'T do a big sales pitch about your product as part of your speech.

- DO create a story about how you created your product or perhaps a story about the advantages somebody received from your product. When I'm selling my book *The Comedy Bible* I use a compelling story about one of my readers, Jimi Land, who wrote me from prison. Jimi had a hard time getting off drugs and dealing with his anger so they put him in solitary confinement. His mother had ordered my book for him, and right before they shut the door to his three weeks in solitary confinement, the book arrived. Reading materials were not allowed in solitary, except for one, a Bible. So, the guard threw my book at Jimi. "Here's your Bible." He had three weeks with my book and he took all his anger, frustrations, and pain and turned it into a stand-up act. After leaving prison, comedy helped him deal with his rage and he learned to turn his problems into punch lines. It also gave him a career when he got out of jail. Jimmy now performs all across the United States and he's managed to stay out of jail all these years. You better believe that when I tell that story, my audience links my product with an emotional event. They associate my message with my book and rush to my sales table.

If you want to include a "product story," I suggest you include it with your Action Steps so you can connect your product to your solutions. You can also say something at the end of your speech, like "I'd be happy to sign copies of my book."

HAVE A GHOSTWRITER WRITE YOUR BOOK

No time or desire to write a book or develop a DVD? No worries, as you can go to MarketYourSpeech.com/publishing for lists of people who can do that for you.

- DO have free stuff that they can pick up. I like to give away a free T-shirt with a funny message for the first ten buyers of my book. That gets them to the table *fast*.

- DO have something to give people if they give you their business card. Promise them a free download of tips and advice. People love free.

- DO have bundles. You can't really sell a book for more than twenty bucks but bundle it with a DVD or a great gadget and you can double your intake.

- DO have a way to take credit card payments quickly. I have an attachment that turns my iPhone into a credit card machine that even lets them sign. Go to MarketYourSpeech.com/services as a resource to find materials and information on how to turn your Smartphone into a credit card charger. Then, its swipe, sign, book, and sell.

After reading this chapter on everything you need to do to market yourself, you might feel exhausted. I so understand. Speaking for a living is a full-time job. It's a stressful combination of 85 percent grunt office work, 10 percent creativity, and 5 percent glorious appreciation for a job well done. For those of you with patience and persistence, you will succeed. If you are the ambitious sort who can delay gratification, then you've got what it takes to succeed. But some of you might not want to become a professional speaker and that's okay, too. It doesn't mean that the work you put into finding and honing The Message of You is wasted.

In fact, your journey is just beginning.

CHAPTER NINETEEN

LIVE THE MESSAGE OF YOU

The Message of You can create a ripple effect that rocks the world.

If The Message of You is in sync with what the world needs, then you don't need to wait for speaking gigs to share and receive The Message of You. There is an audience waiting for you just outside your front door.

Shakespeare said, "All the world's a stage," so life provides us with plenty of audiences. You can make a difference in someone's life whether you're speaking in front of 1,500 dentists at the Vegas Hilton or to one person at your neighborhood dry cleaner. There are plenty of one-on-one opportunities to make a difference in someone else's life—not only by speaking, but by actively listening. Matter of fact, each time we take the time to truly listen to the stories around us, as well as speaking our message, we become a part of the ripple effect of self-improvement.

If there is one truth that can't be denied, it is this:

You can't just breathe out. You must also breathe in.

What I mean by this is, you must learn to be more than a great *talker,* but you must learn to become a great *listener* as well. We've spent the vast majority of this book learning to become an expert about ourselves, turning our critical and investigative eye on our own lives in order to express who we are to the world. Yet there is a world of stories outside of yourself that not only can motivate and nourish your soul, but put you in touch with what people are thinking and feeling.

If you get tired of your own stories, or find yourself stuck in a creative block, then seek out other people's stories. I'm asking you to become a collector of experiences, to see yourself as an anthropologist digging for the larger messages that are layered underneath the surface of those stories. I'm asking you to not only live your message but to help others do the same by simply . . . listening.

TURNING THE MESSAGE OF YOU INTO AN EMPIRE

When your message is in sync with you as well as a larger audience, The Message of You can turn into a speech that becomes a radio piece that becomes a blog that becomes a book that becomes a web series that becomes a TV show that becomes an International multimillion-dollar empire. Just ask financial speaker, TV host, author, and millionaire Suze Orman.

As a waitress she *listened* to her customers having a hard time making ends meet. As a stock broker, she *heard* the concerns of her clients trying to plan their retirement. Then when the world was plummeting into economic recession, Suze found her message of financial freedom right on the pulse of the American public. Now, her books have sold millions of copies; she has her own TV show and even her own Suze Orman–brand credit card.

Suze gave away her *message* of help and assistance long before she became a media darling. She made her audiences feel as if she truly cared, whether they were buying a cup of coffee or a thousand-dollar financial program. How? Because she had *listened* to their concerns and created easy-to-understand solutions.

Now, when she speaks, *others* listen.

Remember when you started developing your speech by asking your client the problems facing their audience? Well, there is a larger audience than the one that meets at the chamber of commerce. It's the audience of strangers that live beyond your front door. It's your mail person, the person at the gym on the next treadmill, the people in the grocery checkout line. They all have messages for you if you are willing to actively seek out their stories. If you truly listen, you will find out their needs which lead you to find your next speech topic, a better

Action Step, your next Heart Story, or even some great advice to enhance your own life.

For example: One day in the express lane at the grocery store, the line was held up by an excessive coupon cutter. As the shoppers waited impatiently, the elderly woman behind me started up a conversation. Within one minute she had shared, "My husband had a stroke, and we don't have sex anymore. It's been three months!"

I have long ago made peace with the fact that I am a "message magnet"—there is some vibe about me that makes strangers want to share the most intimate details of their lives in public places at the most inopportune times. While most people might have smiled politely and turned the other cheek, I responded, "Tell me about your husband."

She then told me the remarkable story of their forty-year love affair. It was a tale of passion, romance, and the difficulties of intimacy as the senior years approached, then ultimately took over. I was actually disappointed when the line began to move. Right there, in the "Ten Items or Less" line, I received a Heart Story that inspired me to go home and enjoy the time I have with my loved one. A great Action Step, free of charge, right there at the supermarket: enjoy the time you have.

Stories are everywhere if you open your eyes and ears to hear them and ask questions.

Each week, my Weight Watcher leader, Elaine Berman, inspires the group with her stories of weight loss, transformation, and how to make a low-fat potato latke. From Elaine I've learned to make my goals important. At the hair salon, I asked the woman who painted my nails where she was from. She then shared the moving story about her family's escape from Vietnam, and I learned the lesson to appreciate what I have. When a homeless man asked me for money, I stopped and asked him for his story. He told a Heart Story worthy of any hall of fame speaker that made me realize there is a core at which we can all connect and never have to feel alone.

These brief encounters can be considered a time suck or they can be seen as opportunities to create a larger movement of message from person to person, creating a ripple effect of inspiration. I incorporate what

I learn from the people I meet and they become part of me, part of my message, and part of my speech. We speakers carry on the message.

As a speaker, whether or not you have a booking, you still have a job to do every day—living The Message of You. It's your job to practice what you preach whether or not anyone is paying you to do so. That means reading books, taking classes, and consciously practicing your own Action Steps.

For me, living my message means that I have to always remember to turn problems into punch lines, to find a way to transform stressful situations into laughable memories. If a salesman at the register of a store says, "I need your phone number please," I can either flat-out refuse and embarrass him or I can make a humorous response: "I'm so flattered but I'm married. Thank you for asking." Then we both share a laugh and the issue's resolved with a smile instead of a stare.

I'm not saying this is easy to do. Living The Message of You is not always convenient. If your message is about treating animals with the kindness they deserve, you may find yourself having to make tough choices: Do I report my next-door neighbor to Animal Control for neglecting their dogs, or do I keep the peace because I have to live beside them? One thing is for certain: The surest way to crash and burn as a speaker is to say one thing publicly and do another privately. Just look at any "family values" politician who's been caught cavorting in a public bathroom, or tweeting graphic photos of himself, or being outed as Client X for a high-end escort service.

There will always be things that get in the way of you living The Message of You. Fear, cynicism, and burnout will challenge your commitment. I have clients who, in the middle of working on their speeches, have just disappeared. The sad part about this is that they really had a great Message of You to give to others and now the world will never hear it.

Don't let your fears stop you from being a part of the ripple effect, so here is a new way of looking at your creative road blocks—they're selfish. They're narcissistic self-preoccupations that get in the way of giving to others. And this is what I have to say to you: "Snap out of it!" Change the direction of your concerns from "I'm scared that people won't like me" to "I care enough about others to give them inspiration." Or, if you are not a "people person," there certainly must be one person you care about enough to help. Think about them, because what you give to others when you speak your Message of You can create a ripple effect you cannot even imagine.

Know this: your fear level has nothing to do with your talent. Talented and successful people deal with fear on a regular basis. Martha Graham, who was an American modern dancer and choreographer, received the highest civilian award of the USA: the Presidential Medal of Freedom. Until she was ninety, she was known for delivering spellbinding lectures, yet she was often overwhelmed with fear. However, her lifelong friend and fellow dance legend Agnes DeMille remembers a letter Graham wrote to her, a portion of which bears repeating here:

> There is a vitality, a life force, a quickening that is translated through you into action, and because there is only one of you in all time, this expression is unique.
>
> If you block it, it will never exist through any other medium and be lost. The world will not have it. It is not your business to determine how good it is; nor how valuable it is; nor how it compares with other expressions. It is your business to keep it yours, clearly and directly, to keep the channel open.
>
> You do not even have to believe in yourself or your work. You have to keep open and aware directly of the urges that motivate you.
>
> Keep the channel open. No artist is pleased. There is no satisfaction whatever at any time. There is only a queer, divine dissatisfaction; a blessed unrest that keeps us marching and makes us more alive than the others.

Here's how the ripple effect works. Graham fought her fears and showed up. My mother became a dancer because she studied with Martha Graham at UCLA. Although my mother's career as a chorographer got sidetracked by having a disabled child and other family issues, she instilled in me the motivation to pursue creative expression and go beyond my fear. It was the same advice Graham gave to DeMille that my mother gave to me: "Keep the channel open and get out of your own way for the sake of others."

Here you are reading my book, which means I actually finished writing it, which at the time of writing was a scary process with an inner critic throwing insults at my brain with every page I wrote. To help me finish, I thought of you, the reader. I thought of you bringing your Message of You to the world, and how by writing this book I would be a part of a larger movement for change. I got out of my own way, so now you can get out of yours!

Remind yourself of your intent and remember you are writing this speech because someone out there, in some audience, needs to hear what you have to say. I remember doing a stand-up set at a club in Tampa, Florida. It was to a horribly drunk audience of businessmen. They weren't laughing. I came off stage feeling like a failure. Then a woman came up to me and said, "You really made a difference in my life!"

I was shocked. What kind of difference could a horrible show like that make in someone's life? Then she told me a story about her life and how she was living in a battered women's shelter. That she was here with a few of her new friends and she saw my strength. She said, "I felt that you handled the men so powerfully. I've never seen a woman do that before. And I realized watching you that I have that power in me, too."

Wow! Now every time I feel scared, panicked, and insecure, I imagine her sitting in the back of every audience. I play to her.

Who is in your audience? Whom do you need to be a hero for? How important is it that your Message of You gets out? What can your Message of You do for others? Is it important enough to get out of your own small, narrow world of self-doubt?

If it is, then get out there.

Do it.

Make me proud.

Book that first speaking gig—because I have the sneaking suspicion that you *still* may have skipped that part!

Find the courage to step onstage.

Take the microphone in hand.

And speak.

RESOURCES

TheMessageofYou.com
Your ultimate Web resource for becoming a paid speaker, including—tips on getting your first gig, speaker services, gadgets and aids, new exercises, commitment contracts, templates, speaker software, and free insider tips and stories.
　　Facebook: TheMessageOfYou—Join and share your stories of triumph!

KeynoteU.com
You've read the book, now get personal coaching from Judy Carter from the comfort of your couch. Enroll in the ultimate online professional speaker university with enhanced exercises and courses designed to further help you achieve your dream speaking career. Also available—personal one-on-one tutoring, TeleSeminars, and free MP3 downloads.

MarketYourSpeech.com
Everything you need to market your speech and become an expert. Find on this site—fee schedules, sample contracts, book writing services, and up-to-date information related to Bookable Topics.

MySpeakerBuddy.com
Need to find your creative soul mate? Visit this site to find the perfect person to collaborate with you to find your message and write your speech.

SpeakerDemo.com
Create your Electronic Press Kit (EPK) for free—in only ten minutes!

JudyCarter.com
Complete listing of Judy Carter products and services, including, specialized speaking products and coaching for CEOs, executives, doctors, lawyers, teachers, and comics.

Keep up with Judy on Facebook (JudyCarterComedy) or Twitter (JudyCarter).

HireJudy.com

For your next event, why have a boring speaker when you can hire Judy for a LOL inspiring speech that your staff will be talking about for years to come? Or, hire Judy to create a custom workshop for your staff that uses comedy improv to teach presentational skills. Go to this site to view videos and get more information on Judy's speaking services.

Follow Judy on Social Media

Facebook: JudyCarterComedy

Twitter: JudyCarter

YouTube: ComedyGoddess